PENGUIN BOOKS

A FAMILY PLACE

Leila Philip is the author of *The Road Through Miyama*, a memoir of her apprenticeship to a master potter in Japan, for which she won the 1990 PEN/Martha Albrand Special Citation for Nonfiction. She teaches creative writing at Colgate University. Philip lives in New York state.

Praise for *A Family Place*

"In *A Family Place*, Leila Philip manages to seduce the reader into wanting to know what's happened for centuries behind the doors of her family's house, Talavera . . . an unpretentious, subtly shaded story of the importance of understanding the ghosts and heroes that reside in every ancestral home."
—*The New York Times*

"Leila Philip's view of her family's land is, in part, sweeping and romantic, a panoramic view much like the luminous paintings of the Hudson River School, yet nothing in her detailed narrative of this cherished place dwarfs the lives of those who have lived here. They live again in her telling. Philip grafts history, natural history and autobiography into a stunning performance, as tempting as the Golden Delicious apples that grace the trees of her orchard."
—Maureen Howard, author of *Big as Life*

"An exquisite rendering of a Hudson Valley family farm, as detailed and colored as a Persian miniature. Philip's family history is alarmingly transporting, and her sense of place so rich you can taste it."
—*Kirkus Reviews* (starred review)

"Mesmerizing . . . Both narrative threads are profoundly personal. Braided together with insight, they pay homage to the ideals of home and family with a resonance that should extend beyond her home region."
—*Publishers Weekly*

"In this eloquent memoir, Leila Philip deftly braids elegance and struggle, memory and loss, past and present, place and time. With wit and insight, she probes the intricate ties of landscape and history, finding in her family farm deep reserves of meaning and mystery."

— Alan Taylor, author of the Pulitzer Prize–winning *William Cooper's Town*

"Riveting . . . one of the most finely written family histories available."

— *Library Journal*

"The writing is poetic, haunting, the subject riveting, the research prodigious, the people just wonderful. . . . I read this one over a few sunny afternoons and have been thinking about it ever since"

— Bill Roorback, author of *The Smallest Color*, in *The Hartford Courant*'s "What Was the Best Book You Read this Year?"

"Leila Philip understands better than anyone just how complex our ties to the land are. In deliberating over mysteries of her family's history and questioning her own dreams and responsibilities toward the family orchards, she has created a rich and textured world for a reader to inhabit. *A Family Place* is full of intelligence, gracefully written, and guided by a devoted heart."

— Jane Brox, author of *Five Thousand Days Like This One*

"Like the house at its center, Leila Philip's *A Family Place* is elegant but also generous, full of feeling but never sentimental; more than once its subtle moral shadings reminded me of Forster's *Howards End*. Larger in scope than a memoir but more intimate than mere history, Philip's genealogical ledger expands with each new chapter, reflecting and readjusting American notions of family, land, lineage, service, and country."

— Dale Peck, author of *Martin and John*

"Through letters, journals, conversations and speculations, Leila Philip teaches us how to eavesdrop on the past. *A Family Place* should be in the library of everyone who has marveled at how family history connects us to the place we call home and the place we discover through the secrets they left behind."

— Nancy Willard, author of *Things Invisible to See*

A FAMILY PLACE

A Hudson Valley Farm,
Three Centuries,
Five Wars,
One Family

Leila Philip

PENGUIN BOOKS

PENGUIN BOOKS
Published by the Penguin Group
Penguin Putnam Inc., 375 Hudson Street,
New York, New York 10014, U.S.A.
Penguin Books Ltd, 80 Strand, London WC2R 0RL, England
Penguin Books Australia Ltd, 250 Camberwell Road,
Camberwell, Victoria 3124, Australia
Penguin Books Canada Ltd, 10 Alcorn Avenue,
Toronto, Ontario, Canada M4V 3B2
Penguin Books India (P) Ltd, 11 Community Centre,
Panchsheel Park, New Delhi – 110 017, India
Penguin Books (N.Z.) Ltd, Cnr Rosedale and Airborne Roads,
Albany, Auckland, New Zealand
Penguin Books (South Africa) (Pty) Ltd, 24 Sturdee Avenue,
Rosebank, Johannesburg 2196, South Africa

Penguin Books Ltd, Registered Offices:
Harmondsworth, Middlesex, England

First published in the United States of America by Viking Penguin,
a member of Penguin Putnam Inc. 2001
Published in Penguin Books 2002

1 3 5 7 9 10 8 6 4 2

THE LIBRARY OF CONGRESS HAS CATALOGED
THE HARDCOVER EDITION AS FOLLOWS:
Philip, Leila.
A family place : a Hudson Valley farm, three centuries,
five wars, one family / Leila Philip.
p. cm.
ISBN 0-670-03013-9 (hc.)
ISBN 0 14 20.0145 7 (pbk.)
1. Columbia County (N.Y.)—Description and travel.
2. Columbia County (N.Y.)—History.   3. Hudson River Valley
(N.Y. and N.J.)—Description and travel.   4. Hudson River Valley (N.Y.
and N.J.)—History.   5. Country life—New York (State)—Columbia County.
6. Philip, Leila.   7. Philip family.   8. Columbia County (N.Y.)—Biography.
9. Fruit growers—New York (State)—Columbia County—Biography.
10. Orchards—New York (State)—Columbia County.   I. Title.
F127.C8 P47   2001
974.7'39—dc21   2001025391

Printed in the United States of America
Set in Bembo/Designed by Ginger Legato

Contents

INTRODUCTION: IN THE BEGINNING   ix

1. ONE   1
2. THE COUNT   5
3. CLAVERACK, 1732   31
4. AFTER   38
5. YESTERDAY'S HARVEST   44
6. TALAVERA, 1969   58
7. WILD BEES   65
8. IN THE HOLLOW OF HIS HAND   72
9. WRITING TO THE WIND   97
10. TALAVERA, 1866   115
11. HOUSEHOLD ACCOUNTS   118
12. HARDLY A HASTY WORD   139
13. TALAVERA, 1913   149
14. THE LIVES OF AUNTS   153
15. ANNA   199
16. ANOTHER WAR   203
17. IN THE ORCHARD   240

Sources   273
Acknowledgments   275

On May 27, 1649, the Mohican Aepjen, or chief, Keesieway began to exchange his lands in Columbia County—what would become thousands of acres of verdant rolling hills, winding creeks and sheltered inlets that led onto a shimmering tidal river—to the Van Rensselaers for a payment of ten fathoms of cloth, ten kettles, ten axes, ten adzes, ten swords, ten necklaces of strung beads, ten knives and one firelock gun.

In the Beginning

BEFORE ME STOOD TALAVERA, but all around was darkness. Light was spewing out from so many of the tall windows that the house could have been a ship sailing the night sea. But instead of feeling cheered by what I saw, I felt frozen. Talavera, that grand vessel of the past, how much of it was illusion, a house of cards, precarious, hostage to the slightest breeze?

Even now I could shut my eyes and see each room as it had been. On the uppermost floor in the west room sat the mahogany cradle that had rocked generations. My sister and I had found it a perfect place to nurse the baby rabbits that we sometimes found abandoned in the fields after the mower had gone by. Determined to save them from the dogs and the cats, we wrapped them in old sweaters and nursed them with tiny droppers of milk, feeding them every two hours. The rabbit kits never lived more than a few days, but we would always try, stroking their impossibly small ears and frail, quivering bodies with a finger until they fell still, asleep in our palms.

In that same room was the strange armadillo basket, a Victorian horror made from an armadillo shell, the nose wired to the long tail to form a handle. Boredom was never possible on rainy days at Talavera. It was an adventure merely to open the huge old doors and wander through these rooms. Each was filled with strange old things to finger and collect or just to stare at from a wary distance. Downstairs the curio cabinets were stocked with prehistoric and Mohican arrowheads collected each season in the upturned plow furrows. I loved to look at them and at the shelves of relics from an ancestor's travels. Medals, bits of stone, a tiny shoe with a message written on the sole, a stone lantern, a piece of Roman tile, the broken edge of an old relief, a square of embroidered fabric, a pile of coins, a strange torpedo-shaped Civil War bullet: so many things that each time you looked you could find something new.

My family saved everything, a habit that would make my search possible when it came to digging up the past. I loved the funny silver and porcelain thimbles, the faded, falling-apart packets of needles and thread and blanket binding, the old quill pens and nibs and the glass inkwells that I painstakingly strove to use when I was twelve, blotching ink all over the white pages of my leather-bound journal. The books were old; the wastebaskets were old; the drapes were old; even the bottles of alcohol and Pepto-Bismol in the medicine closet were from a time long before I was born. Once I went looking for a Band-Aid and pried open the rusting metal box only to find that the Band-Aids inside had withered. I dumped out a dozen yellow strips that crackled and broke to the touch like dried cicada shells.

⁂

Talavera was not just a house and not just the past. It was not just my father's dream, and it was not just my aged rival. Somehow Talavera had absorbed my own childhood, becoming me. Once I walked out of the house, across the lawns and onto the farm's land, time would conflate, and I was not just the age I was then but all the ages I had ever been. I was five years old and climbing on, then falling off our Shetland pony. I was nine years old and riding my first new bicycle, down the big hill faster and faster until my wheel caught in a rut and I came to a stop, smack against the boxes of a beehive. I was twelve years old and proudly backing up a tractor and trailer. Then sixteen and racing my horse, faster and faster without a saddle or a bridle, across the meadow.

I walked slowly back up to the house and crossed the north porch. All around me the tall Corinthian columns spired up, echoing the tripartite structure of the house with its north and south wings and its central pavilion, designed to appear as if a temple lost within a grove. I reached out to open the door. Beneath my fingers the brass door handle felt solid, reassuringly smooth and cool. But as soon as I began to turn the knob, I felt myself grow weak. The knob turned and turned, but the door would not open. Broken, the inside mechanism separated from the catch. A simple matter, but at that moment my insides split into panic. I couldn't get in, I couldn't get away.

I thought back to the psalm that my mother and I had chosen for my father's funeral: "You sweep us away like a dream; we fade away suddenly like the grass." Then, as if on cue, the knob on the front door caught and turned. I pushed the door forward and walked in, listening to my footsteps echo in the now-darkening house.

One

My father is trying to teach me how to prune a tree. "Here," he says, holding the center section of a young tree in one hand and angling the clippers toward it with the other. "See these two terminals growing close together. That won't do. They are competing. One has to go."

His large hands hold the clippers easily, almost carelessly as he bends his tall frame over the young tree. I watch his fingers squeeze over the orange grips. The blades snap. A long, slender branch slides down the length of the tree. "You have to find the leader, make a decision, then cut.

"There, now we'll just top the one we've left a bit." He bends the tip of the tree's new leader toward me and fingers the silver, bullet-shaped buds. "You always want to cut just above a bud." His clippers snap again. This time the length of tree falls onto his boot. He bends down and grabs it, then flings it over his shoulder. The cut wood lands with a thud in the broken winter grasses, startling the dog.

"These trees got away from us last year," he says, still holding the clippers up as a pointer. "Look at all this side growth—"

My father interrupts himself to begin pushing down some of the side branches, or scaffold limbs, so that instead of angling up around the trunk of the tree, they jut out from the center of the tree at right angles. He studies the tree for a moment; then his clippers begin again, snapping a limb off here, another one there, twisting around the soft new growth, to cut the wood clean and close to the trunk. Each time he makes a cut, my father flicks his wrist so that the newly cut wood twists away from him, rustling down into the tree. Sometimes branches fall against his chest, but he just brushes them away without looking down. He has a vision for this tree: the strong limbs studded with red apples, the entire tree a green spreading focus to produce good fruit. No excess limbs to cut the light, a leader rising straight and tall.

I rub my gloved hands together in an effort to keep them warm and continue watching. My father's clippers flash silver in the cold winter air. Only when several more branches lie at the base of the tree does he step back to look. So much of the bushy side growth is gone that the tree looks awkward, shorn. The limbs and trunk are dotted with white marks where the soft underwood has been exposed. For really deep cuts on the older trees, my father will coat the surface with tar and turpentine to prevent disease, but for clipper cuts on a young tree like this, he will count on the tree's vigor to heal over the wounds. A leader now rises; evenly spaced side branches push out on all four quadrants.

"That's enough for now," says my father. "Next year we can work straightening out some of those side limbs, but I don't want to cut off any more fruit buds since this is its first bearing year."

While I pull the branches away, piling them in the center of the row so that they can be scooped up by the brush picker, my father pulls his gloves off and adjusts the wire guard around the tree's base. Then he pulls a handful of mouse bait from a coffee can and scatters it around the tree's base. "If we can just keep the mice and deer off of them, these trees should be okay."

I look down the rows of young Empires that now line the slope of the meadow as it cuts down from the garden.

"Here"—my father hands me the clippers—"you try the next one." He walks back to the tractor with its wooden pruning tower and pulls out a saw.

I move down the row to a short tree, dense with limbs. I see only one central branch shooting up, no competition to clean out of the way. But the central terminal seems crooked and stunted. Sometimes my father looks at trees like this and decides to get rid of the weak leader and restart the tree. He cuts the old leader back and chooses one of the lower branches to be the tree's new leader. Should I do that, letting one of the lower branches, already beginning to spire up, become the tree's new center? I decide to go with that idea but then can't decide which lower limb to choose as the new leader. The branches are all about the same size, all vigorous. I try pushing down the side branches, as I have watched my father do, to get a handle on which scaffold limbs should stay, but that only confuses me more. I want so much to get this right. I know it will please my father. When he heads out for the orchards, he is always glad when I come along.

But there are too many branches, each one twisting this way, that way. I tell myself I will just have to begin, start cutting somewhere. I bring my clippers up against a limb, pushing them close to the trunk to make a clean cut as my father has shown me, but just as I am about to squeeze the handle, I am overcome with fear. What if I make the wrong cut? I back up and study the tree again, but even then I can't decide where to begin. I try a new tactic. I push myself into the center of the small tree so that I can look at the branches from that angle. But now I am simply wedged into the chaos of branches.

When I push my way back out of the tree, a branch snaps in my face. The sudden sting makes me only more determined to begin cutting in somewhere. I raise my clippers, but it is no use. I am stumped again. All the bottom branches look identical. What if the one I choose to be a leader becomes stunted? Then I will have cut away the tree's other possibilities and chosen the wrong one.

My father, busy cutting a split limb off a nearby tree, doesn't seem to notice that I am just standing there, clippers poised. Everything seems to depend upon a kind of confidence I don't feel. Knowing how to prune a tree, like knowing how to handle a horse, is important here. I am already a competent rider. I will learn how to prune an apple tree. Tomorrow.

I push myself back into the center of the small tree and resume cutting the sucker growth off limbs. I know it is not real pruning, those cuts that determine the fate of a tree, just cleanup work. I snip quickly and decisively at the forest of suckers, thin, upright terminals that shoot up from each limb almost parallel to the leader. I hate the sense of defeat that I feel, but I will not admit to my father that I have no idea how to prune a tree. He makes it look so easy, like something I should already know.

Suddenly the dog leaps up and runs across the meadow and onto the frost-heaved expanse of back lawn, chasing a rabbit. His feet clatter through the large heart-shaped catalpa leaves. I look up for a moment at the borders of old shade trees that ring the huge yellow house. Lined with snow and ice, their unpruned shapes etch a mysterious calligraphy across the blank winter sky.

CHAPTER TWO

The Count

I am standing at the edge of the world. All around me young apple trees spread down and out in obedient lines. But if I look across the meadow below, past the pond, past the road leading up the far slope to the enormous house, shouldering in among tall white pines, and past that too, the mountains begin, their smooth blue flanks crowding the sky. I have arrived just in time. Waves of yellow light are spreading over the land, so much orange today that the clouds begin to throb, the dark outline of the Catskills looming closer, pushing back the foothills that rise up and down in green waves to the river, five miles away.

The sky shudders, suddenly gone neon, psychedelic, wild with color. It won't be long now before that final diving down and the drawn-out afterglow, that famous Hudson Valley light that drove landscape painters wild. Soon the trees around me are glowing too, absolved somehow of all responsibility to bloom and produce, to grow tall, not to falter. I watch the gray bark turn purple in the softening rose-colored light. Their limbs, still leafed out and loaded with red fruit, shimmer. The brisk October air is musty with rent pollen and the slightly burned smell of falling leaves. I take a deep breath. I will never grow tired of this drama, just as I will never not love this land. I whistle for Danny, my father's dog, and walk back to the silver truck to finish the closing-up chores.

My family has owned this land since 1732, but that is only European time. For generations before the arrival of Henry Hudson and then my own family, Mohican Indians lived here, hunting and fishing along Claverack Creek and farming in a small way. That is, until 1649, when the Mohican chief Keesieway began to exchange his lands in Columbia County to the Van Rensselaers for the pathetic payment of ten fathoms of cloth, ten kettles, ten axes, ten adzes, ten swords, ten necklaces of strung beads, ten knives and one firelock gun.

Soon after that historic land deal, Admiral Adrian Van Ness set sail with a broomstick tied to his mast, indicating his intent to sweep the English from the seas. Back in Amsterdam, he might well have known Kiliaen Van Rensselaer, who, having recently acquired 850,000 acres of Hudson Valley land, had begun to establish Rensselaerswyck Manor and himself as the first lord or patroon. In the library of the large house on the hill hangs a framed sheet from the log of one of Admiral Van Ness's seventeenth-century voyages. Growing up, I had no idea what the strange faded sheet of almost illegible Dutch writing was or why it was hanging by the library closet where we always kept the green cashbox of harvest money. My father's middle name was Van Ness, as his father's had been, and his great-uncle's had been. Before that, Van Ness had been the surname of men whose names were listed on the deed for this land.

For years my family has grown apples and pears here, running a commercial fruit orchard named Philip Orchards. We sell the entire crop to customers who come to "pick your own." Now that my father is sick, my sister, my three brothers and I are taking turns managing the orchards on weekends throughout the ten weeks of harvest. I don't have time to linger because it is time for me to begin the orchard check, driving through the various orchards to see how many last-minute customers are still picking and to look over the remaining fruit so that my father can plan where to send customers the next day. By the end of October, or by the first frost, whichever comes first, we need to sell eight thousand bushels of fruit.

I had parked the truck on the main farm road so that any remaining customers could see it if they were on their way out. Most of our pickers have picked here for years and would know to stop and find me in order to pay for their fruit. Still, I walk quickly now, cutting along the top of the ridge so that I can look over the whips of Harrow Sweets, planted in an effort to reenergize flagging pear sales. Harrows are a new breed of pear that should ripen later than the sweet, juicy Bartlett, which always comes on too early in September for the Pick Your Own crowds. I see that over the summer the infant trees have pushed up two and three feet of new terminal growth, just as they should. My father will be pleased. But when I look closely at the young side limbs, I see that they are growing too close to the slender trunk, the angle of these new scaffold branches more like forty-five degrees instead of the strong right angle desired. Unless side limbs emerge from the trunk at the proper angle, once loaded with fruit, they will snap. The trees need shaping, the still-pliant growth pushed away from the leader with toothpicks or small props of wood or pulled down to the correct angle by weighting the limbs with stones tied on with string. Normally my father would have done this by now, for in a few weeks the plant tissue will be too stiff. Given a few days, I could do the work too, but I don't have the time, and neither does my mother. It would just agitate my father to mention the wayward trees to him. I head down the slope so that I can scan the Empires. A perfect set here, the apples large and low to the ground for easy picking.

Soon I am in the M-Nines, a block of semidwarf Red Delicious trees. My family called this sorry-looking section of

7

trees the M-Nines after the name of their rootstock, and they were something of a family joke. Back in the 1970s, my father's idea had been to replace the large old orchard trees planted by my grandfather with semidwarf stock that produced significantly more bushels per acre. Basically, his strategy worked, for within eight years the orchards were producing as much as they had once done on twice the acreage. But the M-Nines were an exception. The tentative rootstock didn't like the rocky feel of our hill, and the root base spread out far too slowly for the ambitious apple cultivars that had been grafted on to them. The trees began to produce magnificent purple-red apples, but just as they reached maturity, they began to topple. Still, my father would not give up on the trees. Instead of cutting them down, he'd be out on the hillside, endlessly staking leaders, wiring and pruning limbs in an attempt to keep them upright. When I came home from boarding school at Christmas and Easter, we'd head out and work on the M-Nines together.

8

I grab a leaf from one of the trees and pull it off with a flick of my wrist. Crazy old fools. They are like old family pets, naughty, untrainable, but impossible to get rid of. Still, as I pass the trees now, I see several good bushels of large red fruit peeking out from the leaves. The caravan of Chinese families that drives up from Queens every fall and heads straight for these trees will not be disappointed when they get here tomorrow.

The truck starts easily, and I turn right onto the farm road, heading away from the mountains and the house so that I can make a quick loop of the back orchards. I haven't gone twenty feet, however, before I come across a yellow sign with orchard directions lying facedown in the grass. I stop the truck, grab the heavy steel mallet and, holding the sign with one hand and the huge hammer in the other, gently tap the sign back in. I had painted many of these signs myself the summer after I graduated from high school, and now many need replacing. The wood splinters a little when I step back to give the sign a final whack, but it stands firm.

Back in the truck and I'm on my way. No customers and no deer. I am moving along in good time. Danny runs alongside me, and I rev the engine, racing up the hill so that he has to run full tilt in order to beat me to the next ridge. There, at the hedgerow, I slow down to pass into the next orchards, to scan the trees on my right. They all are Mutsu apples, most of them planted on my eighteenth birthday. Now they produce some of our fastest-selling and most lucrative fruit. Almost every tree I see is picked clean. I drive on, following the road down now into a mature orchard bordered on all sides by plantings of oaks and maples and conifer trees. Just before the next hedgerow I pass an enormous hemlock that my mother had always called the wild bee tree because wild bees nested in its top. The trunk was so wide I could not get my arms around half of it, and trillium grew beneath its draping limbs.

Soon I am in the backlands, where long lines of trees spread to the woods and the old railroad bed where the Hudson & Boston line had once passed through. Stone walls bound this orchard on all sides, although the woods have crept up over them so that the only use we ever put them to was to head our horses over them as we rode, way too fast, through the trails my father and uncle had cut through the woods.

The truck bounces easily along the soft orchard grass, and I can't help speeding up a little, remembering how my horse, snorting in the spring air, would always take off the minute we came bounding out of the woods and his feet touched this springy orchard turf and how I would let him. In the center of this back orchard rises a twisted oak tree, which, like the hemlock, has a trunk far too wide to stretch one's arms around. I park the truck on a level area near the tree and head out to walk the back rows by foot. During my childhood one of the last vestiges of my grandfather's many farm improvements had stood here: a corncrib, which by then was empty, the weathered gray boards slanting like an enormous dilapidated rib cage.

I walk down long rows of ten- and fifteen-foot trees,

thirty- and forty-year-old McIntosh, Red Delicious and Cortland trees that my father considered too productive to replace with semidwarf stock. On either side of me the tall trees here are acrobats, strong limbs arching up and over, down and out. They are beautiful, like huge silver spiders, and a short history of pruning shows in their arched and jointed limbs. When they were young, the trees were open-center pruned according to the thinking of the day so that they rose in perfect storybook apple tree shape, the top of each tree a green globe of leaves. But one year, after he attended a pruning workshop at the Geneva Agricultural Experimental Station, my father had decided to top the trees, bringing the fruit down low for Pick Your Own. That winter he spent days in the orchard with a chain saw and several men cutting off the upper limbs so that the trees were forced to spread down, letting light into the center to color the fruit.

Most of the trees look pretty well picked over to me, with only scattered pockets of fruit in the upper limbs. I make a mental note to tell my father to have some ladders set out here tomorrow, and I whistle for Danny. Soon a white and brown blur appears. Delirious with the scent of deer and other animals, he races back to me, pretending that he can't stop and must crash into my legs. This time I let him jump in the cab with me, and we ride back together, each of us sticking our head out our side window to get a better view. I drive to the opposite end of the orchard and exit there, crossing the hedgerow by a small wooded pond that had a pump in it to fill the spray rig when I was growing up. Because the water was used to fill the spray rig and the sprays were added to the tank there, we weren't allowed to swim in the back pond. But the bank was gradual enough and firm enough for our horses to walk in without slipping, so we would often ignore our parents' warning and take our horses swimming there.

As we drive by, a duck flashes up, and I have to lunge for Danny's collar to keep him from leaping out the window of the moving truck. In a few minutes we are heading up again, over the hill, through the hedgerow and back to where we started. A huge white pine tree towers over the road here, and I stop for a moment under its swaying limbs to look across the meadow at the house pond. In the settled light, the water shimmers, a bronze gray disk framed with willows. Danny and I study the smooth surface.

The pond is a place where things happen. When the ice breaks in spring, the open water provides a rest stop for blue herons, migrating geese and wild ducks. Flocks of red-winged blackbirds love to perch in the swaying willow limbs, where they squabble. By late summer the edges blaze yellow and red with jewel and fireweed. All winter wild turkeys would leave their tracks across its surface. It is a spring-fed pond, dug thirteen feet deep, and was designed by my uncle as an engineering project when he was still in graduate school. It was our childhood swimming hole, but these days only a muskrat family and at least one large snapping turtle swim in its murky water.

Nobody there today. I put the truck back in gear and let the wheels pick up speed as we roll down the long hill, around the meadow, then another hill and back to the house and barns. As I pull into the barnyard, I catch up to a green minivan, the last customer of the day. Once the van stops, two children leap out and run across the barnyard, then down the hill, chasing each other, falling and laughing through the bright leaves. A man gets out next. I hear the kitchen door slam.

"Got it, Mom," I shout toward the house, and walk over to add up their tally. It doesn't take me long to take their pair of crisp twenty-dollar bills and hand back change, but the man doesn't seem in any hurry to leave.

"How old are these barns?" he asks, looking toward the three barns, built at right angles to one another, forming a large open barnyard.

"About the same age as the house, I think," I answer. "The house is almost two hundred years." It occurs to me that I don't really know when the barns were built or by whom. It will be a long time before I discover that kerf marks in the timbers indicate that they were milled before 1820. Or that the triangular martin holes cut into the south side of the loft indicate an early Dutch barn-building practice. We both look at the barns for a moment.

"Still run by your family, right?" asks the man.

"Yes," I say without hesitation.

"Good. Keep it that way."

"We're trying," I answer with a laugh, which he echoes.

Then he adds, "You know, I do a little building. I like to work with wood. Those barns"—he nods toward the complex—"they're old, that's really something."

As if on cue, a lemony band of fading sun moves down through the trees to strike the siding along one barn. It is as if this last glance of sun has found the long-forgotten colors in the graying barns, and for a moment they don't look so dilapidated, the long boards so old they seem ready to slide off. Even the black lines of strap hinges, forged sometime before the Civil War, look blacker, more definite where they secure doors and windows.

The man calls his children, and when they pile into the van, he turns the key and they zoom off. I stuff the twenty-dollar bills into the blue vinyl bank bag and quickly pull the zipper. Long stripes of shadow have begun to pull away from the resting ladders like peels of fruit. I hurry toward the packinghouse and pull the enormous doors shut.

In the open shed area of the farm office, I stop to pull out a tarp to throw over the apples, although we no longer have animals we have to worry about getting into the fruit. Jostled by the thick canvas, an apple rolls out of the box and stops at my feet. An Ida Red, *Pyrus malus,* as large as a small grapefruit. A good half pound. I recognize it as one of the Ida Reds we had picked in early September to show in the fair. It had been left behind because it had a slight bump on the bottom. Fair entries must have size, color and perfect conformation. I had picked the fruit with my mother and Willi, the man who now does all the tractor work—spraying and mowing, plowing and disking—for the farm. My father, unable to walk far, watched from the truck, bending over to choose from among the apples we brought in. When looking over a pile of apples, my father had an eye for choosing a winning plate, the set of six that complemented one another, making the whole group glow. On the tree, however, it was my mother who could spot the winners.

I brush the dust off the smooth surface. There on the bottom is the small bump, like a callus, the touch of scab that roughened the surface and disqualified the apple. Back in March, when the blossoms were setting, warm, wet days had sent scab spores migrating across the orchards. Spraying was not possible until petal fall because the sprays that could kill the scab would also kill the blossoms. Scab that overwintered in the fallen leaves had a heyday, setting out with each warm wind, infecting and blighting entire orchards, while farmers waited, helpless until the rain stopped so that they could get their rigs through the orchards and apply a spray. We had been lucky and were saved from the epidemic that had hit most Columbia County growers. Our orchards had been clean the year before, so few inocula were present in the dead leaves wintering over under the snow. This scab had probably blown up from the abandoned orchard that now bordered ours to the south among an emerging housing development.

Generally, winds here come from the west and don't blow too much inoculum up from the South Place. Still, a spore inoculum must have penetrated this apple's blossom, pushing its way inside the sepal of the flower and moving down through the fruit bud. Perhaps it came on the feet of a pollinating bee. By May the spray rig had made its rounds, shooting out fungicides to kill the scab, but where spores had landed on this tiny, yet-to-emerge apple, the fungus had blemished the skin.

No one knows exactly how flowering happens, that mystery by which some plant cells are chosen and instructed to develop as flowers rather than as stems, leaves or wood, although botanists have identified a hypothetical plant hormone that they call florigen. I am not consumed by the desire to know more about the mystery by which vegetative cells change to those with what botanists call floral initiation, but I am deeply envious of the synchrony that whispers to each cell, "Get ready, expand, flower." On St. Patrick's Day I had walked out to check block thirteen. That orchard, planted on a west-facing slope, was a warm pocket, and sure enough, the tiny, bullet-shaped fruit buds on the Ida Reds had cracked, revealing layers of leaf and blossom still covered with a silver fuzz. The swollen buds were just opening into silver tip. One week later pussy willows had sent up their own silver points, the back pond was yellow with marsh marigolds and the apple blossoms were in full silver tip, green tip and then tight cluster.

In late April the bloom began in earnest. The orchards were dizzy with bees, and along the sides and in the woods, the ground was feathered white with wind anemones and bloodroot. To walk in the orchards was to believe that there could never be a winter. Thick green grass was overtaking the brown stalks of winter grass. Birds were delirious. I put my ear to the cool ground and heard it buzz.

I stood on the top of the ridge and let the soft wind travel my face. When my father turned seventy that April, we had the first of our apple blossom parties, a large picnic in the orchards with dozens of friends. To celebrate his birthday, my family gave my father Danny, an English springer spaniel, like the kind his father had kept for hunting. My father and his brother had spent summer evenings chasing spaniels across the lawns in order to kennel them in their runs by the smokehouse. He was delighted with the wriggling pup. My father was recovering from his mysterious collapse the previous summer. None of us knew yet that his body was struggling to breathe with only 30 percent of his lungs still functioning, the rest damaged by years of smoking and by the tanks of Guthion, Lannate, Alar, Captan and Manzate that he himself had sprayed on the orchards to save money during those years when the farm, recently divided, could not yet afford to hire a man to apply the sprays. Unwilling to believe that the sprays were really that lethal, my father didn't take seriously the need for protective clothing.

Within two weeks of the orchard picnic, the silver apple buds were green pearls. By June they had blown up to the size of golf balls, still green but showing the promise of size and beautiful shape. Weeks of rain and heat through July swelled the fruit to fantastic size. By mid-August, while we battled mite infestations, my father worried that if the days of perfect August sun that followed were interrupted by any more rain, the fruit cells would expand too quickly, resulting in mushy fruit. Just in time the August haze lifted, and September days were clear and, most important, cool. As soon as the temperatures dropped, the leaves responded, producing ethylene, which signals the fruit to ripen. Each night along the branches where clusters of apples hung, starches turned to sugars, pectic compounds changed shape and flavor esters were produced. Then a farmer's dream. Snappy nights the first week of September that put a stop to chlorophyll formation so that the shy pigments—anthocyanin, carotene and xanthophyll—were revealed and the apples turned pink and rosy, mauve and scarlet, russet, burgundy, tawny and, like the apple now in my hand, the parrot colors of bright yellow and fire engine red.

I have a sudden impulse to bite the apple in my hand, crunch down into those vibrant colors. But I have already eaten so many apples since breakfast that I have lost count. I throw the apple into the box with the others and secure the tarp over its top.

Out of habit I glance at the house, where by now my father is certainly waiting. Talavera, William W. Van Ness's old mansion, glows between the trees. I have a lot to tell my father about how the day has gone in the orchards. We need four more good weekends for the farm to break even. As late as 1935 more than four hundred orchards existed in Columbia County. Today fewer than forty remain. The price of ap-

15

ples is just too low to keep up with the costs of spray and fertilizer, labor and taxes on this increasingly valuable land.

I grab the bank bag and the basket of tallies and turn to look west for a moment, out and down the farm drive. The light, chimeric now, flattens the blue mountains until they seem mere cutouts pasted against the darkening sky. Reassured by these harvest colors, by the rosy orange light, by the boxes of red, red fruit, by the barns standing the way they always have and by the money bag, now fat with bills, I stop worrying about the farm's ongoing struggle to pay its bills. What a good day we have had in the orchards, each row cascading with the sight of bright red fruit. I feel the way I did when I was fifteen and had just come back from riding, sweaty and tired but completely at ease. Talavera, that familiar place, that resting stop, always the same, always there. A place where dream and reality never collide because there is no distinction. Like the shadows, stretched confidently out into the barnyard, striping the cooling dirt, I know where I am when I am here. I am home.

By the time I head up to the house, my calves ache from the constant walking, and my arms circling the basket of tally slips and receipts feel tired too, but I don't care. I think about my next job, the day's count. As I get closer to the house, however, I see that my father has been waiting for me on the back porch. Is that really my father? His bent figure could be a hunched silhouette in an Edward Hopper painting. The face is half hidden, chiseled with blue shadows. But even without looking, I can tell you every detail of how he sits there, his large hands clutched around his drink, the knuckles chapped and scraped from work. His face, gaunt, worried, brightening when someone appears, but otherwise still. There he sits on the porch, staring out over the view he loves. If I follow his gaze, my eyes take in the sloping lawn, the meadow punctuated by the round pond with its willows, the rise of the hill, the parklike hedgerows and plantings and the lines of hearty young dwarf apple trees, but what is the landscape that my father sees? After fifty years of running the orchards, does he think of the land in fruit-growing terms? *Leaf color bad on the plums by the pond, remember to add nitrogen this winter. The top row of young Delicious, outperforming the others, plant more there. A bad frost pocket on the dip where we put the young Macouns.*

Or does my father feel something less direct, less tangible or considered, his own father's heavy touch upon the land, an expectation, an obligation? Does the sight of the round pond in the meadow that my uncle designed cut my father with sadness, as he thinks of that happier time before his brother became ill? Is it the soft reach of my grandmother's voice he hears there, her poems every holiday, the parties, her blue dresses? Petunias and asters cascading from crystal vases placed throughout the house? Tall orange gladiolus under the banjo clock in the hall? The knowledge that wherever they lived or traveled, they would return to Talavera, their home? Perhaps it is nothing coherent, articulated or even thought. No specific memory or memories at all, but that complicated sense of belonging to a landscape, of knowing the press of light on the hills as surely as one knows one's own palm. I will never know exactly what holds my father to this place so strongly, but I will always wonder.

The October evening has already grown cold, and my father should be wearing a sweater over his blue flannel shirt. But he will not think to check if he needs one before he sits down, his evening drink in hand, and once seated at the round picnic table on the back porch, his long legs scrunched up under the bench, he will not want to get up and go back inside. Neither will he call into the kitchen and ask my mother, who is busy making dinner, to get a sweater for him. I have never known if my father did not mind discomfort or if he grew up so attended to that waiting patiently to be served has become a habit that he has never outgrown. But perhaps my father is so glad to have completed his day of mandatory resting and to be enjoying his

17

end-of-the-day ritual that he does not mind the chill already making its way up his back.

As I get closer to the house, I see my father's silhouette more clearly, and anxiety rises through me. How thin and frail his shoulders look under his blue flannel shirt. His thick hair, tousled as usual, is more gray than I remember. And his face, with its long family cheekbones, square jaw and prominent nose—the old patroon's face is gaunt. My perpetually tanned good-looking father is old. Out of habit I begin to rush. I clutch the basket with receipts and the money bag a little tighter. It must have been a record day.

Ahead of me, Danny bounds across the lawn and charges up the back porch stairs. Without hesitating, he rushes to the kitchen door and claws at the screen door enthusiastically until it opens enough for him to squeeze his body through. The door bangs after him. I can hear my mother, busy stirring dinner, greet him. I do not follow but ascend the steps, two at a time, and walk over to where my father sits at the table outside the door to the office.

"Hi, Dad." Immediately I fall into my childhood role as my father's eager helper. "Empires are picked clean except for a row by the M-Nines, and there's not much Red Delicious left in the far back. I'd say we had a good day."

Although I have been reporting on the progress of the harvest since morning, my father nods and looks pleased. His eyes, a deep smoky blue, hold no worry. How I love it when his eyes look that way, clear and satisfied. He takes a sip from his drink.

"I'll do the count," I say, putting the bank bag down on the table and pulling up a bench.

"Why don't you take a break? We can do that later," my father says. His voice is quiet. I look at him and smile. My father could bark out orders one minute as if he were still a U.S. Marine, then surprise me with his gentleness.

"All right," I say, and sit. We are silent the way we often are, sharing a kind of intimacy that is not about the exchange of information. As usual, my father does not ask me about myself, and only the extremity of his illness makes it seem okay for me to inquire about him. It has always been like this, and what makes this moment feel close and not cold or distant, I couldn't say exactly, but I know it has something to do with the way we both love the place around us yet feel the heavy weight of its past as well.

"How are you feeling, Dad?" I finally ask.

"Not bad, it's just the breathing." My father shakes his head slightly and clucks as if observing bad weather, not the state of his failing lungs. "I've got to get some breathing lessons. Then I think I can beat this thing."

"What about seeing a specialist?" I ask, hopeful. "There must be an emphysema institute somewhere; they probably have new treatments—" Midsentence I stop myself, realizing that I am talking faster and faster. That my father is not really listening. That I am falling into my other role of wanting to fix everything.

"Yes, that's a good idea," my father says vaguely, but I can tell that he is saying the words only to make me feel better. I promise myself to make some phone calls when I return to Cambridge.

Yet perhaps my father's quiet this evening is of a different order. He has even less to say than usual. For a while I accompany him, the chill of the evening swirling around us, the soft chirr of insects and the busy calling of birds filling the gaps where words might be. It seems as if we sit there forever and for no time at all. Then I notice that the sunset has faded to a whisper of light. It is late.

"Dad, I better start the count," I say, louder than I intend. "I've got a long drive ahead."

My father nods. "Sure, let's get started." He looks down. It's an ambivalent gesture. I know that he is disappointed.

The screen door bangs as Danny leaps out onto the porch, bounds over to my father and pushes his head into my father's lap.

"Hi, Danny boy." My father's large hands stroke the springer's head in generous fumbling gestures, and the dog

19

wriggles in pleasure. I hear the tenderness in my father's voice as he speaks to the dog, and I forget about my life in Cambridge. I am ten years old again.

"Lift," shouts my father, and I do. I am sitting on the wheel guard of the old Case tractor, one hand holding on to the metal seat where my father sits, the other grasping the rope that operates the lift mechanism on the hay rake. Sun presses through my T-shirt and my perfectly worn blue jeans. A stalk of hay is caught in the toe of my favorite blue Keds with the hole above the toe. We come to the end of the row and this time, right on cue, I yank the rope so that the hay rake lifts with a screech of metal and a tawny hump of straw falls out. My father turns the tractor and we start back across the meadow. My left arm has begun to ache with the effort of hanging on to the back of the metal tractor seat while the tractor bumps along, but I don't care. My ears fill with the powerful grind of the engine on each turn, and I love the smells of sweat and oil and exhaust as much as I love the hot sun beating down, turning everything golden. I am working with my father and that is all I will ever need.

"I guess I'll get some tea first," I say, and go into the kitchen. When I come back out with a steaming mug of tea for me and a plate of cheese and crackers for my father, I see that he has already begun to list figures on the page and has completed a rough count of the money that I'd brought up from the barn over the course of the day.

"Dad," I say, putting the tea and crackers on the table, then sitting down, "I've been thinking. Next spring I want to come stay for a couple of weeks and paint the barns. I can take some time off if I really work hard now."

"That would be great," he says simply, and takes a piece of cheese.

"I think June," I say, and in that moment I am only thinking about how good it would feel to run a brush over the beat-up old boards, leaving them a dark russet red.

My father balances another piece of cheese on a cracker, then puts the whole thing awkwardly into his mouth. He does not disturb my daydream, even though he knows what I know. My idea is absurd. Painting the barns would take far more than two weeks even if I did devote that much time to working here. I am the one who finally changes the subject.

"What was the rough count?"

"Up from last year, I'm sure," my father says, and I immediately understand the buoyancy in his voice. Earning more on the harvest than the previous year is always our goal, and this year we have made it. I am thrilled. I look at my father and know that I am grinning.

"Let's do the count here," I say.

My father answers without hesitation, "Okay."

I go inside to get the other bundles of today's cash from the green box in the closet where they have been stashed. We will each count the total amount of cash brought up from the barn, then compare our figures. It is a long process that begins by sorting, then counting the number of bills in each denomination so that they are ready for the bank deposit bag. We will each do this to avoid mistakes.

Usually my father would have never permitted us to do the count there on the porch, where a late customer, driving up to the back porch, could see the money. "Don't get sloppy," he might have said. But things are different today.

This has been a better harvest. For the past two years a frost in May, then rains during the fall have killed Pick Your Own sales, so that the farm didn't meet expenses even with my parents working without wages as usual. But this year has been miraculously rain free. Days like today with its warm wind and constant sun inspired people from Westchester and Manhattan, Queens and Long Island to drive north. Many of our customers have come to pick at our farm since the sixties, when my parents first had the idea of having people come in to pick as an alternative to packing out wholesale with Jamaican picking crews. Many have come for two generations or more. Just as many speak English with heavy Italian, German and Polish accents or come from places like Korea, the Philippines, Thailand and Vietnam.

21

Over the years we have come to know which groups prefer what apples and pears, and these preferences tend not to vary. Asian pickers want sweet apples like Red and Yellow Delicious and Mutsu. These are given as gifts, eaten as dessert fruits and prized for appearance and size. Italian pickers, many of whom have families that emigrated to the Hudson Valley in the late nineteenth century to work in the iron mills, seek a good pie apple like a Cortland and most of all want Bosc and Seckel pears.

Beautiful Bosc pears with only a touch of psylla fly damage had delighted the Italian customers this year. "You still got Boscos?" I had been asked all day, and when I led them to the rows of tall trees still loaded with brown fruit, they hurried out of their cars to set to work.

Periodically I had driven up to the house to give my father reports on how the day was progressing:

"The only good Cortlands left in number eleven are too high to get without ladders. I think it's time to move to the dogleg or orchard sixteen."

"The Filipinos are spread out on their usual spot at the top of thirteen. Danny's been there all morning filching food from the picnic. This year they're roasting meat!"

"The pickers just can't keep out of the Mutsu, so I've taken the new boy out and posted him there as orchard patrol."

"A group of Italian women want to pick watercress from the irrigation ditch. Said you told them they could last year. I couldn't think of why they shouldn't, so I said yes. They're down there now."

But today my father had been only mildly interested in such news. That alone should have told me everything, but I was too rushed to notice. I hadn't stayed inside with him long. I told myself that I was on orchard duty, that he wanted me busy on the farm the way he would have been, on the move all day. But now I realize that this is only half the truth. I couldn't stand to see my father the way he was, head back in a chair, feet up, resting. I rushed back out to join the crowds of cheerful pickers, reveling in the glorious October weather and the rows of trees studded with fruit.

All day customers had asked me about my father. "Best apples in years," they'd say, "but where is that man who we usually see? Where is the tall man? Where is your father?" I had mumbled that he was resting, then changed the subject.

By afternoon I was encountering the usual problems. So many cars had parked in one spot that a traffic jam had ensued. A bunch of nine-year-olds were throwing apples. The ladders I had just placed in block eleven for people to reach the pears had dropped in the grass. At three o'clock the bus from a Baptist church in Queens arrived right on schedule but then promptly drove to the exact spot where they got stuck last year and had to be pulled out by a tractor.

But all in all, as if in response to the gorgeous weather and the fine fruit, customers had been better behaved than usual. When I made early evening rounds, I found that the picnic crowds had carefully cleaned up their garbage. No hastily flung diapers had to be fished out from under trees. The ladders that I had reset in the afternoon were leaning neatly against the trees, and I found no piles of fruit dumped by an overzealous picker who then decided not to pay.

On my way back I had stopped to look at the McIntosh whips and had encountered a strange and wonderful sight: a blue minivan parked by the ridge with its doors open. Inside sat four saffron-robed Thai monks busily eating apples; their driver, a man dressed in black, waved from where he was still picking under a tree. The monks waved when I drove by and kept on eating and chatting, their saffron robes glowing as they sat hunched in the back of the minivan. I knew not to try to talk to these monks, although I wanted to know where they were from. In Thailand I once brushed the robe of a monk by accident on a crowded Bangkok street. He immediately prostrated himself. By touching him, even accidentally, I made him unclean because I was a woman. The thought of some of our Red Delicious piled high on the altar of a gilded Thai Buddha seemed like another fine omen.

23

Most notable this year perhaps was that my three brothers, my sister and I were working together without our usual bickering. Were we sobered by our father's collapse or responding to the great optimism of this harvest? Whatever the case, he was different too. When each weekend one of us stepped in to run the Pick Your Own operation, he was uncritical of our efforts, staying out of the way and letting us do the job. In previous harvests his silver truck would have been heard zooming through the orchard rows. All day he would have been on the move, looking and fretting, moving ladders, talking to pickers, fussing over the placement of signs, annoying all of us with constant commands. Back at the house, the weather radio would have been on full volume, blaring out hourly reports of weather in the Hudson Valley. But this year my father has only turned the weather radio on each evening to listen for frost warnings. His silver pickup sat idly by the back door.

This time, when I step out onto the back porch, my arms are full of money, packets of bills held by a rubber band. I drop the bundles on the table in front of my father, and some of them bounce slightly, as the rubber bands hit the hard wooden surface. My father reaches over and pulls the band off one bundle, then begins to sort the bills. I pull the dollars out from the blue bag. The change spills on the table.

"Put the bag count in first," my father reminds me.

I nod and count out thirty dollars of ones, fives and coins and put that back in the bank bag so that it is ready for making change for customers tomorrow. Now I begin to sort through the remaining pile of money. Quarters, dimes and nickels get stacked into rows. Then I begin to lay the bills out on the table, one pile for each denomination. My father takes a stack and makes his own piles. He lays each bill down carefully, each one facing the same way, right side up. Soon he comes across a piece of paper with initials and an amount written on it and squints at it, then scowls.

"I can't read this damn thing," he says, and hands the paper to me.

I take it and read an IOU for forty dollars signed by my mother.

"I wish people wouldn't do that," my father says grumpily. "We have to keep the house expenses separate."

"Mom just didn't have time," I say quickly, hoping to head off my parents' age-old fight over two different styles of bookkeeping.

"That's no excuse," he says.

In a way he is right, but as usual he is also forgetting about all the demands on my mother, most notably the fact that he is now disabled. I knew that she had hurried off to get groceries while I was there because she does not want to leave my father alone.

We resume sorting. When the table is covered with faded green faces—Washington, Hamilton, Lincoln, Jefferson—we begin the count. My father leans over and grasps the pile of twenties, then shakes it slightly like a cook weighing a piece of meat.

"Eighteen hundred," he says, then puts the pile down.

I look at him and smile. I know this game. I pick up the stack and weigh it in my own hands; then I also guess at the total of the twenty-dollar bills there.

"Seventeen hundred and eighty." I put the bills down. "Hey, Mom," I shout into the kitchen, "can you come here?"

"What?" she calls back.

"The count," I say, speaking shorthand.

My mother appears with her "I'm busy" look on her face, but she doesn't hesitate to come over to where we sit.

"Here," I say, handing her the stack, "take a guess."

My father is grinning, wide and boyish.

My mother shakes the wad and purses her lips. "Exactly nineteen hundred," she says, squinting, "and just watch, I'll be right."

The phone rings and my mother disappears. My father and I begin to count our piles of bills. When I was ten, eleven, twelve, even thirteen, this ritual of the harvest

25

seemed magic. We couldn't really be poor with so much money piling up. All day the money poured in as if from nowhere. And the harvest with its endless bounty lasted weeks. I eagerly helped at the barns, hurrying up to the line of waiting cars, counting bags of fruit, identifying varieties, answering questions. Then came the hard task of writing up receipts, counting up numbers while customers stared, scrutinizing my addition. I tolerated their glances. I rarely made mistakes, and I knew that in a moment they would hand me a twenty or a fifty and then I'd get to run to the small table and make change, dipping my fingers into the bowls of change and grabbing a fistful of ones that I would dispense slowly into the hands of the waiting adults. By the end of the afternoon my throat would be burning dry from the dust swirling up from car tires, but I felt elated. I would push the money from apple sales into the pockets of my blue jeans until they bulged so high the cloth tightened around my legs, making it hard to walk.

When we gathered in the library in the evening, emptying our pockets was the start of the count. What heaven to pull out handfuls of the hot, crushed bills and to do it confidently, carelessly so that they fell to the floor, scattering like leaves. Sometimes when the bills were scooped up and carefully unfolded, a hundred-dollar bill was revealed. I would finger it in amazement. Enough money back then to buy the ten-speed I was saving up for, but it never occurred to me to take any of this money for myself. So many bills soft and loose under my touch, and I wanted oh so many things. But harvest money was not like the quarters I filched from under the table where my father emptied his pockets at night, always spilling a little change onto the floor. Harvest money, like everything else at Talavera, was of this world but not of it too. The past sanctified everything. I also knew, without knowing anything about that history and without anyone's saying so, that this past meant everything. Harvest money was farm money; it was sacred.

After the count, done by the fire in the library, it would

be time to call the dogs and drive the money bag to Hudson to drop it in the night deposit chute at the bank. I usually volunteered to go along as a lookout, just in case of robbers. "Get the six-shooter," my cousin would shout if he was there, and insist on getting out the six-chambered pistol that my father had carried in World War II from where it was locked in the gun closet. The dogs jumped in the car, grinning and drooling. The drive to Hudson and the night deposit chute took only ten minutes, and in that sleepy part of town meeting a mugger was about as likely as stumbling upon a great horned owl, but I'd be getting ready for my dash to the bank deposit chute, one hand on the car door handle, the other clutching the locked canvas bag. Under the glare of the high-intensity streetlamps, the silver door marked "Hudson City Savings" glistened dangerously.

While the driver waited, I'd sprint as fast as I could to the box, jam in the key, turn the lock, pull open the heavy metal door, then push the bag in and slam the chute closed. Only when I heard the bag's satisfying thump at the bottom of the chute did I breathe a sigh of relief. Then I'd climb back in the car, pat the dogs and begin trying to convince whoever was driving, either my father or one of my brothers, to stop at Dunkin' Donuts on the way home.

Time was nothing then, unlike today, when the counting has begun to feel like yet another chore I have to finish before I can leave. Before I realize it, I am thinking about my long drive back to Cambridge and the pile of work waiting on my desk when I get there. I have counted my stacks twice, and I am still waiting for my father to finish counting his stack of ones and fives. Methodically he sorts the bills with his large hands, but periodically one or two bills fall off the table and float to the floor. I lean over and pick them up, but my father is so busy squinting in order to see the numbers he is writing down that he doesn't notice. How tired and cold I now feel.

I tell my father that I am going in to get a sweater. When I come back out, I bring one for him as well.

"Thanks, Lele," my father says, using my pet name as he takes the sweater. He pulls the sweater over his head and continues counting, but not before I hear it: the hoarse rasp of his breath caused by the small exertion of putting on his sweater. Seventy percent of my father's lungs are filled with fluid. He is slowly drowning. Is there really nothing anyone can do?

My father has gone back to his counting without bothering to arrange his shirt, and it sticks out in an uncomfortable-looking bunch at the neck. He looks old then and weathered like the boards of those falling-apart barns. Once again I feel overwhelmed: the young trees that need training; the signs to be fixed; the barns nude of paint; my father, who can hardly breathe. Why can't he at least fix his collar?

"Dad, your collar," I say, and even though I try, I can't keep the frustration from my voice.

"Oh, thanks," he says absently.

Finally, he is done with his count, and we compare figures. I read off mine first. "I get one thousand eight hundred and sixty in twenties—hey, Mom's the winner. What about you?"

"I get—" my father squints down at his writing and studies it. Suddenly he pushes the paper toward me. "I can't read these numbers."

"I can," I say quickly, and lean over the paper. My father's handwriting, always long and slanted with decisive angular strokes, has become faltering. At first I can't read the numbers either; the sevens look like ones and the fives could be eights. I rapidly study the lines until I can make out a series of figures that match mine.

"You got one thousand eight hundred and sixty as well. Looks like Mom's the winner," I say quickly. My father chuckles.

I compare the figures from our separate counts. The total for the day comes to $2,955. When I flip back the pages of the black-bound farm journal, it appears that we have made at least twice what we did last year.

"A record day," I say, closing the book.

"Could be," my father says, and begins to arrange the piles of bills into stacks for the bank deposit, "but I don't think so. Mutsus came on a week early this year. You can't go just by the calendar."

"Still, it's good, isn't it?"

"Very good." Then my father adds, "Thanks for all your help today."

His words catch me off guard, and I say only a mumbled "You bet." Still, I am pleased and surprised by his remark. Then my father begins to cough, and again everything in me cracks. He doesn't cough long or hard, not nearly as deeply as when he smoked and his hacking cough would echo through the house. But even this shallow clearing of his throat is enough to leave him panting for breath. And it is as if I too were drowning, in frustration and grief and fear. They rise up and engulf any feeling of sympathy that I might have for my father. I am mad at him for fifty years of smoking, for never seeing a specialist, for ending up sick. Under the table my fingers clench and I tell him that I had better get myself ready to leave. All I want right then is just to get in my car and drive away.

29

⁂

What would we do differently if like Cassandra, we could see the future? I do not know it, but this evening will be the last time that I see my father alive. In two weeks he will call me at the number where I am staying in Brooklyn to say that he just wanted to make sure we were on for meeting the next day. Such a call was unusual for my father, and putting down the phone, I will be pleased, thinking that finally my formal, old-world Dutch father was reaching out to me instead of the other way around. And he was finally going to see a lung specialist. I was planning to meet my mother and him in Manhattan the next day after his appointment. We talked about the prognosis. My father's voice was thin; mine was eager and hopeful.

"Dad, I'm really glad you're coming down. There's a whole emphysema institute now doing research, new ideas about treatment—"

"Well, I hope so. I have to lick this thing."

"You will. Maybe it will take some time, but you will."

"We probably won't be done until after lunch."

"Okay, I'll be here, just call when you're free . . . Dad?"

"Hmm?"

"I'm really glad that you're coming down."

"Yes, well, see you tomorrow then."

"Yes, see you tomorrow."

We will never meet. A half hour after he puts down the phone, while my mother is helping him get ready to leave, my father will lean down to reach for his boots and his heart will constrict, once, maybe twice, and then stop. My mother will hear him fall and rush back into the bathroom with his socks. By the time the rescue team races upstairs, they only confirm what my mother already knows. My father is dead.

30

☙

Only. That moment with its crushing awareness has not yet come. I am still back in time's sweet web, sitting with my father while the sunset fades, while birds and a light whisper of a wind signal the coming of night. Leaves are dropping from the trees, each one glazed with sun. But I see only the aftermath: bright swatches of color on the lawn. These will be the last moments that I share with my father. How I wish I could say that I am cherishing him, but I am not. I am worried about a bunched collar, some dropped dollar bills, irritated by his handwriting, which I cannot read. I wait impatiently for him to finish sorting the bills. I feel pursued by the silent yellow house looming up around us, by the hopelessly old barns and especially by the relentless work of the harvest. I am not conscious of history, or if I am, it is simply that escalator back to a better time, back then, when the family was rich and the farm prosperous.

CHAPTER THREE

Claverack, 1732

*I*n 1732, Willem Van Ness (1711–1790), the son of a well-to-do farming and merchant family from Halve Maen just north of Albany, married the daughter of an equally well-established Dutch family some forty miles south, in Claverack. Willem was the great-grandson of a brewer named Cornelius Van Ness, who acquired fame in New Netherlands for feuding with the sheriff. This feud took a new turn when Cornelius's wife knocked the sheriff off his horse with a broom. The family packed their belongings and the already parched sheets of paper recording Admiral Van Ness's sea voyages and moved to a location somewhat south of Beverywyck, or Albany. Willem Van Ness inherited his ancestor's travel account and his great-grandfather's intolerance for authority.

The young woman whom Willem moved south to marry was Gertrude Hogeboom. She was born into a landed family in Claverack, meaning that they were definitely not tenants, those at the bottom of the economic spectrum of the manor system in the Hudson Valley. But they did not have lordship privileges either. Interestingly, Willem Van Ness and his bride did not set up their household on Hogeboom land. Instead, they began to clear a 294-acre reach of land along the Old Post Road, not far from the Mohican hunting camp of Pot Koke on Claverack Creek.

Traditionally understood to be the southernmost tip of Rensselaerswyck Manor, although in eighteenth-century New York, property borders could shift depending upon who employed the mapmaker, this land may have been initially leased by Willem. By 1790, however, his will clearly passed ownership of the land down to his son William. *"Mack ik aen my soon Willem Van Ness en syn erfgename en assins al myne stad . . ."* read the faded will, written in Hudson Valley Dutch, which went on to delegate one plow to his son Peter but the house and land, barns, tools and other livestock to the eldest son, William, who was responsible for caring for his mother.

When I finally found the old will, I studied it carefully, looking, among other things, for any mention of slaves. It was the practice of early Dutch farmers in New York to hire laborers to help clear land and work their farms. Many owned slaves. By 1714 the Claverack census listed a population of 216, 19 of whom were black slaves. I suspected that descendants from Van Ness slaves still lived in the area, for I knew of several black families just north in Kinderhook who had the surname Van Ness. But I found no slaves listed in Willem's will at that time, a fact that, for the moment anyway, filled me with relief.

Farmers like Willem were motivated by the demand for wheat and potatoes coming from New York City. Wheat from the Van Ness farm may have also found its way onto Livingston Manor trading ships bound for the West Indies. These ships, loaded with wheat flour and grain, among other stuffs, traded such products for more exotic items, including slaves. Willem Van Ness could well have made an increasing profit each year. He soon built what for that time was a large Dutch-style farmhouse and raised a barn complex nearby.

This early founding date of 1732 for the Van Ness farm

was significant, for most of the valley at the time was divided up into huge manorial estates, an Old World model of tenant and manor lord rather than the ideal of the yeoman, or independent farmer. Rensselaerswyck Manor was largely disbanded by then in the Claverack area, but just to the south of Claverack Creek began Livingston Manor, a holding of almost one million acres. Livingston tenants generally worked hundred-acre parcels and paid rent in schepels of wheat. Robert Livingston, the first manor lord, calculated that by the late 1700s the average tenant farm was producing an income of eleven to fourteen pounds or twenty-eight to thirty dollars. A take of ten bushels of wheat per acre was considered good.

Tenants and manor lords lived at the opposite ends of an economic spectrum. While a typical tenant farmer would have eaten dinner in a farmhouse that probably had a dirt floor, the Livingstons dined on seven-course meals, attended by the many servants who also lived with the family in their Hudson River mansion.

33

As a landed farmer, however, Willem Van Ness inhabited the middle ground and was thus well suited to act as something of a go-between, as he did. This was the practice among the landed Dutch families of Claverack, such as the Hogebooms, the Van Nesses and the Van Alens. In the role of landed farmer Willem and later his son William collected rents, advanced the claims of the Livingstons for new lands and, at times of tenant unrest, directed militia forces. It was an affiliation that enabled Van Ness sons to receive gentlemen's educations. Unlike tenants, whose burden of high rents prevented upward movement, Van Ness sons could raise their fortunes. They inhabited the beginnings of America's middle class, a place of opportunity but also of instability and risk. By virtue of hard work, the right marriage and individual talent, they could attain wealth and status. But unlike the sons of manor lords, who had the land to pin their status on come what may, Van Ness sons could also fail.

Talavera, the grand house on the northern end of the

farm, was built in a moment of Van Ness family fortune. By 1807 Willem's grandson William W. Van Ness had risen to considerable acclaim as a lawyer and was appointed judge of the State Supreme Court. Not surprisingly, he decided to build a house that would reflect his passionate belief in the ideals of the new Republic and his social and economic rise. That house was Talavera, a Federal-style mansion whose ornate columns and grand public spaces incorporated diverse and ambitious elements of classical architecture. At Talavera one can see the ideas of Benjamin Latrobe and other leading architects of the day, put together in a personal, at times idiosyncratic way, probably by William W. Van Ness himself. He did not engage a professional architect to plan his house, and the elegant and exotic arrangement of rooms that some scholars attribute to French influences deviates considerably from the Federal-style patterns that would have been typical of that time.

34

It is not possible to date Talavera or the barns exactly for a fire in the Hudson City Courthouse in 1909 burned most of the early property transfer records and Van Ness ledgers that might have detailed payments for bricks, nails, wood and carpenters' fees also did not survive. The house may have taken as many as five years to complete, for Judge Van Ness first mentioned moving into his new house in a letter to his friend and fellow Federalist Colonel Solomon Van Rensselaer, dated November 23, 1812.

Colonel Van Rensselaer had just returned from the War of 1812, during which he was wounded in the attack on Queenston. William W. wrote from Kingston, where he was presiding over the court.

Dear Sir,
In a paper which I have just seen while holding court
in this place, I have with heartfelt satisfaction read the
above, your safe arrival at your own house. . . . As
soon as I have moved into my new house and can
leave home, which will be in about a fortnight, I shall

go to Albany, to tell you in person how much I re-
joice that you are still in the land of the living, and in
the bosom of your family.

With unabated affection and friendship,

Yours &c.

W. W. Van Ness

By the winter of 1812 then, Judge William W. Van Ness
was settled in his stylish new house, which, through the setting out of grounds and the building of a long, curving
drive, signaled the establishment of a country seat in the English tradition. What had begun as a Dutch farm took on a
villa overlay that also signaled a way in which William W. was
choosing to separate from his roots, by then the much-
maligned Dutch tradition of the valley, and to identify with
the rising English establishment. He named his new establishment Talavera, after the Battle of Talavera de la Reina in
Spain, Napoleon's first land defeat. With this exotic name for
his new residence, William W. further established his allegiance to British culture. Now that he was a venerated judge,
no doubt he also chose the name to help correct his earlier,
youthful exuberance in initially supporting the ideals of the
French Revolution.

In keeping with the villa tradition, Talavera was sited on
the top of a hill overlooking a panorama, the Catskill Mountains to the west and the Berkshire foothills to the east. Gardens, initially of Italianate design, were laid down as a series
of terraces that marked a clear separation between the house
grounds and the agricultural lands. Yet these farmlands continued to be farmed. From 1812 on Talavera became a *villa
rustico,* a self-sustaining agricultural estate.

With the building of Talavera, then, Judge William W.
Van Ness signaled not only his desire to live in a house that
reflected the ideals of the new Republic through its very architecture but also, in concrete ways, his family's rise from
landed farmer to landed elite. Not long after the building of
Talavera, his daughter Analiza married Henry Livingston,

the younger son of a manor lord, John Livingston of Oak Hill, and the couple moved into Talavera.

Henry and Analiza Livingston had so many children that soon several more rooms were added to the house. Emma, Herman, Catherine, Henry, William Van Ness, Ancram, Anna and Cornelia were born at Talavera and spent their early childhood there. In a noted portrait by Charles Inman, all eight children are depicted "on the piazza of their father's house," with the Catskills looming up through the trees, a stylized version of the view from Talavera.

Henry Livingston died young, leaving Analiza a widow at Talavera. When she remarried, one year later, ownership of Talavera and much of her husband's Livingston lands in the Ancram area passed on to her son Herman, only eleven years old at the time. Mystery surrounds what happened next. Analiza, the children and her new husband lived at Talavera for several years, but when they moved, they dropped out of the family record.

When Analiza's father died some years earlier, his lands had been split into north and south parcels. The north farm, which Analiza and Henry Livingston had taken over, became known from that point on as the homestead, since it contained Talavera and grounds, while the southern section, on which the original Van Ness farmhouse still stood, was called the South Place. Analiza's aunt had taken over ownership of the South Place after her father's death, but not long after Analiza's remarriage, her aunt's name was on the deed for Talavera as well.

For the next thirty years the family clearly endeavored to keep Judge William W. Van Ness's grand house and the surrounding Van Ness lands in the family. Ownership was transferred back and forth between cousins many times. In 1847 the north and south sections were reunited by Abraham Pierce, a cousin on the Livingston side, and run as one large farm for more than ten years. But by 1855 it had been split into north and south farms again with different branches of the family living on each place. Perhaps even then maintaining the exotic house was more than most family members could afford. Then another cousin, this time on the Philip side, appeared on the scene. He left his rising career in the navy and moved north from Annapolis to throw himself into restoring Judge William W.'s fine house and to seek his fortune by running the farm.

In my father's papers I found notes that my father had made about a letter written by his great-uncle Lieutenant John Van Ness Philip to his mother, Catherine Douw. The letter was dated 1855. According to my father's penciled notes, Lieutenant John Van Ness, then teaching in the newly founded U.S. Naval Academy, had proudly announced: "I can no longer serve my nation through teaching. I am returning home to buy *that* farm." That farm was Talavera, his mother's family homestead, the vast columned house, landscaped grounds and 120-acres plus my father envisioned keeping together by running Philip Orchards.

CHAPTER FOUR

After

After my father's funeral, my mother, my three older brothers, my older sister and I met in the sitting room to decide what to do. We didn't usually gather in that room of the house, a sunny place just to the right of the formal south entrance. We usually gathered in the library, sprawling over the arms of the worn armchairs, one of us sitting in my father's straight-backed chair at the octagonal writing table, one of us pushing aside the dog beds to make room by the fire.

The sitting room was in good repair, for just a few years earlier my parents had replastered the walls and painted them a rich sunflower yellow. The armchair and Georgian sofa had been recently recovered in burnt umber velvet. Perhaps we knew intuitively that we needed the distance, the formality of this room to begin to work out a way forward, a way that didn't include our father. We also needed more chairs, for gathered together we filled the room.

I took a place on the footstool, as if following an instinctive role as the youngest to seek low ground. I didn't mind: My back was to the fire, and that way I didn't have to look at the portrait of Leila Whitney Stott, my grandmother's mother.

Leila Whitney was only nine years old when the artist sat her down and began to sketch her plump rosy cheeks, still smooth and open with childhood. In the picture she is smiling in a charming, delicate way that changes from child to young woman depending on the angle from which you gaze. It is a bewitching, impish, ambiguous, almost Mona Lisa smile. Her clothes only increase the effect. She is dressed to perfection in a gray coat with an elegant fur ruff. Pearl drop earrings hang from her small ears.

But that day I took no pleasure in looking at one of my namesakes. Instead, the fact of her being on the wall above left me feeling even more scruffy and uncomposed. My then-long hair was pulled back in a hasty, half-tangled ponytail, and the cuffs of my pants were wet and muddy from my mad rush to get to the meeting in time. That morning I had walked out along the farm road, east toward the back orchards, then on through the woods. Brush had grown up over our childhood riding trails, but I pushed through until I came to the sudden rise and the long, elevated roadway, the abandoned railroad tracks. There I walked along the even road, soothed by the rhythm of my feet, by the tawny browns and reds of late fall, by the foggy November air.

Now, back inside Talavera, my shoulders to the fire, I wished I were still walking along that road. Everything in the house seemed to oppress me just by the fact of its being there. So much stuff. So much old stuff, and all of it needing tending. Even Leila Whitney, behind her beautiful smile seemed to have joined the other portraits in judging us from her place on the wall, her very elegance bearing witness to our fallen present. My father, the oldest son, my grandfather's namesake, had struggled to keep Talavera from being sold out of the family. He had succeeded, but I was sure that the effort had been a large part of what had killed him. Now he was dead, and we were supposed to carry on. The question was how.

My father had believed that the farm could be made to

39

support Talavera, and for many years his plan had worked. But the national trend of small-farm bankruptcy had arrived in the Hudson Valley. All around us fruit growers were buckling under high taxes, the cost of labor and the bottomed-out price of fruit. To keep Talavera now, we would have to find a way to support the farm, not the other way around. Anyone looking from the outside would have probably advised us to sell the house and land and salvage what we could. But I knew that wasn't going to happen. I wrapped my arms around my knees, hugging them as I waited for the meeting to begin.

My eldest brother, named after my father and my grandfather and my great-great-uncle and my great-great-great-uncle, passed out copies of my father's will. I accepted one, although it would be weeks before I could make myself read it.

At the funeral it seemed that my three brothers had ascended to take on highly sanctioned, if invisible, roles as the sons of a dead father. When the time came, each had stepped forward confidently and read the eulogy he had written. Each of them memorialized my father in a different way, but each described him in clear, loving terms as a patriot, as a business pioneer and a farmer, as an uncompromising individual. Their eulogies had placed them as the sons of a successful, landed father. Since we were reading in order, I stepped forward last. But when I looked out over the crowded church, at the gleaming polished red wood of my father's casket, flooded with yellow flowers, words seemed impossible. For minutes that seemed like hours, I stood there, rocking wildly in an uncharted sphere. Then I took a breath and read a short poem in which I described my father trying to teach me how to prune a tree. When we left the church, my eldest brother had made the sign of the cross and, in the Presbyterian tradition, bent over and kissed his father's coffin.

Historically the transfer of an ancestral place in an established landowning family like mine, in keeping with the English tradition that it followed, would have had nothing to do with me or my sister. Perhaps we still felt that even though we inherited equal shares of Talavera. At the meeting my eldest brother, who, as the coexecutor of my father's will and as a lawyer, had drafted our trust agreement, did most of the talking. My sister and I were quiet.

I was trying to listen, but at first I couldn't hear a word. Moments from the previous week, surreal, disorganized, came flooding back. The day after the funeral, my eldest brother, my mother and I had driven my father's ashes down to Washington, D.C., where the family gathered again in the Oak Hill Cemetery to place them in the Van Ness family mausoleum there.

For most of the way, I had sat in the backseat next to the little brass box with my father's ashes inside. It was unbelievably odd to be sitting there amid tree wire and loose tree tags, things that only recently my father had tossed into the back. If I reached my hand out, I could touch the blue velvet bag that held the brass box engraved with my father's initials, JVNP. When we stopped for coffee in Maryland, I was worried because the doors to the car didn't lock properly and I thought someone might try to steal the box, thinking it was gold. Besides, it didn't seem right to leave my father alone. For a moment I considered taking the box with me into Roy Rogers, but then I lost my nerve. Once someone was dead, how did you know anymore what was the right thing to do? In the end I stayed in the car and let my mother and brother bring me a cup of coffee for my turn at the wheel.

When I brought my attention back to the meeting, my brother was saying words like *trust, lifetime, our mother, legal transfer*. Unanimously and with little discussion, my three brothers, my sister and I agreed to form a land trust to keep the house and the farm together for as long as my mother lived and for three years thereafter. After raising five children, working in an office in Manhattan, helping my father found his business newsletter, then participating on the farm each weekend, my mother was retiring to the relative leisure of

41

only running the farm. "I've always wanted chickens," she joked, showing us through her humor the fine steel from which she was cast. "Now I'll be able to get some."

Soon our meeting was over, all of us supportive, together, intact. But for me, that meeting only confirmed my confusion. In many ways, what we just agreed to made no sense. None of us had the kind of income needed to maintain a Federal-style mansion or to subsidize a farm. How would we ever manage? Even if the larger economic picture for farming in the valley improved and the farm had a chance at solvency, we had a more important challenge. Could we learn to cease our sibling spats long enough to own and operate a business jointly? Like most brothers and sisters, we could provoke one another so that even the clank of a glass in the dishwasher could hit a nerve, starting an argument.

Yet we had not discussed the words *sell, divide, withdraw* with any seriousness or conviction. Such conversation was taboo. We could rail at Talavera or despair over what could seem like a vain pretense of heritage, but we could not sell the place and feel that we had done the right thing.

"Five years," my mother said simply. "Let me see if I can make it work in that time."

*

The night after the meeting, I walked out along the drive and looked back at Talavera. For a moment I felt a thrill as I looked up at the enormous house, at the tall white pines spiring up on all sides. All that I did not yet know about Talavera only heightened its mystery. Gaston Bachelard says that we spend our lives trying to dream our way back to the house that was our childhood home, but what if this house still exists, still encompasses your family, what then?

In many ways the meeting had made me realize all that I loved about my family. Perhaps, although we didn't have a plan or money in the bank, our instinct of keeping together, of staying put would carry us through. But I was worried. I was pretty sure that my mother was the first woman in the history of the family to manage the larger farm, and I was proud of her. But could she live at Talavera alone and avoid the despairing loneliness that I had seen come over my father?

I was filled with unsettling questions. All this was supposed to be worth it because of the past. That was our inheritance: this history, our sense of place, Talavera and all its glamour. Certainly Judge William W. Van Ness, who had built the house, had been both eminent and rich. But that was so long ago. What of the family since then? What of the family aunts, women like my great-aunt Bessie, who had fled Talavera? What of us? If we were poor when we appeared rich, couldn't this grand elusive past be bankrupt as well? I hated thinking such things, as if I were betraying my father even to ask such questions. But it was worse not to. We were at a crossroads: Either commit to saving Talavera or accept its loss. The fact that our dilemma stemmed from great privilege only made it feel worse.

CHAPTER FIVE

Yesterday's Harvest

I had come up with a plan. Maybe I couldn't change the dismal economics of small farms in the Hudson Valley. Maybe I could not prevent the strange paralysis that came over my brothers and sister and me when we tried to think about Talavera's future. But I could find out about Talavera's past, that elusive force driving us forward. My plan was this: I was going to dig out all the old papers from the house and barns, pull these clues out and study them. Yesterday's Harvest. I wanted to find out exactly who had lived at Talavera and when and what their lives had been like there. I wanted to find out if the farm had ever been profitable, and if so, when and how. I wanted to uncover Talavera's secrets.

I told myself that I was sick of being bullied by a past I didn't even know. But really I was scared, scared that like my father, I would get sucked into a way of living that revolved so much around Talavera that it lost touch with the larger world. If I looked, I could see signs of this in my own generation, in me. We all were a little too comfortable with Talavera's state of disrepair, that slippery state of mild neglect and denial. Success in the outer world involved a strange sense of betrayal.

I knew the myths. That my family had lived here as if forever in splendor and elegance. That the orchards, with their yearly renewal, were as resilient and holy as thousand-year-old olive trees. That if we cared for the land, we would be caring for ourselves. What I didn't know was how much of this remembered past coincided with historical reality. If I could understand what Talavera had been, then maybe I could find a way to Talavera's future, and maybe I could set myself free.

My mother had left for a week of much-needed vacation in Vermont, and I was at Talavera house- and farm-sitting. On a previous visit I had mapped out the location of trunks and boxes and closets full of papers: the scrapbooks and files, the boxes of letters and rows of farm journals, the piles of unsorted papers that filled places like the library closet where each harvest we kept the farm's cash. I was going to read through these things and map out Talavera's history. I would begin with the library closets. On my yellow pad I could see the words *Library closet, left side—top shelf.* But that had been three days ago. I still had not opened the closet doors.

Instead I cleaned the kitchen, weeded the flower beds and washed the dogs, who had rolled on a dead woodchuck. A thick, humid heat spread over the land, over me. Each evening I walked out into the cooling rows of trees with the dogs. Animals that we did not usually see appeared like omens at unexpected moments. Along the leafy tunnel of the railroad bed, we came upon a snapping turtle so large that at first I thought it was an abandoned tire that someone had flung onto the road. The next morning a red fox came sauntering up to the edge of the back lawn, then drifted, red smoke, back into the woods.

When it grew too hot to be outside, I walked the cool interior of the house, around and around as if circling a mandala. Library, kitchen, dining room, parlor, hallway, sitting room, boot room and up the curving stairway. Nursery, blue room, hallways, then the third-floor landing, the east room, the west room and down through the north wing and back to the library. Talavera was a game of Clue. Mr. Mustard in the ballroom with the revolver. Mrs. Peacock in the library with the candlestick. Up in the cavernous west room, I looked out through the windows at the massive columns of the porte cochere, then turned to notice a rope of cobweb draping from the corners like the dirty ends of Miss Haversham's gown. I opened the doors of the dark armoire and dug my hands into the thicket of men's coats: scarlet riding jackets for fox hunting, black-tie jackets and tails, cummerbunds, silk-lined dress pants, then a row of my father's floppy tweeds. It was just like my family to have a closetful of dead people's clothes and no room to put our own.

Soon I simply began to trace my steps from room to room, feeling my way like a blind person, the pads of my fingers touching the chipped places in doors and windows, the broken ends of furniture, the delicate patterns of wear on the arms of brocade chairs and sofa covers, the brittle husks of lampshades. Another cup of coffee. Another loop around the house. I had become a kind of rapt pilgrim, only I wasn't arriving anywhere. I began to shrink from the outside world. I stopped going to the village in the morning to pick up the mail. When the UPS truck arrived with a package, I ran upstairs. Willi arrived one windless evening to apply the first of the apple mite sprays, preventing me from taking the dogs into the orchards for twenty-four hours, so I piled them into the truck and headed for the local cemetery. There, while the hot evening dwindled down, the dogs leaped and played in the oval stone-lined pond while I walked among the gravestones. Only three days alone at Talavera, and already I was more comfortable with the dead than the living.

I found myself calling a local stable to make an appointment for a riding lesson. I hadn't ridden in years. Only when I had finally completed the long process of sorting and reading through my family's long and complicated history at Talavera would I see how in desperation I was invoking a historic family passion, horses.

"Okay, canter right," shouted the instructor. I pressed with my outside leg, the usual signal, but the pony just began a begrudging trot, then, when I kept signaling, trotted even faster. I was being jerked so roughly I could feel sharp spears of pain along my spine. I was not riding; I was being bounced around the ring like a sack of meal. If the pony had chosen to fling her head down, the kind of trick our old Shetland Bimbo would have tried, she could have sent me sailing. I pulled her back to a walk, took a deep breath and tried again. Once again, I signaled, but the pony ignored me. She was bored. Stop. Start. The riding instructor said nothing, but I could tell she was not impressed. Neither was the pony. Her walk was sloppy; she stiffened when I signaled with the outside leg. We were at an impasse. Could it be that I had really forgotten how to ride? The thought was so mortifying that I stopped the pony for a moment and re-collected my reins, eyes blinking.

Peter, his mane flying, his eyes wild with delight, is galloping hard across the meadow. I am on his back, crouched down, bareback, the pressure of my legs urging him on. We reach the end of the meadow, and when he feels the touch of my hand across his neck, he turns right, heads up the final hill, legs still moving at that thundering pace. I bend down like a jockey until my face is almost level with his mane. He smells sweet and salty, sweat beginning to dampen his copper hide. I will never fall because he will never let me. He is Pegasus, one wing dipping as he turns, racing through the clouds.

47

This time, when I moved the pony out, I did so with a more determined pressure from my calves. Her walk picked up a little, and I increased the pressure in my legs but held her back when she tried to trot. She woke up a little. I pressed my calves even more firmly and still held her back by checking her with the reins. Her head began to lift; she began to feel frustrated, to want to move. I kept this up, pushing her forward, holding her back until I was sure that she knew what was coming. At the next corner I made sure that I was sitting back, then signaled her to canter. This time I focused everything I had on the gesture. I imagined my calf pressing into her side. I looked only at the point in the ring at which I was headed. I insisted through the position of my body that she follow my command. But it was still not enough. She started to canter, then broke into a trot. She was all pony, sizing me up, figuring out what she could ignore.

I didn't hesitate. Little flares of anger shot through my brain. I remembered this contest of wills. *Canter, canter.* I could think of nothing else. I sat back and imagined her front leg, reaching out, finding the correct lead. *Canter, canter.* This time, when I pressed her with my legs, I did so hard, and this time she sensed my resolve. Miraculously, incredibly, it happened. She listened, decided to follow and threw her front leg out to find that even, rolling stride. I was overcompensating a bit, overeager, and she sensed that too and sped up, her canter becoming a gallop. I pulled her back, tried to relax my seat. My legs had all gone to hell. One foot had come entirely out of the stirrup. I couldn't get her moving and keep my hand steady and my legs in the proper position. Even now one circle of the ring, and my legs were on fire with the strain of trying to keep my balance.

But I didn't care. Everything now depended on whether I could control this animal, convincing her to follow my will. The pony was moving, smoothly now, her back relaxing into her stride, and for one more circle of the ring I was riding, that incredible sense of power, of communication with an animal more powerful than oneself. It was simple really. Once you resolve in your own mind where you are headed, a horse, even a willful pony, will go there too.

That night, when I shut my eyes to sleep, I could still feel the steady, pounding beat of the pony's hooves as she circled the ring. Each hoofbeat, the steady rising pulse of my own childhood.

"Want a ride back?"

"Sure."

"Hop on in front, here. You jump, I'll pull."

My cousin pulled her mare up and made her stand while I poured the water out of my sneakers and put them back on, preparing myself for the walk home. We had spent the morning swimming the horses in the back pond, all of us trying to stand on the back of my uncle's huge gelding, circus style, falling in the stinky pond. It was my sister's turn to ride our horse, and she had gone on ahead with the others. I looked up at my cousin with adoration. She was four years older than I was and an excellent rider. Her horse was a fast, hot-tempered mare that my cousin could convince to do almost anything. The mare stamped her feet impatiently but held still while I bent my legs and leaped up with all my might. My cousin caught the back of my shirt and helped guide me up in front of her. I twisted my fingers into the black mane to steady myself, and my cousin tightened her hold on the lead rope attached to the horse's halter. It was a point of honor to be able to ride without a saddle or bridle, what we called Indian style, on an excursion like this one. As soon as my cousin turned the mare toward the barn, she headed off in a smart walk.

We followed the grassy road through the orchard and began to climb the first of the hills that led up to the ridge and the hedgerow above the meadow. The horse's walk was rough. I could feel the sharp ridge of her withers under my seat, but it was much more fun to be riding home with my cousin than walking back on my own. Suddenly, at the first of the low hills, when we turned onto the dirt road, the mare threw up her head and gave a loud, anxious whinny. Within a few sec-

49

onds, from the other side of the hill, came an an-
swering whinny. The next thing we knew, she
was off, running as fast as she could to catch up to
the other horses. We reached the crest of the hill
in a blur of dust, both of us managing to stay on.
But worse was yet to come. The big hill that she
had just galloped up was about to lead down in a
steep incline. We swept past the first hedgerow,
past the huge white pine. My cousin was bent
over me, pulling on the lead rope with all her
might. Her efforts were to stop the horse, but her
arms were forcing me down so that my head was
level now with the horse's withers. All I could see
was the road, hard-packed dirt and stones. Time
stopped. I was past terror and into a strangely
calm, prescient state. I found myself thinking
only one thing: I am going to fall, and I am
going to die.

Then miraculously, just beyond the hedgerow,
I felt the horse swerve to the left and off onto a
grassy orchard road. My sister and the others had
not continued on to the barn without us. They
were there on the left, waiting, the horses busily
munching grass. By the time I slipped down to the
grass, my legs were so wobbly that when they hit
the ground my knees buckled. I looked down and
opened my clenched hands. Bits of black horse
hair were still sticking to my palms. My cousin
and I looked at each and began to laugh.

50

When I fell asleep later that night, I dreamed that I was
back in Japan and once again a potter's apprentice. But something was wrong. I sat at my wheel afraid to touch the clay.
My teacher, Nagayoshi-san, came into the workshop, saw
me sitting at the wheel frozen and handed me a piece of
white Shinto paper like the kind found decorating shrines.
He handed me a pair of scissors and walked out. I didn't

know how it happened, but soon I was cutting the paper into the most amazing shapes. The paper fluttered in my hands. I cut and cut and felt nothing but joy.

જ્ય

The next day I drove to the Columbia County Historical Society just north in Kinderhook, resolved to begin. The librarian there directed me to Franklin Ellis's 1878 volume on early Columbia County. When I turned to the sections on Claverack and Philmont, plates of men with names like John Van Ness Philip startled me with their physical resemblance to my own brothers. But there was no indication of who had lived at Talavera and when. Only one thing was clear: Whatever family myths existed were braided into a long and continuous involvement in actual events in early American history. Unraveling the strands was not going to be easy. On one hand, I felt relieved, even a bit proud to be flipping pages of description about these early men who seemed to have been eminent enough to have been included in an official history. On the other hand, it was depressing. If the past really had been grand and important, what had led to this great dive into the present, when nothing about my contemporary family seemed as grand or rich or entwined with history? I didn't learn until much later that at least as far as regional history was concerned, Ellis's book had been sold by subscription. Families that wanted biographies and plates included could purchase space. Sure enough, later I even found a letter written by my great-grandfather in 1878 to Everts and Ensign, Ellis's Philadelphia publishers in which my great-grandfather inquired about the price of including a short biography of his dead brother Lieutenant John Van Ness Philip.

I pushed the Ellis book away and looked over to catch the gaze of a slight, nervous-looking man who had been staring at me. He wanted to know what I was researching and, after I told him, explained that he was of Mohican ancestry, a descendant of the Rensselaer people. They had recently organized a protest of the building of a Wal-Mart on their ancient burial ground near Saugerties. With his light brown hair and marble blue eyes, any connection he had to Mohican tribes was clearly thin, tenuous, so long ago. Couldn't one say that some gap in his present was making the past, that glamorous once upon a time glisten just a little too gold? Might the same be said about me?

As I began my next task, reading through the clipping files labeled "Philip" and "Van Ness," wasn't I also looking to the past to explain the present? However, so far what I was riffling through seemed too distant from my own experience to explain anything. There had been a Cornelius Van Ness who had been a brewer and merchant in Albany. His wife had knocked the sheriff off his horse with a broom. A Peter Van Ness who had built a mansion in Kinderhook named Lindenwald, which had been acquired by the eighth president of the United States, Martin Van Buren, then later had become a state park. Lists of other Van Nesses in the Red Hook and Rhinebeck regions. Then so many John and William Van Nesses followed in the genealogy that I became hopelessly confused. It was fun reading through the lists of seventeenth-century Dutch names—Martinus, Annetje, Catharina, Jacobus, Petrus, Hennik, Henrius, Hezkiah—but I felt no connection to them as early family.

I was about to close the file, weary of this litany of names and dates, when out of a sense of duty I turned over the last piece of paper in the file and uncovered a photograph. A man was standing on a tractor, an old Case that looked as if it belonged in a tractor museum, except that we still needed it on the farm. The man had one hand on the wheel, the other dropped by his side. His face, averted from the camera, looked shyly to one side. He gave a look both good-humored and embarrassed at being the subject of a picture. But his shoulders were full of pride. It was my father, heading out after a day at his desk to do what he loved most, mow the orchards. If the camera had looked down and to the left, it would have taken a picture of me as well, dressed in blue jeans and a T-shirt, looking on. The photographer for the newspaper had wanted very much to get a photograph of my father on the old Case. "What a shot," he kept saying. This had irritated my father, who refused to pose. But finally, when the interview was over, he had become so impatient that he told the man to get his camera out; he was going to start up the Case to head out mowing.

Looking at the black-and-white print above the story of Philip Orchards, I saw now what the photographer had been after. Dressed in his Brooks Brothers shirt and corduroy blazer, my father looked like a gentleman farmer. Only he was too familiar with the broken-down tractor, the khaki of his pants too stained with tractor grease and grass from pulling weeds out of jammed mower blades. He looked like what he was, a man who could make the transition from gentleman to farmer in the late twentieth century.

Clipped to that 1974 article about the orchards was another, smaller one, without a photo, that read: "John Van Ness Philip, Jr. Fruit Grower, Publisher, 70." My father's obituary, carefully clipped from the *New York Times.* Back at Talavera, my father hardly seemed dead. His boots still sat in the downstairs closet, as if waiting for him to pick them up and, as was his habit at five, to drop them with a bang on the kitchen floor. But someone at the historical society had clipped the obituary and added it to its Van Ness file. History was washing over me. According to the file that I had in my hands, my father had been the fourteenth generation of Van Nesses in New York. That made us the fifteenth generation. Fifteen generations: That was close to three hundred years. Could my family possibly have lived at Talavera that long?

* handmade divider*

That night I took my yellow pad and sat at the octagonal desk in the library where my father had spent his days writing. According to family lore, it was the same desk where Washington Irving had once tutored an earlier generation. Outside, the cicadas began to moan, that great sea of yearning. Tonight I was determined to begin. Everyone dreams of finding that trunk of letters in the attic, to be able to flip back the lid of history and be in the presence of the past. Underneath the study of history, especially family history, must lie some primitive totemic need.

If this were Japan, we might believe in ancestor worship, the dead swirling around us, informing the present. We could give them a bit of sake, some salt and rice, even new clothes if we were in the mood, and ensure that they would not make trouble in the present. But here in the West we don't believe in ghosts. We believe in God or we believe in information, the truth as solace. I was no different. I too wanted to discover that one fact that could explain it all. Only paradoxically, now that the possibility was before me, not just the opening of one trunk, but an entire closet, then more closets, an entire basement, the lofts of barns, I felt dread. It was true the sheer amount of information was over-whelming, but I knew that was not the real problem. *What if I open the closet and find nothing? What if I find out what I do not want to know?*

54

Before I could lose my nerve, I reached out to grasp the Delft vase on the library mantel, dug my hand in and took hold of the smooth metal key for the library closet door. That familiar coolness in my palm, only this time I wasn't opening the closet to put the day's take of Pick Your Own money in the cashbox. Quickly I stepped in and pulled the frayed string that hung down from a lightbulb. I shut my eyes against the explosion of light. When I opened them, I looked out over stacks and piles and boxes of papers.

Each shelf was crammed: papers, records, books, things, all waiting. Behind a collection of glass soil sample tubes and the cashbox, I could just make out a row of hardbound jour-nals. One peeling label read "Talavera Accounts 1911." Other books, with disintegrating leather bindings, were lined up along the shelf. I pulled one out and on the inside cover read the words *W. H. Henry Philip, Cash Accounts, 1855.* Relief flooded through me. How could I have feared there would be nothing? For a moment I simply stood there and looked in a state of shock and awe. It was as if I had just opened the door onto the brain of the house. Surely I would find in this mass of papers some of the answers that I sought.

After an hour I filled several sheets of my pad. My list began: "File Folders: Orchard Work Plans 1913–1916; Old Deeds and References Pre-1900; William H. Philip, executor of the Estate of Gaston P.; South Place; Stark Estate." Stark Estate? I blew dust off the old folder and opened it quickly. On the top was a newspaper clipping with the headline FEMINIST PIONEER. The file was about my mysterious aunt Bessie, whose paintings hung in several rooms throughout the house. According to the file, May 31, 1975, was the first Elizabeth Philip Stark Day in Jacksonville, Florida, established to recognize her work during World War I organizing the Cherokee Rose Girl Scout troop that patrolled Jacksonville's beaches on horseback in search of German spies. With great excitement I flipped through the file, but there was no time to read in detail. I noted the location of the file and placed it in a box for removal.

The archival principle of provenance states that before removing any materials from a site, one should note the location and condition of the papers being removed, the idea being that the way things are stored can tell as much as the items themselves about the people who put them away. In keeping with this idea, I carefully noted where I had found everything before I placed it in a box to be removed for later sorting.

Soon my list contained things I had not expected: "Spray records 1955–1960—6 files, 3 blue hair curlers, pennies, box of shotgun bullets, letter from President Roosevelt to grandfather, small can of chimney solvent, mouse skeleton, six loose bullets, soil sample kit." Hair curlers, chimney solvent, stray bullets, plastic tubes for rolling quarters, a stack of quarter- and dime-size paper rolls for coins, glass soil-sampling tubes, five pennies sticky and blue with spilled ink. What did such things tell me about my family other than that the closet reflected the confusion that I felt? On each shelf, there seemed to have been no attempt to distinguish what was of value from what wasn't. I had the impulse not to record these details, but to revise history as I went. Who would ever know? This is the nonfiction writer's greatest temptation, tinkering with the facts: "If it's not there, put it in . . . If it doesn't seem to fit, take it out." But I reminded myself that I was not here to make a story. I was here to find the story that waited. These details, however painful, would lead me to it.

I forced myself to write down these uncomfortable notes. From a file box containing notes on my grandfather's pure-bred hunting dogs, I extracted a signed invitation to the inauguration of President Roosevelt. Then I pulled out the mouse skeleton and marveled at the tiny, grasping paws. Digging in had become fun. I was Helen Mirren now, a detective hot after a lead with not a minute to waste.

Time stood still, until I realized that I was exhausted. Dust from the old papers crawled on the back of my neck as if tiny midges were dancing there. The idiotic dive-bombing of moths into the lampshade had become intolerable. I no longer felt like a detective. I felt more like Cinderella, cleaning up while everyone else was at the ball. As soon as my chair legs scraped against the floor, the dogs leaped to their feet. They rushed out ahead of me. We walked into a night swirling with heat, the rasping beat of cicada wings.

Psychoanalysis has revised Freud's evocative idea of the psychoanalyst's work as that of an archaeologist, pulling up sheaves and remnants of memory, then sleuthing through clues to reconstruct the past. Perhaps it is impossible to reconstruct or even remember a past faithfully or even truthfully. In that case, such clues can only partially explain the present. But one of Freud's greatest achievements was to show how both memory and dream stem from desire. Freud understood what literature has always known: that for the writer, each act of memory is an act of redemption, a transformation driven by want. Elizabeth Bishop's hard blue river of knowledge: our search for the truth. What is the analytic process anyway but that crude digging up of stones and pebbles, then the slow turning of a memory or a phrase over and over until it begins to gleam?

I had no choice but to try to make sense out of the mess of papers before me, those fragile tokens of lives that time had welded into totems. Although I was not on the analyst's couch here, I was in search of the story or stories that could set the record straight. I needed to know who these people were who had kept these files, those unsmiling faces on the walls, this place that always whispered, "This is who you are."

CHAPTER SIX

Talavera, 1969

My parents stand on the front porch dressed for a costume ball. My father wears my great-uncle's Rough Rider uniform: tan riding breeches, gorgeous brown leather boots, a khaki-colored shirt and a banged-up U.S. Cavalry hat. Seventy years earlier his uncle wore the same clothes to Cuba, then following Teddy's lead, charged up Kettle Hill. In his right hand my father grasps the Civil War sword of his great-uncle, after whom he and his father, my grandfather, were named. My mother wears something more contemporary, a flowing scarlet gown. Draped over her shoulders is a white silk shawl. Her hair is jet black; her lips are ruby red. Standing there, framed by the white pillars, each one rising twenty feet in the air, she could be Scarlett O'Hara. I am in awe of their transformation from parent to fairy tale.

My grandmother is settled into her room by the kitchen for the night, and her cook, Betty, is on

call in case we have an emergency—only in case
of an emergency. She has drawn the line at preparing dinner for the grandchildren. All eight of us
are there: my three brothers, my sister, me and
our three cousins. We don't care. We hate it when
Betty cooks for us anyway. The kids have to eat
separately, in the kitchen. Every now and then we
hear the tinkle of the little bell that means my
grandmother is calling Betty to bring something to
the dining room table from the kitchen or to serve
the next dish. Betty hates that bell. She scowls
and wipes her hands on her frilled apron and
clomps out through the hall in her enormous shoes.
When she comes back, she expects to see that we
have finished the food that she scooped into our
bowls. When I complain that I don't like my
chicken and my peas and my mashed potatoes all
mixed up in a bowl like that, Betty says, "It's
just going to get mixed up in your stomach anyway, and aren't we a fussy little miss?" So when
Betty puts food in my bowl, I eat.

59

Betty thinks we are spoiled. When she was
growing up on the farm, her family never had
shoes, never had anything. They had so little to
eat that in the mornings, Betty explains, they ate
fried cow snot. I think Betty is marvelous. I usually wake up before anyone else and slip down to
the kitchen. While I sit on the stool, Betty cooks
bacon and tells me stories about when she was a
kid. One time her father got so mad at the bull,
which was making trouble, that he punched him
in the nose. Calmed that bull right down. No
doubt Betty's father had to be tough. Later I will
think about Betty's name, Scofield, and with a bit
of research, discover that in the early 1900s her
father bought their small farm in East Taghkanic.
It was hardscrabble land, too rocky for profit, land

that in a previous generation had been farmed by a tenant of Livingston Manor: ten schepels of wheat as rent for eighty acres. Betty came to work as a fruit packer down in our barns when she was in her late twenties. Then word got out that Mrs. Philip was looking for someone to work in the big house. Betty went to work up there and stayed through most of my childhood.

But back to that evening, which I can see as vividly as if I were still there. Some memories are so painful it is hard to call them up; others come swooping down like barn swallows, winging circles in the air. My childhood memories of Talavera are like that, emblems of a time when life was not divided into categories of bad or good, moments to be regretted or moments to be grateful for. What happened was accepted and lived and believed in like the fried cow's snot, which of course I knew wasn't true, but which still made Betty my hero.

As soon as the wheels of our parents' cars crunch down the long, curving drive, we begin. First is croquet, which we love but which inevitably brings out the worst in us. When I skunk my cousin's ball into the tall grass, he calls me a bloody fool and begins to chase me with his mallet swinging. I think it is funny and dance away, flaunting my competence. I am winning, you see. Then I realize that he is seriously intending to brain me. I run to my older brother, just then taking aim at his own ball, which he is about to send through the final two wickets, finishing the game. My brother wants to hear that satisfying thunk of the ball against the wood. We are bugging him as usual. He grabs my cousin's arm and tells him to cool it, but my cousin, a whirling dervish by this point, hits him in the shin with his mallet and calls him a bloody fool too. So my brother grabs him and gives him a wedgie he'll remember and ceremoniously hangs him by the underwear from a knot in a nearby pine tree.

I don't remember how long it takes my cousin's underwear to stretch out enough so that he can get his footing and wiggle free, or maybe my brother takes pity on his shouts and lets him down. But it doesn't matter because I am not fool enough to stick around. I am long gone, down to the barn to watch the funny bay colt that just this spring arrived. He is learning how to drink water, and while I watch, he sticks his small, rubbery nose into the water barrel, then snorts in surprise, springing back, quick as a deer, flicking his black flop of a tail. My parents named him Peter, after Peter Van Ness, who built Lindenwald, and although he is to be a family horse, I have already made him mine. When I watch his spindly legs gather under him to run back to his mother, I imagine us leaping over fences as high as those that my father jumped when he was a boy my age. Well, maybe we'll jump a little lower. In the photographs in the library, my father is riding a huge dark horse and leaping over solid wooden fences, not over movable gymkhana poles. Wind sweeps his hair back because he is not wearing a riding cap. Such confidence, such risk. In the room my sister and I share are the ribbons he won in the horse show that day. Even at eight I know that I can't quite live up to the past.

Soon it is time for dinner. When our parents go out to one of their cocktail parties, we have spaghetti if Betty relents and decides to cook. If she doesn't, we make pancakes from the huge bowl of batter that my mother has left in the refrigerator. We soak the pancakes in syrup. My

61

cousin, no longer mad about the wedgie, has joined me in proposing a pancake-eating contest. I eat twelve and am sure that I am the winner, but then he stuffs two more in his mouth. "No fair, you have to swallow," I say. I know this trick. As soon as the count is done, he will go and spit them out off the back porch. But we don't get to resolve the matter because Betty appears in the kitchen, telling us that we are making too much noise, we will disturb our grandmother. We quiet down immediately and decide to play monster in the basement. We don't put the dishes away or clean up. I imagine that when my mother gets home, she will do that, hoping to fend off Betty's tirade of complaints.

Betty clumps back upstairs, and we troop down into the basement. One or the other of my older brothers is the designated monster. We turn out all the lights and hide. The chase begins. The monster comes roaring through the darkness. We race away from him, through the wine cellar, the fruit cellar, the old kitchen with the enormous iron pot, a real witch's kettle, still hanging on a hinge over the Dutch fireplace, through the laundry room and the furnace room. Someone is on a bicycle. My older cousin, who always has great ideas, has put on a pair of roller skates. I can hear the whir and skid of the wheels, ball bearings screeching as she races from room to room. Laughter, screams. In desperation for a new place to hide, one cousin and I push through the small opening into the coal bin. We scramble over the slippery sharp coal, safe. But being safe soon becomes boring. We crawl back out and join the fray. Then I am wearing the skates. I can remember their sudden speed where the floor abruptly tilts down by the old furnace, shooting me forward into the dark. The dogs are barking and chasing now too, biting our clothing in their excitement at joining the melee. It is a miracle that no one cracks his head or breaks any bones. Those on bicycles don't wear helmets—none of us even has a helmet then—and the floor is smooth concrete in the main areas, dirt in the wine and fruit cellars under the wings. Periodically we bang into pipes and insulation that release clouds of dust. Only when we're exhausted do we stop.

It is time to climb the steep steps up to Betty's room. I would have been too scared to do such a thing on my own, but my older cousin, the one with the great ideas, has told us that she knows Betty has a stash of candy in her room. Three of us troop up and knock at the door. We can hear the sound of the television and the recognizable rustle of a cellophane bag. To my surprise, Betty seems glad to see us. "You look like vagrants," she says, and this seems to please her. "Well, come on in." We do. "Wash your hands," she orders, and we do that as well. Then she lets us climb up on the bed. She continues watching the western, and soon we are too, staring at the small black-and-white television perched on her bureau and munching on Snickers bars while we follow the shoot-out.

Soon someone is shaking me awake. The movie is over. We head out to run through the fireflies, another evening ritual. The lawn is ablaze with flickers of green light, and we run through them, quickly beginning a game of king of the sundial, climbing up and pushing one another off the stone sundial in the center of the lawn.

We are filthy by the time my parents get home. None of us has worn shoes all evening. Even visiting the horses, I simply have hopped over the

63

piles of wet horse manure, toes curling in the dust. Of course I'm not supposed to be walking down there barefoot among the rusty nails and piles of old machinery. I know the risk too. I have already cut myself on rusty nails and have had to have the gigantic tetanus booster more than once. But who is there to tell me no? That is one of the incredible joys of being at Talavera, the freedom that comes of life in a big family and the infinite number of places to explore. We get to do things that none of my friends ever do. It is, I think, part of why I have come to have this sense that somehow we are special.

When our parents return from their party, we know they will not make us take baths or scold us if we are not in bed. They sit on the wicker furniture on the south porch and talk in quiet voices. Maybe they have a few more drinks. I love going to sleep upstairs hearing the murmur of their conversation on the porch. It doesn't matter to me that they are probably smashed. They came of age in the forties and lived through a terrible war. What could go wrong now? Their pockets bulge with the slim outlines of Camel cigarettes, and each evening their glasses tinkle with ice, cocktail time. These are the good days. I snuggle myself down into the sheets, safe.

CHAPTER SEVEN

Wild Bees

Months, then a year before I could return to complete my excavation of family papers. When I arrived at Talavera on a hot July day, my mother was glad for company, for someone to share her worries about the fruit. The valley was in a drought, only six inches of accumulated rainfall when by then there should have been twenty-six. July was when the fruit produced all the fruit cells that it would make and the hot, sunny days gave the trees time to photosynthesize huge overloads of carbohydrates. Size should be fantastic—that is, if we had rain. At this point it could be an extraordinary season or a terrible one, depending on how much rain fell between now and August. The taste should be above normal as well. Apples are like grapes in that hot, sunny days help them develop an abundance of fruit zesters. The more fruit zesters, the more complex and rich the final taste. This is a matter of survival for apples and pears. The better they taste, the higher the likelihood that they will be consumed by animals that scatter their seeds, ensuring the next generation.

Like most farmers, my mother has seen too many summer

hailstorms and too many dry seasons to count on good weather until it has already come and gone. But something more than the weather was troubling her. The wild bees that lived in the old pine tree by the back porch were gone. Woodpeckers had pecked so many holes in the old tree that sections of the trunk resembled a colander, and the mostly hollowed-out core was perfect for bees. But this summer they had disappeared. My mother and I sat on the back porch and listened: silence. If the hive had been alive, the bees would have been coming and going from the dark hole. They would have buzzed for a moment at the entrance, the seven thousand facets of their lateral eyes taking in any relevant information necessary from bees that passed them by as they readied themselves to dive into their home. Careful to fold their four wings, they would have slipped into the darkness, that intricate city where thousands were working, tending the brood, cleaning or grooming their beautiful queen. She would have been busy as well, laying as many as three thousand eggs in one day. As long as the queen remained in the hive, they would never behave irrationally, robbing and engaging in other self-destructive acts. What had happened to the hive? Had it starved?

Starvation seemed unlikely, for we had had a mild winter. Even if they had run out of food, workers would have starved themselves in order to save their last bits of honey and pollen for the queen, hoping to save the unlaid eggs that she contained. On the coldest days they would have surrounded her like a living bee blanket, huddling their furry bodies together and fanning her endlessly in an effort to keep her warm. The brood, tucked into their hexagonal chambers, would have been similarly protected, surrounded by their nurses even when the hive was in a state of emergency. Something must have happened to kill the queen, and since it had not been a harsh winter, the probable cause was pesticides. We were careful not to thin the fruit with chemicals like Sevin, which kills bees. But they could easily have journeyed into a sprayed bed of clover somewhere else. Sometimes even a beehive, that place of architectural, political and economic perfection, cannot be saved from disaster. Their queen must have died. And if something had killed the wild bees, what was the state of my mother's predators? The ladybirds and lacewings and blackflies that she counted on for mite control?

After my father died, my mother attended Cornell fruit schools and took a spray applicator's course, then studied and passed the exam. She intensified my father's initial experiments with integrated pest management (IPM) strategies to replace traditional spray methods. IPM meant spraying for what pests you had, rather than what you thought might be there. The aim is to achieve biological control of marauding pests. It required checking the trees weekly, sometimes daily with a magnifying glass to identify what insects were there and at what thresholds. Then you could begin to consider how to use good bugs, or predators, to prey on those that harmed the fruit and trees. The risk was in missing an infestation and losing your crop. The old way was comforting. Each week Cornell sent out bulletins listing which insects were hatching at the Hudson Valley Experimental Station and which chemicals were recommended to kill them. You could follow those guidelines and know that your fruit was not going to get pocked and scarred or killed by infestations of mites and curculios, banded leaf rollers and the nasty psylla flies.

The problem is that those same chemicals wipe out any natural means of defense as well. They kill natural predators, such as ladybugs and blackflies. So once you got started that way, your orchards were hooked on a steady stream of chemical bathing. Breaking the cycle is not easy. It takes careful watching, and it takes guts. But my mother, with her appetite for risk, was an IPM natural. She could walk out into a block so infested with aphids the tips of the branches writhed green and shrug, saying, "I've seen worse. Give the ladybugs some time."

I helped my mother with the scouting whenever I could.

During the peak times we'd prowl the fruit trees two or three times a week, magnifying glasses in hand, looking for trees with a yellow pallor or curled leaves, those that were slightly off color. If a tree looked off—the leaf canopy thin or the usual green tinged with yellow—we collected leaves from four quadrants, turned them over, then began to scan, midrib to outer serrate edges, counting bugs and bug eggs of all shapes and sizes. Sometimes we'd just see their trails of frass, bug poop, and know they had been there. Or we saw the white stippling where leaf miners had been. Aphids are greedy and would leave whole sections of the leaf brown. We looked for good bugs too, the haphazard and finicky red-and-black spotted ladybugs and the busy black ants, which herd up colonies of aphids on certain leaf quadrants to use as food supplies for the colony. Once the aphid "corrals" were established, with guard ants posted to keep them there, orderly lines of ant workers marched up to feed on them at regulated times.

But if something had wiped out our bees, chances were good that it was also affecting our predators. Aphids and mites could be having a heyday in the orchards. My mother and I decided to drive out to check. Sure enough, back in the far orchards, mites had begun to bronze the trees, especially the blocks of Red Delicious, which they particularly loved. They were sucking the nutrients out of the leaves to such a degree that the trees had taken on a brownish tinge. The young pears were covered with aphids, so many piling up on the young terminals that I was worried, but my mother didn't want to spray. She pointed to the lower leaves, where an ant colony was already busy devouring the juicy aphids. The leaves on the young pears weren't curling yet. She would give the ants a week before she decided whether to spray. But the apples were a worry; we had better start a mite count.

We started in the block of young Red Delicious, a variety that must have sweeter foliage, for they are always hit with the worst concentrations of mites. Four leaves from each quadrant, north, south, east and west, meant sixteen leaves to collect per tree. Four or five trees from each block meant examining eighty leaves. By 11:00 A.M. the orchards were steaming with heat. We quickly bagged our leaves and drove them back to the house. For the next hour I sat on the back porch, counting red mites and bright orange eggs. My mother was edgy, another spray would cost seven hundred dollars. But that wasn't all: Having bronzed trees was a fruit grower's shame. She began to wonder what she had done; perhaps she'd miscalculated her predator population or put on the preventative spring oil spray too late. Worse yet, the bronzed leaves were a sign that some undetected soil deficiency had left the trees vulnerable to mite predation.

But we were in luck, at least for the time being. Despite the bronzed leaves in the back orchards, I counted only an average of four motile mites per leaf, one below the July threshold. My mother had a few more days to let the lacewings and ladybird beetles and syrphid fly larvae have a go. If the mite count was not down by Monday, however, she would have to spray. At this point in the cycle, mites could not only wither this year's fruit but also affect next year's crop as well. Already the trees had chosen which cells would develop into next year's fruit, and the tiny buds were there, growing alongside this year's crop. If the trees encountered too much stress in August, next year's fruit buds would not be strong enough to withstand the winter. Both drought and mites are August worries for the fruit grower.

ॐ

By the end of the week twenty-five boxes of papers were stacked in the south hall, a huge cache of letters, diaries, journals and other farm and family papers. My husband and I would drive them back to the university where I taught so that I could begin to clean and sort and catalog them. Together with almost fifteen thousand items that had been removed from the house in 1973 and were now housed in the New-York Historical Society, they made up a collection of farm and family papers that stretched back to the early 1800s. Surely in that mass of information I would find answers to some of the questions I was seeking.

While we waited for my husband to arrive, my mother and I sat on the back porch, watching the evening light. All along the river, fog was descending, but here the light was still rosy. We wondered if the clear skies would hold through tomorrow. The weather radio announced rain. That morning my mother had driven down to the Germantown agricultural cooperative to buy Apollo, one of the weakest of the mite sprays. We had found a growing number of predator black mites and even some Ti pyri (*Typhlodromus pyri*), mite killers capable of consuming quantities of red mites a day, but even so, the mites were regenerating too fast. If she allowed the next generation to hatch out, she would risk losing complete control. Ironically, while at the co-op to conduct her depressing errand, my mother picked up some news that had cheered her considerably. Mites were out of control all across the valley, and Cornell was blaming the warm winter, which seemed to have allowed an unusually high number of eggs to overwinter and hatch out. It was not that my mother enjoyed other people's misfortune, but now she could stop worrying that her mite predicament was the result of her bad management.

We seemed to sit there for minutes, simply enjoying the breeze, while we waited for my husband's car to pull up. Then we heard it, that distinct high-pitched buzz. My mother and I both looked over to my right, where a bee zoomed along the porch rail, sighting us with its third cyclopean eye. A wandering bee out hunting pollen would never zoom so close and in such a bumbling, almost confused manner. Soon another bee flew by in an equally erratic pattern. It looked like a drunk, buzzing this way and that, coming toward us, then veering away.

It was my mother who pointed to the bee tree. A thick cloud of insect bodies was suspended over the hole, then began to funnel itself inside. Within minutes the bulk of the

swarm was gone. Six or seven thousand bees were now sorting themselves out inside the trunk, workers heading one
way, drones another. The queen, surrounded by her nurses,
was settling down, safe in the darkness of the tree. Only the
guard bees swirled this way and that across the entrance. We
had just watched a swarm of wild bees descend into the old
tree.

My mother was thrilled. After dinner, my husband and I
told her some other good news. She had another grandchild
on the way. My work on the project took on a new urgency.
I no longer needed to resolve my quest for answers about
Talavera just for myself. In seven months my son would be
born. What did I want to pass on to his generation?

CHAPTER EIGHT

In the Hollow of His Hand

Ever since I uncovered my father's notes about an earlier John Van Ness Philip who wrote his mother to announce that he was returning home to make money through farming Talavera, I have been determined to find the letter. The irony of his proclamation was simply too great. Here was my own family, struggling to hang on to a farm that by 1992 we needed to support, while in 1855 a young man could consider building his fortune through it.

My mother had never seen the letter herself, so she could only advise me to search through the Philip–Van Ness papers at the New-York Historical Society, but she did think I might be interested to know that she had found Lieutenant John Van Ness's sword. Rather, the sword had found her. The man who bought it recently from an antiques dealer had contacted her, and they had begun an exchange. He had come to see Talavera and to meet her. Now I was on the way to Washington, D.C., to meet him.

When I arrived at the gleaming Reagan International Airport, Ronald B. Moser was waiting for me at the gate. I spotted him right away, a tall, lean man who was scanning the crowd, looking for the woman from New York whom he had advised to locate him by means of his blue ball cap. Even dressed in civilian clothes and sporting a North Carolina ball cap, Mr. Moser looked like what he was: a retired U.S. Navy officer, once the commanding officer of the ocean surveillance ship USS *Alacrity* and the guided missile fast frigate, USS *Antrim*.

Mr. Moser greeted me warmly, and soon we were driving down Interstate 95 in his silver Jeep Cherokee, past the Pentagon, past Crystal City, where he sometimes worked while on the job as a senior analyst for EER Systems, a department of defense consulting firm. He drove the speed limit, south toward Virginia and his home in Woodbridge. Along the way we talked about one of his favorite subjects, the Civil War. Mr. Moser collected Civil War items, especially those used by the U.S. Navy. In March 1997 he saw a particularly beautiful U.S. naval officer's sword that a dealer purchased with him in mind. Mr. Moser was impressed by the sword, but not enough to pay the thirty-four hundred dollars that the dealer wanted for it.

One month later, at another gun show, he saw the sword again and this time knew that he had to have it. The sword was similar to a standard issue 1852 Ames naval officer's sword, one of which Mr. Moser already owned, but this one had an imported German blade from Solingen. Mr. Moser couldn't get over the quality of the blade and the fine condition of the brass detailing on the handle and quillon and the sword's sharkskin grip. But mostly he was impressed by the scabbard which bore the inscription "presented to Lt. John Van Ness Philip by his fellow townsmen of Claverack, Col. Co. NY May 20, 1861." This time he bought the sword, then began to wonder about the man whose sword he had come to possess, the man who happened to be my great-great-uncle.

"It's an absolute miracle that we are talking," Mr. Moser said when I first called him earlier in the year. "I had never even heard of Claverack. I just took a long shot one day. All

73

I had was the inscription on the scabbard and the sword. I called up the Claverack Town Hall and said that I had purchased the sword. I asked if they could give me any information on the family of J. Van Ness Philip. They said, 'Why don't you just call up Julia?' I said, 'What?' They said, 'Yeah, she lives there.' They gave me your mother's number. I had some trepidation. But I called your mom up and said, 'Do you know John Van Ness Philip?' and she said, 'Yes, I'm looking at a picture of him right now.' I tell you, I just about fell out of my chair."

My mother meant she was looking at a photograph of my father, but that was before Mr. Moser knew that three generations of men named John Van Ness Philip had come along since the owner of the sword that he now owned. Lieutenant John Van Ness Philip, my great-grandfather's brother, had signed up for the Union cause six days after the first shots of war had been fired at Fort Sumter. He was thirty-eight at the time and had retired from a career in the navy to return to Talavera and take up farming. Life at Talavera in the Arcadian vision of a gentleman farmer seemed to have been his life's dream, but he was no sooner settled in at Talavera, and the farm, revitalized by his interest and investment, had been transformed into Claverack's third largest dairy, than news of war traveled north.

John Van Ness reenlisted in the U.S. Navy and that night gave a rousing speech in the Hudson City Hall, where he called upon all able-bodied men to uphold the Union. The next day the *Hudson Daily Star* considered his talk the lead war news item. "The addresses were full of ardor for the cause of our country," proclaimed the paper, "the principal one being from our noble citizen J. Van Ness Philip, who though retired to the quiet pleasures of his farm and his home, like the illustrious Washington and Cincinnatus of old, leaves his plough at the call of his country and braves the hazards of the sea and the hostile foe, to sustain the honor of the old flag under which he has served for twenty years. All honor to such noble patriotism as this say we."

Quinctius Cincinnatus, that fifth-century B.C. Roman hero, was summoned from his fields to aid a trapped Roman army. In fifteen days he triumphed over the enemy and laid down his sword to return to his plowing. The comparison fascinated me. John Van Ness's decision also raised so many questions. Why would a man with a rising career in the navy have quit at age thirty-eight to take up agriculture? Why would the farm he chose to cultivate be Talavera?

I was more determined than ever to find that letter. Certainly it would offer clues to what I had come to see was a key moment in the history of the farm. John Van Ness's portrait had been hanging in the dining room at Talavera all along, but I had never taken much notice of it. The only thing I knew about him was that he was one of Catherine Douw's three sons. As soon as I could, I began searching through the files on John Van Ness Philip in the New-York Historical Society. Day after day I read through the files of parched letters, each a hieroglyph at first, then gradually a discernible, often highly ornate script. Lieutenant John Van Ness's formal prose seemed a foreign language to me. Only slowly, under the dim lights, did the swirl of letters become so familiar that I could discern words, sentences, a distinct writerly style. The story of his life began to unfold.

Influenced by his uncle General John P. Van Ness, who seemed to have taken a special interest in the nephew named after him, John Van Ness left home at the age of eighteen to seek his fortune as a midshipman. From the beginning he was in love with life on the sea. His early logs describe his sense of the romance of walking the decks at midnight watch and his horror at watching sailors flogged for insolence. Within ten years he witnessed the planting of the U.S. flag in California in 1846, then joined the USS *Mississippi* to sail to Constantinople to help free the Hungarian rebel Louis Kossuth in 1851. Once I saw his logs from his time aboard the *Mississippi,* I understood the inscription on the thick gilt-edged volumes of Archibald Alison's four-volume history of Europe, published in 1849, that I had found stored in the barns at Talavera.

He had signed the first volume "Midshipman JVNP, USS Mississippi." In all likelihood, it was these books that he read while crossing the ocean to Constantinople.

Soon after the historic rescue of Kossuth, John Van Ness developed an interest in life onshore. On August 8, 1852, he married Laura Johnson, the daughter of the wealthy John Johnson, the last chancellor of Baltimore. His ship, USS *Mississippi,* was soon to head out on another historic mission, this time sailing for Japan under Commodore Matthew Perry. In July 1853, she arrived in Uraga, the southern tip of Tokyo Bay, to begin persuading the Japanese that it was better to begin formal relations with the United States than to resist. On that day, two hundred years of self-imposed isolation ended and Japan was soon forced to open to the West.

John Van Ness did not mention any regret in having left the *Mississippi,* although he later purchased Commodore Perry's handsome volume about the mission to Japan. In letters to his mother he sent detailed and happy accounts of his new post, teaching mathematics to young recruits in the newly founded Naval Academy in Annapolis.

Letter after letter crackled under my fingers like dry leaves. Each slim, carefully bound ship log revealed more and more of John Van Ness's interest in travel as well as his intense love for his Columbia County home, a place he described with reverence as "the mansions of magic." But read as I might, through boxes and boxes of correspondence, I still could not find the key to his connection to Talavera, the letter in which he linked his fate with the land and the farm. I began to think that my father must have been mistaken. It would not be surprising. I was getting used to a disparity between family history and fact.

One afternoon, as I was about to leave for the day, I forced myself to look through one last folder labeled "Miscellaneous Correspondence 1850's." At first I didn't even realize that I had found the letter. Lieutenant John Van Ness began by talking about his delightful discovery of a pay bonus, but in his close, he made his legendary proclamation. I had found it! Of course, the wording was not exactly as my father had remembered it, but it was more interesting yet. The composed elegant writing explained John Van Ness's reasons for coming home, and they were decidedly financial. "Two horses and an *expensive* wife add a little to a fellow's expenses," he had written to his mother the previous year on March 11, 1854. Was he trying to convince her that farming was not a mistake? Was he bragging about his fancy wife, or complaining? One of the horses was his beloved Kossuth, named after Louis Kossuth, who, to judge from the copious notes about him in his ship's log from that time, had had a strong impact on John Van Ness.

I soon forgave him mentioning his pedigreed horses and his wife in the same line. Before I knew it, I became swept up in an unexpected soap opera of events at Talavera. Later, on April 1, 1856, he signed a deed with his cousin Stephen K. Hogeboom, purchasing Talavera from him for fifteen thousand dollars. His mother, then living on land she had inherited from her grandfather Peter Van Ness of Kinderhook, was delighted that her eldest son was returning home. "Lord bless you and keep you as in the hollow of his hand," she wrote back when he informed her that he intended to be the next master of Talavera.

Within months, she and John Van Ness's younger brother Martin Hoffman and his family were happily settled in at Talavera. Catherine Douw's slim red diary soon recorded the comings and goings of family members, sleigh rides and dinners and always, in keeping with her devout faith, how "the joys of each Sabbath with its exalted privileges has passed away."

Soon after, John and Laura Van Ness moved north to Talavera, taking along three black servants and a slave named Tom whom Laura had taken as part of her inheritance from her father earlier that year. "It would kill him to be sold away from us," John Van Ness wrote to his younger brother William Henry (my great-grandfather) about their decision to bring Tom north from Maryland with them. His tone was apologetic. Whether this was because taking Tom was a poor business decision or because he was ashamed at having inherited a slave is not clear. "He will never leave us I am certain," added John Van Ness, "and then we will have a good servant. He can do almost anything and I am sure that he can earn his money in a short time." Presumably, since John Van Ness writes of money that he will pay Tom, he intended to free him by bringing him north. But the status of southern slaves in northern states was still unclear. The famous Dred Scott case of 1857 had decided that a slave, even if freed, could not claim U.S. citizenship. Moreover, African Americans had been emancipated in New York State by 1827, but slavery was not abolished in Maryland until the final months of the Civil War.

Once north, John Van Ness initiated a flurry of improvements. His letters from this time to William Henry, then starting his law career in Washington, D.C., mentioned the arrival of new china and glass, new carpets and the tidy sum of $125 for ornamental trees. From 1857 on, William Henry began visiting Talavera for lengthy stays each summer, foreshadowing his eventual purchase of the farm from Laura in 1869. Familiar with life on southern estates, Laura would have felt at home in the Palladian feel of Talavera's columned porches, the grand porte cochere and its long, curving approach.

Under Laura and John Van Ness's stewardship, the original gardens at Talavera—a series of terraces of simple Italianate design that led down from the south lawn of the house— were given the definition I grew up with. The entire garden was outlined and framed by plantings of ornamental trees and bushes. Lilacs were planted to establish walkways while a cedar lane soon bordered the garden to the east and a hawthorne hedge divided the whole into upper and lower sections. Varieties of trees were planted to create areas of light and dark in accordance with the ideals of the picturesque as espoused by the American landscape gardener Andrew Jackson Downing. When I walked the grounds at Talavera, I could see those efforts: white pine, hemlock, fir, spruce, maple, elm and that aristocrat of shade trees the American beech, a tree that 115 years later became my favorite climbing tree.

The basic concept of the picturesque—that one could shape the land so that it resembled a picture, particularly those pictures made by early landscape painters that evoked in the viewer poetic moods of nostalgia for purer, more bucolic pasts—was fascinating in itself. In the Hudson Valley, during John Van Ness Philip's time, what was especially interesting was the ways in which these ideas of the picturesque were extended to agriculture as they had been in England decades earlier.

At Talavera, as on other Hudson Valley estates, this aesthetic was not limited to the twenty-five acres surrounding the house. John Van Ness was equally concerned with the design of the farmland. Nothing summed this up better than the huge misshapen hemlock at the far edge of orchard thirteen, the tree that my mother called the wild bee tree because spring after spring it was filled with wild bees, bees she counted on to help pollinate the fruit:

Back in the mid-nineteenth century, when it was planted, the hemlock would have been expensive, a fancy imported breed fashionable at the time for its expressive, drooping limbs. Carolina hemlock reflected Downing's emphasis upon striking, irregular and spirited forms. A shade tree, planted for the utilitarian purpose of providing shade for horses, men and oxen doing fieldwork, would never have been planted at that location just up from a hedgerow. No, the tree's role on the farm was aesthetic; it served to punctuate the view, what in landscape gardening is called a visual marker, probably chosen for its deep forest looks, an emblem of the former wild state of a landscape now tamed.

Similarly, in 1857, the front meadows that began at the edge of the lawns, now kept open as fields of wild grass and wildflowers, were planted with hay. Within American ideas of the picturesque, beauty and agricultural function were to be integrated as they had been on British estates for decades.

Once you were aware of these ideas, you couldn't walk any-where at Talavera without seeing more and more vestiges of that romantic landscape: a spreading horse chestnut tree, stands of maples and hemlocks, sudden lines of larch trees, clusters of catalpa, the copse at the corner of the drive. Trees everywhere, spreading and lifting in the wind.

Not surprisingly, once I thought to look in the Talavera library for books on landscape gardening, I found an 1844 edition of Downing's *Treatise on the Theory and Practice of Landscape Gardening* sitting on a shelf crammed with the books on agriculture. Reading through the preface in the fragile, gold-leafed book, one and a half centuries after John Van Ness's time, I was struck by the connection between Downing's emphasis upon home and John Van Ness's return to Talavera.

Downing had most certainly been influenced by the Christian home movement that flourished in antebellum America. In his preface, he established the connection be-tween home and country: "The love of country is insepara-bly connected with the love of home. Whatever, therefore, leads man to assemble the comforts and elegancies of life around his habitation, tends to increase local attachments, and render domestic life more delightful; thus not only aug-menting his own enjoyment, but strengthening his patrio-tism, and making him a better citizen."

Such words must have had a profound resonance in my great-great-uncle, who had forged a career of military ser-vice, especially as they affirmed what on a personal level he wanted to do: to concentrate his wealth and his efforts on the cultivation of a rural life at Talavera. To beat his sword into a plowshare, retiring at the height of achievement like Cincin-natus. To serve his country by farming.

Of course John Van Ness also intended to serve himself. He was not being sarcastic when he said that he wanted to farm because he needed more money. Once settled in at Talavera, he would certainly appear to have joined the upper class of gentleman farmers in the Hudson Valley, although for him, the bottom line was different. The farm at Talavera needed to make money.

Luckily, in 1855, this was possible. Farming was still the major industry of the state, and several factors contributed to make it extremely profitable. One of these was population. Between 1820 and 1860 the population of New England and the Atlantic seaboard doubled. Columbia County went from thirty-five thousand people in 1790 to seventy-six thousand in 1850. As population rose, local areas as well as the nearby cities of New York and Boston needed poultry and eggs, and butter and milk. Hay and grain were in demand for the growing number of horses.

Meanwhile agriculture was being transformed by new machinery that increased production. Plows, harrows, planters, cultivators, reapers and threshers all were invented and perfected during the 1820s and 1830s, making them available for widespread use by 1850. Farmers could produce more and sell more. The era of scientific agriculture was well under way.

John Van Ness threw his efforts and modest inheritance into making improvements on the farm. The barns that we played in as children were built in quick succession, probably by a team of itinerant barn builders from the Berkshires, just to the east. Straight-timbered English-style barns, they signified a scientific departure from the low-roofed, heavily timbered Dutch barns that had been raised by John Van Ness's Dutch predecessors. A silo and hogpens completed the seven-building barn complex.

Within the next two years John Van Ness spent $321 on cattle, $82.50 on a pair of oxen and $100 on a pair of workhorses. He also splurged on another fancy horse, this time a fine gray mare for which he paid the exorbitant sum of $146.

Farm machinery included a hay press and a newfangled mowing machine, a new horse plow and saw and several hundred dollars' worth of tools. By 1865, when the next state agricultural census was taken, these improvements had raised the farm's value to twenty thousand dollars. John Van

Ness had invested a total of eleven hundred dollars in stock and one thousand dollars in tools and implements (a figure that presumably included the new barns): The farm was running 75 tons of hay and harvesting 500 bushels of winter rye and 150 bushels of potatoes. In addition, there were peas, beans, Indian corn, buckwheat and barley. One hundred apple trees produced cider, and some twenty hens were raised for eggs and meat. Four horses lived in the barns along with two working oxen, but the primary residents were twelve milk cows. Just down from them in newly built hogpens wallowed seven pigs.

Just nine years after John Van Ness had initiated improvements, Philip cows produced three thousand gallons of milk per year. A sizable hog operation, grown from the original seven pigs, produced two thousand pounds of pork. The farm had been transformed from a declining agricultural enterprise into the third-largest dairy in Claverack. In the process John Van Ness had transformed himself from Annapolis naval officer to Hudson Valley gentleman-farmer. Sort of.

The more I read letters between John Van Ness and his brothers, the more I realized that this transformation had not been easy. If there had been a glorious age of wealth and ease for my family, it had not been in 1855. John Van Ness had returned home to confront a considerable domestic problem. His youngest brother, Martin Hoffman, who had stayed at home to manage the Philip family's carpet mill in Philmont, had managed to run up ten thousand dollars' worth of debt, quite a remarkable sum, considering that the standard navy widow's pension for the time was thirty dollars a month.

At one point John Van Ness conjectured that his brother had not earned a dollar in over ten years. Why John Van Ness did not know of Hoffman's financial duress earlier is a story in itself. But it is one that perhaps even John Van Ness did not want to know about, for far from criticizing his brother, he threw himself into straightening out Hoffman's affairs.

The other brother, William Henry, was called on to help as well, but in every letter John Van Ness was surprisingly protective of Hoffman. According to family notes, their grandfather on their father's side, George P. Philip, had made a fortune building the first dam in Philmont, thus helping to found the town that took his name, Philip's mont. But a massive mill fire, then the bank crash of 1857 and what seems to have been Hoffman's screwball judgment had resulted in financial ruin. John Van Ness had used up his entire inheritance from Laura's father, and still there were debts to pay. William Henry began sending money north. I couldn't help wondering as I read: Would a family today, would my own family, come together so dramatically to take care of one of their own? Conditioned by life in the twentieth century, wouldn't we be more likely to let an irresponsible family member rely on governmental programs like unemployment and welfare or to take a Darwinian approach and let that person reap his own folly?

Something else was going on besides a nineteenth-century approach to family. For when John Van Ness wrote to William Henry in 1857, he expressed unveiled contempt for the carpet business and urged him not to criticize their younger brother. "My Dear Brother," the letter began, "I have just received your letter and I can only thank our father in heaven that your affairs are so that you can send us $8,000." He proceeded to write that Hoffman was a little better and had been to church, then added, "As to Hoffman's management, there is a screw loose somewhere. I will have a good talk with him after these matters are cleared up. But say nothing about it in your letters. Remember this poor fellow has not only sacrificed every dollar that he had, but spent the best years of his life in a business and a community which is horrible to contemplate." Clearly too close an affiliation with the scourge of industrialization was not considered gentlemanly.

John Van Ness went on to reassure his brother, writing, "I

have stopped all improvements and all fancy work. The only money I intend to expend now will be for the purpose of putting things in the ground. I am in for hard work and making money, and I think we can do it." The only luxury he admitted indulging in was a full-blooded Newfoundland pup, which he bought for the modest price of five dollars. He then added, "I believe that is all. Send the money by return mail by all means. Send it all to Hoffman in a letter to him. It makes no difference to me. His reputation is at stake. People even think I am immensely rich."

A year later John Van Ness was less patient with Hoffman's lack of progress. Usually the brothers took great pleasure in commenting on each other's "fast hosses." But when they were angry, they would insult the others' mounts. The first clue that John Van Ness was unhappy with his brother was the way he described Hoffman's horse as that "pitiful excuse for a horse." Then, in a letter dated March 11, 1859, he complained to William Henry that he was paying Hoffman's debts all over the county. "Don't say anything to Hoffman about striking off somewhere," he wrote peevishly. "He can't strike off. He must remain here. He has nothing to strike off with. It will kill ma to speak of it. No, our duty is here and here we must work and live."

Talavera, duty, work, live, debts, here. The words could have been written by my own father, also named John Van Ness. Had he known about his great-uncle's return home to take up responsibility for Talavera? If so, had his own decision to do the same been modeled on this past? I felt as if I were reading a novel and could recognize the themes: loyalty among brothers, a fierce, compelling desire to hang on to a family place, the need to settle inherited debts, the struggle to live up to the past, that glorious age of family wealth and achievement gone mythic. Only it wasn't South, it was North. I wasn't amazed by what had changed since 1855; I was dumbstruck by what seemed to have remained the same. Everything centered on Talavera. We were still this landed, aristocratic family. Sort of . . .

ↄↄ

It took four years and all of John Van Ness's inheritance from his father-in-law, but he finally succeeded in bailing Hoffman out of debt and paying the mortgage on Talavera. The new barns were completed, and the dairy was in full operation. Talavera, renovated as John Van Ness's country seat, was perhaps even more resplendent than it had been when first built as the showpiece of John Van Ness's forebear Judge William W. Van Ness. John Van Ness threw himself into his new pursuit of agriculture. Engaging the interest of nine other county men, he founded the Columbia Agricultural and Horticultural Society and served two terms as president. The association was to organize Hudson's first agricultural fair, displaying imported cattle, agricultural innovations and a mammoth workhorse named Gentle Jim.

Throughout these years Talavera bustled with family. Catherine Douw's diary records her domestic joys of visits and visitations, dinner parties, luncheons, the flowers she planned for the garden and the births of Hoffman's three children. Each day she read the Bible, then selected passages from her thick but compact volume by Dr. Hook titled *Meditations for Everyday.*

By the close of 1860, however, her entries had begun to document the threat of war. Catherine Douw herself was not ignorant of the northern system of slaveowning that had existed in New York until 1827. As a baby and young child she had probably been reared, at least in part by a black slave woman named Sattin. Her grandfather Peter Van Ness had willed Sattin to her father in 1804, describing her as "the slave woman now in the possession of my son-in-law, Martinus Hoffman."

But when the war began, there was no question but that two of her sons would fight to uphold the Union. As soon as I opened the slim leather-bound volume and began to read, I could hear her voice, a mother speaking of the tension and drama of life in a country about to be torn by civil war.

JANUARY 30TH Van Ness and Hoffman have just left for Albany to attend a Democratic Convention—God save the Union.

MARCH 15 I have just had another letter from William Henry. Oh, if I could only see him. Lord bless him and keep him as in the hollow of thy hand and commence thy blessings to rest upon him.

MARCH 22 Our country is still in an unsettled state. I was in hopes that "Old Abe" would be able to heal our difficulties and bring peace to our unhappy land, but we are still in an unsettled state. There is no telling what will be the result of all this trouble

APRIL 7 This has been a delightful day. I do love a pleasant Sabbath

APRIL 18 The ground still covered in snow but not very cold. I have said nothing about the state of the country for it is a relief to me to get away from the newspapers and the sound of war. I feel so uneasy about my absent son William Henry down there in Washington among all the turmoil and excitement. Oh, that peace and quietness may be restored.

MAY 4 A bright pleasant day. I have been so anxious and excited of late that I have not felt like writing, our poor unhappy country

MAY 29 Tom just left with Van Ness's trunks and also his own. Hoffman has just taken him down to Hudson to put him on the Oregon, which goes down the river tonight.

JUNE 4 The RR Cuyler sails today and my dear Van Ness is gone. May the Lord keep him in the hollow of his hand.

Claverack was five hundred miles north of Richmond, but the war had reached north to Talavera. Within days John Van Ness was cruising the thousand-mile coast, pursuing Confederate ships that had broken the Union blockade of southern ports. Her younger son, William Henry, busy in

Washington, D.C., had already joined the Army of the Potomac and would serve as aide-de-camp to General William Buel Franklin. For the most part, John Van Ness's splendid sword remained in his stateroom along with his books on European history and the small dog that he had taken with him on board and named "Cuyler." But every evening, John Van Ness polished the long blade, then, in keeping with his mother's wishes, read a passage from his worn black Bible.

⁂

By the time Mr. Moser and I arrived in his handsome Woodbridge home, it was clear to me that his great interest in the Van Ness sword had to do with Lieutenant John Van Ness and the way the sword connected the Civil War to Talavera, to the land there and to my family. As soon as we walked into the house, Mr. Moser led me directly into his study. He put his briefcase down and slipped behind his desk to lift down a long sword from its place on a bookshelf in the center of the room. While I watched, he turned the sword-point down and carefully drew it slowly out of the scabbard. As soon as the sword was unsheathed, he handed it to me gently, the reverse side of the blade toward me so that when I reached out with my right hand, I could grab the hilt.

"Usually you get something and have no idea of whose it was," he said as I looked down the length of the gleaming blade, "but this sword had his name right on it. It's a very tremendous sword."

I grasped the handle, feeling the textured grip, and immediately my arm dipped. The weight surprised me. I decided to lay it on the desk while Mr. Moser began to point out details. "Look here," he said, pointing to the brass pommel. "You can see the thirteen stars, one for each state in the Union." He traced the naval pattern of oak leaves and acorns carved into the knucklebow, explaining that U.S. naval officers' swords always carried the motif of acorns to represent oak, the strongest wood for boatbuilding. As he talked, I fingered the brass dolphin heads carved into the quillon, comparing them with a similar dolphin head design decorating the tip of the scabbard. The black leather scabbard had two brass rings as well, for it was suspended by straps rather than carried in a sleeve called a frog.

Mr. Moser bent his head to point out the faint but intricate designs etched into the blade. Where his finger reached, I saw stars, floral sprays, a fouled anchor and a ribbon inscribed with the words *US Navy*. Any detail of the design that he did not know, Mr. Moser looked up in a thick volume on American swords that he kept nearby.

I asked him if naval officers carried swords today. In answer, he lifted a short sword from its place on a rack nearby. Again, his handling of the sword was precise, a practiced movement full of respect. He pulled the sword out of the scabbard to hand it to me. "You can see they've gotten smaller," said Mr. Moser, "but the design is the same." As I looked the sword over, I thought, *What purpose could a sword serve in the age of Star Wars?* The sword is ceremonial, nostalgic, a symbol of continuity, and I was struck by the sentimentality and love of ritual that pervades this world I am in.

Abruptly, Mr. Moser turned and said he would be right back. He left me in the room, saying something about giving me a minute to look at Van Ness's sword as he went. He walked out hurriedly, almost awkwardly. I realized that he was leaving to give me time alone to hold and be with this talisman of John Van Ness, an item that for him had great meaning.

I picked the sword up and ran my finger along the tip or false edge. With a start I realized that it was sharp. It was not just a beautiful, ceremonial object but a weapon. And I was struck by a thought so obvious I had never seen it before. I come from a family of military men. General John P. Van Ness, Lieutenant John Van Ness Philip, Colonel William Henry Philip, Major John Van Ness Philip, Lieutenant John Van Ness Philip, Jr. The names that I had come to know from old photographs and letters fell one after the other like dominoes. My great-great-great-uncle, my great-great-uncle, my great-grandfather, my grandfather, then my own father, a marine in World War II: These men had all been in one way or another shaped by the military, and they had all forged relationships with Talavera, so much so that it suddenly seemed as if the history of my home were one of men and land and war. I could see how for a man like Mr. Moser, Talavera equaled a kind of American patriotism. It is my own generation, yes, we with our ripped blue jeans and tie-dyed shirts, my brothers with their once-shoulder-length hair, that had been the anomaly. What would Mr. Moser have thought of us if he had driven up to Talavera in the late sixties and come upon one of my brothers, love beads waving, as he concentrated on walking on high stilts through the columns of the porte cochere?

I put the sword back down on the table and looked around me at Mr. Moser's small study, crowded with books, photographs and awards that documented his own naval career and then the hundreds of items that made up his Civil War collection. Each bit of shelf not taken up by history books was full. I glanced over the lines of pistols, bridle bits, stirrups, powder kegs, photographs. Against one wall were racks of muskets and rifles; on another table rested a collection of swords and the mounted relic of a Civil War rifle that he had found in Gettysburg with his metal detector.

On a side table next to his desk was a framed photograph of Lieutenant John Van Ness Philip, the copy that my mother sent him. This portrait of John Van Ness in full naval officer's uniform had been taken at the Rowles photo studio in Hudson, the same camera shop where as kids we eagerly took our rolls of film taken with Brownie Instamatic cameras and later picked up the white envelopes of out-of-focus prints. Gold stars gleamed on the sleeves of Lieutenant John Van Ness's dark uniform, indicating that when the photograph was taken, he was the commanding officer of a ship. That ship was the USS *Cuyler,* which, during the early years of the Civil War, chased and captured Confederate ships seeking to cross the Union blockade, which stretched a thousand miles along the Atlantic coast. The USS *Cuyler's* mission was to prevent supplies and arms from reaching southern port cities.

Later Mr. Moser figured that given the star on John Van Ness's sleeve and the location of the photographer, the photograph would have had to have been taken in June or July 1862, when John Van Ness returned home for the last time.

That July, on the twenty-third, the *Cuyler* steamed south again, returning to blockade duty off the coast of Florida, and the next month, somewhere near Key West, John Van Ness was bitten by *Aëdes aegypti,* the kind of mosquito that carries yellow fever.

Their first mission was to steam to Havana to inspect a fast-sailing British steamer, the *Oreto,* which had docked there and was being refitted with armaments. Intelligence had reported that the notorious Confederate Captain Raphael Semmes arrived in Havana at the same time as the *Oreto,* indicating that it was probably being refitted as a Confederate ship. John Van Ness and his crew arrived in Havana without mishap, but since the authorities there had refused to allow them to inspect the *Oreto,* they steamed out to wait for her in nonneutral waters. Meanwhile they were on the lookout for two other Confederate steamers, the CNS *Florida* and CNS *Tennessee.*

The *Cuyler* had been on a terrific run since April, capturing first the *Grace E. Baker,* carrying fifteen tons of cotton, then the *Jane,* a twenty-six-ton schooner loaded with pig iron. The *Cuyler* had also chased a large side-wheeled steamer for four hours, but she had slipped into the Bahía Honda under British colors and escaped. In late August, at latitude 30 degrees 23' N and longitude 75 degrees 24' N, the *Cuyler* had captured the *Anne Sophia,* bound for Baltimore and also flying the British flag.

Then, on August 20, just off the coast of Key West, their luck turned. Within two weeks the *Cuyler's* captain, Francis Winslow, then the ship's surgeon, then John Van Ness Philip succumbed to yellow fever.

In 1860 yellow fever was a gruesome way to die, and even

today there is no cure for the disease. It took scientists forty years to conclude that it was carried by mosquitoes and begin to control its spread. As the virus multiplied in the body, it attacked liver cells, producing jaundice, a yellowing of the eyes and skin. In their final days, patients began to bleed internally, vomiting dark, altered blood. Meanwhile patients were dosed with whiskey and brandy to alleviate the pain of their high fever and kept in quarantine. Two days after his death, John Van Ness's sword and his dog, Cuyler, were shipped upriver to Hudson by steamer, but I had not found a steamer receipt for the transport of his body. Possibly it was cremated in New York City as part of yellow fever quarantine. The family held a funeral, however, and had a stone marker erected in the cemetery of the Dutch Reformed Church just down the road. For the next 111 years, his sword rested on the mantel in the library at Talavera. I must have seen it countless times during my childhood but never noticed it.

Not long after Mr. Moser contacted my mother, he had begun to dig up files on John Van Ness in the National Archives and in U.S. Navy records. That fall he drove north to meet my mother and visit Talavera. She told him where he could find John Van Ness's grave, and he went there as well. Next to the portrait of Lieutenant John Van Ness, I could see a color photograph of the tall white stone spire that marks his grave. In the sunny picture, you can clearly see the carved letters of his name and an unusual design of a cross overlaid with a fouled anchor.

My mother's generosity toward Mr. Moser when he visited and Talavera's tall white columns left him with a deep impression of my family. Where I began to see decrepitude, neglect, simply too much to take care of, he saw history. "It's incredible, the stability in your family. People move, and houses get torn down, but Talavera is there. You've got a gold mine of history there, you really do. It means so much more when it's your own family."

But standing there in his study, a part of my family's history enshrined here, I found myself thinking surprisingly opposite thoughts. I glanced over at the sword now on the table. It had been taken down from the library mantel at Talavera during a division of family property after my grandmother's death and had disappeared. I could have felt robbed, either directly or indirectly by the sword's loss, but at that moment I was aware of the sword's meaning, not to me but to the man who now owned it. For Mr. Moser, this sword represented things I could only guess at: tradition, service, the sentimental rituals of the military, patriotism and a way of life he clearly believed in, his own memories of service as a U.S. naval officer on the open sea.

A new story had become folded into that of John Van Ness. The sword had moved from being an object of my family to an object in the world. Questions of ownership suddenly seemed irrelevant. I couldn't help thinking again of those gnawing questions of tradition and history. When did a family's allegiance to a place last so long that it began to suffocate everyone involved? Was hanging on to Talavera really the right thing to do? I wondered if I was practicing a larger lesson for letting go of Talavera. I didn't feel the desire to own my great-great-uncle's sword. What I wanted, now more than ever, was to know his story. There, on Mr. Moser's side table, John Van Ness stared out from the photograph, his eyes dark as the black waterfall of beard that cascaded from his chin.

"John Van Ness is one of my heroes," Mr. Moser said simply when he reentered the room, carrying a plate of sandwiches. He nodded toward the photograph. "He was so patriotic. I've had his picture here in my study since your mother sent it to me. I really admire him and what he did and what he sacrificed. He left his happy life and his family. He didn't have to do that. He had served for fifteen years."

While we ate the sandwiches, he explained the substitution system in place during the Civil War, a practice whereby for three hundred dollars you could pay someone to take your place. "He wasn't going to be drafted," continued Mr.

Moser, "and even if he had been, he was rich enough to pay the three hundred dollars to buy a substitute. Lots of people in his class did just that."

Again, Mr. Moser pushed the plate of sandwiches toward me. Only when he was sure that I had indeed eaten all that I could did he put the plate away, and we resumed looking at the Van Ness sword. I asked him who would have carried swords on ships like the *Cuyler*.

"A jack-tar would not have had a sword like this," explained Mr. Moser, "definitely not, only midshipmen. There was no ROTC then; midshipmen were like officers in training. Enlisted men, they were the jack-tars, would have had cutlasses. Here I'll show you."

He walked over to a rack of swords and pulled out a long blade. He pointed at its curved handle. The sword was as long as an officer's sword but had no ornamentation. Over the handle was a curved brass bar to protect the knuckles. He handed it to me and explained, "Here is a cutlass with the standard soup kettle over the handle. The men who went ashore in boats with John Van Ness when they chased the *Wilder* would have carried these. Maybe Tom had one too. They would have had pistols too, of course."

I recognized his mention of the *Wilder,* a Confederate ship, that John Van Ness and his servant Tom had encountered off Mobile Bay. When I asked Mr. Moser if he had any pistols, he nodded. The next thing I knew I was holding an 1846 single-shot pistol, the heaviest, most primitive-looking gun that I had ever seen. I looked over the slender barrel and dark wood, wondering first how a person could ever fire such a weapon with any accuracy and second, how he could load up in time. To fire the pistol, a man would have had to pull a percussion cap and a ball out of his ammunition bag, slip the cap on the mount and the ball into the short muzzle, then pull off the ramrod to pack the ball in tightly. Only then could he have taken aim and fired.

I handed the pistol back to Mr. Moser, and he held it up to the light. "For all I know," he said, squinting at the burnished pistol in his hand, "Van Ness could have used this in 1846, when he talks about sleeping on the beach with a pistol under his pillow in California."

He chuckled then, clearly enjoying the time we were spending with his collection. For him these weapons opened up times and places in American history. I remembered reading a long letter that John Van Ness wrote home about his 1846 mission to the Monterey Bay. In the navy for only five years at that time, he was proud to have just passed the rigorous midshipman exams. In Monterey, he landed with the naval mission that helped plant the U.S. flag on California soil, establishing its statehood. The legendary General John Frémont had impressed him deeply. So had the reports of Indian scouts that motivated the sailors to sleep on their pistols.

Before I knew it, I was getting a lesson on firearm technology. To illustrate his point, Mr. Moser brought out a Brown Bess, one of the flintlock muskets that were used in the Revolutionary War. When he handed it to me, I was again stunned by its weight. How could anyone stand still for long holding up, arms extended, ten pounds of iron and wood, much less shoot with accuracy? The gun was even more primitive and slower to load and fire than the 1846 pistol. I began to understand why the development of the rifled musket, in which a ball followed grooves carved into the barrel, shooting out straight and fast, was considered the most important innovation of the Civil War. Accurate at 250 yards, the rifle could kill from a half mile away. I also began to understand why the Civil War was called the first modern war. The difference between a flintlock musket and a rifle was like the difference between a bicycle and an automobile. Little wonder that the war left six hundred thousand men dead, 2 percent of the entire population.

Three hours have passed like minutes. As I packed my briefcase to go, Mr. Moser pulled something off the shelf and showed it to me with a grin. "Before you go, look at this," he said, and handed me what appeared to be a brass belt buckle. I turned it over in my hands and read the bold letters *SNY* inscribed on the face.

"A belt buckle?" I ventured, handing it back to him.

"Yes," he replied, "some states had them. It stands for the State of New York." He looked at me a minute, then added with a chuckle, "But of course here in the South we don't call it the State of New York. We say it stands for snotty-nosed Yankees."

I blinked for a split second. How was I supposed to take these words? Then I saw the laughter in his eyes and laughed. I understood his joke for what it was, a show of trust, of our developing friendship. For the first time since I arrived, Mr. Moser had shown me, the snotty-nosed Yankee who had come south to see him, a glimpse of the man behind his southern hospitality and graciousness. He was born and raised in Charlotte, North Carolina. If he'd had ancestors in the Civil War, they would have fought on the Confederate side.

✥

We were driving up into the airport dropoff line when I asked Mr. Moser the question that had been perplexing me ever since our talks began. Why collect military items from the Civil War?

"Oh, I began only about three years ago," he said modestly, then added, "These people made huge sacrifices for us. When you die for your country, you have made the ultimate sacrifice and the Civil War was such a defining moment. . . ." His words trailed off, and we drove for a few moments in silence. I waited, letting him assemble his thoughts. When he spoke, it was clear that he had considered the subject deeply. "I guess we've had three holy wars," he said, "the Revolution, the Civil War and World War II, but the Civil War, well, that was the war that settled once and for all the way we were going to be."

As my plane back to New York took off, vaulting into the clouds, Washington and its landmarks—the domed Capitol, the Mall, the tall white needle—soon shrinking into patterns of green and brown and houses and trees, I thought about something else Mr. Moser said as I was leaving: "You know, you've got a gold mine to write about. You've got John Van Ness fighting off the coast, William Henry fighting down in Yorktown and their mother back at Talavera. If you can connect all that, you've really got something."

That was the question. Could I connect it all? A letter, then a sword had brought me south to Virginia, and I had spent the day talking to a man with whom, before writing this book, I would have had little in common. Now I was heading north again, but it was clear that I couldn't understand the present without diving further into the story of Talavera during the Civil War, the war that tried to settle once and for all the way we were going to be. A war fought so far south had changed forever the configuration of a farm and a family five hundred miles north. A family that had once owned slaves had joined the fight to abolish slavery. The contradictions made my head spin. How to go forward from here? How to begin?

CHAPTER NINE

Writing to the Wind

APRIL 1861

A coating of fine snow hid the green fields, rippling white across the front lawns and gardens, but Catherine Douw noted in her diary that it was not very cold. All the sleighs had been washed and stored in the barn loft, while below the newborn calves, their legs buckling, tried to stand, wobbled, but fell. On the ridge across from the meadow, the apple trees set out by Hoffman were swelling into green tip, and down in the meadow the peepers had begun.

Catherine Douw started each morning as she always did with prayer, then waited eagerly for the newspaper and its daily column of war news. On the seventeenth, William Henry wrote to her from Washington, D.C.

> My dear mother,
> We have got War at last. I presume you keep well posted but you can form but little idea of the excitement here. This city now is going to assume the appearance of a vast camp, orderlies are flying about,

thickets of soldiers are galloping in different directions
and posting themselves on all the thoroughfares and
bridges leading into the city.

. . . There is a rumor today that martial law will be
declared tomorrow, but I do not believe it. It is possible we will come to that but not yet. I fear the south
will bear a terrible destruction before this is over. It
seems to me perfect insanity and madness on their
part to inaugurate a war which in all human probabil-
ity will lead to such fearful results.

A few days later he listed the following in his account
book—uniform coat, $25; epaulets, $18; pants, $11; vest, $6;
sword belt, $6.50; shoulder strap, $6.50, laying out $73 on
his Union army uniform. He had Willi, the large horse that
John Van Ness had recently shipped down to him from
Talavera, outfitted with an army saddle and gear. William
Henry's letter confirmed Catherine Douw's worst fears. A
few days earlier, on April 15, President Lincoln called for
seventy-five thousand volunteers to support the Union. She
knew now that two of them were to be her sons.

John Van Ness was busy for days, preparing to reenlist in
the navy. He wrote William Henry, urging him to appeal directly to Mr. Lincoln to see if the president would commission him to his old ship, the USS *Mississippi*. Still on the sea
after its dramatic voyage into the Tokyo Bay under Commodore Perry, it was, by John Van Ness's reckoning, one of
the most powerful vessels in the navy. In the weeks to come,
William Henry did what he could to get his brother aboard
his old ship but did not succeed. In addition to land attacks,
the federal government was formulating a plan to use the
navy to surround the South by way of the sea. John Van Ness
received orders to serve as second-in-command of the USS
Cuyler, a steam-powered fast frigate being refitted for blockade duty along the Atlantic coastline.

If he was disappointed in his commission to the *Cuyler,*

John Van Ness did not say so. He wrote William Henry that
he was getting ready to depart and planned to take with him
into the war Tom, the slave he had inherited and freed. "I am
getting ready as fast as possible, making underclothes to [sic]
and when my orders come I will leave on the next train. Tom
goes with me as my servant. He is crazy to go."

That Tom chose to follow the man who once legally
owned him into the effort to fight slavery may seem the ultimate of historical ironies. Only five years earlier in Maryland Tom had been listed in the inventory of Chancellor
Johnson's property. It had taken me almost a year to track
down records of Tom, for Lieutenant John Van Ness's father-
in-law had died intestate. But I was determined to find him.
If my family had collaborated in reducing a man's humanity
to a figure of cash on a page, I wanted to see it. Tom was at
the bottom of the estate list after a lengthy accounting of
bond holdings. He was the first entry under the heading
"Sundry household and kitchen furniture": "Negro man,
Tom, slave for life, 21 years of age—$850.00." Reading
those words would leave me feeling sickened.

John Van Ness had decided to bring Tom north to Talavera. Tom's valuation of $850 was subtracted from Laura's in-
heritance. John Van Ness's decision probably freed Tom for
slavery had been abolished in New York by then, and he
mentions wages for Tom, but whether Tom felt able to leave
Talavera and strike out on his own was another matter. It
seems clear from letters that the family wanted to believe that
Tom's desire to serve in the U.S. Navy was a faithful slave's
desire to further serve them.

When Tom was wounded after a particularly fierce skirmish with a Confederate ship, John Van Ness wrote his family
often to detail Tom's recovery. In a letter to his brother some
days after the event, he recounted Tom's desire for revenge.

Tom is getting along very well. There is no danger to
be apprehended from his wound. I went to see him

this morning and asked him how he was getting along. He said "first rate." He would like to be on his legs so that he could "go at em again." But Tom, said I, you must not feel so. You know the bible says you must forgive your enemys. "Love, sir" answered Tom—"I'll forgive the rest of em, but I'll never forgive the fellow that shot me." But, said I, you can't tell exactly who shot you. "But I must shoot somebody else. I got to shoot one of em" said Tom.

I saw that he was bent upon spilling an equivalent amount of blood so I discontinued the conversation.

John Van Ness's letter went on to express concern for Tom but he clearly viewed Tom's role in the navy as an extension of family service. When I read the letter, however, I had to assume something different. Tom wasn't serving in the war to serve John Van Ness, or the family, he was on board the *Cuyler* to serve himself—to fight for the idea of the Union and freedom for all slaves.

In the larger context of the war, the practice of black servants, some of them freed slaves like Tom, following their masters into Civil War battles was not uncommon. Black soldiers were prevented from enlisting in the Union army until 1863, but they could sign up in the U.S. Navy from the start.

Within two years of the start of the war, 339 blacks from New York were listed on U.S. Navy rolls, most of them on the lowest rank as landsmen. Tom was registered as Thomas W. Johnson, using the surname of his previous owner. In the 1862 naval report submitted by the *Cuyler*'s captain, Francis Winslow, Tom is registered as a landsman on the USS *Cuyler*. As far as the family was concerned, Tom's loyalty to John Van Ness, in wanting to follow him into battle, earned him an even more cherished place at Talavera. When John Van Ness wrote of the war news and his own situation at sea, he almost always mentioned Tom. Similarly, when Catherine Douw wrote to William Henry with news of John Van Ness, she often mentioned Tom. The anecdotes were full of condescension but also real concern for how Tom was faring so far from home and at war on the sea.

John Van Ness was eager to be off but concerned about his mother. "Write as often as you can," he urged William Henry when he wrote him next, "and when you do tell Ma that there is no danger of Washington being attacked. She is continuously afraid about you." He was also clearly worried about leaving their younger brother, Martin Hoffman, in charge of Talavera and the farm in which he had so much invested, but as if to reassure William Henry and himself on this point, he wrote on the thirtieth of the month: "I have talked with him very seriously and if the crops will do well I hope he will get along."

Most of John Van Ness's time was spent readying for departure and worrying about how the farm and Laura would get on in his absence. But one Saturday evening distraction appeared in the form of a troop of cadets from the Hudson River Institute in Claverack. They marched up to Talavera along the Old Post Road. It was Laura who spotted them first, proceeding up the driveway to where they assembled and stood at attention on the front lawn. She stepped out to inform them that the lieutenant was not at home. Just then his carriage began its ascent up the front drive.

101

When the carriage came to a stop between the columns of the porte cochere, the boys waited eagerly. Then they caught sight of Lieutenant John Van Ness Philip stepping out, and they began to cheer. They wanted a speech, a speech. A speech from the great patriot. According to the newspaper accounts the next day, "an intense degree of patriotic feeling was manifested." The mood would have been set by the sunset, by the front porches with their commanding white columns. Perhaps already in U.S. Navy attire, John Van Ness, his black beard flowing, must have seemed a schoolboy's dream of valor. One of the cadets returned to the institute to write a poem "in honor of the occasion." On Monday, April 22, along with a description of the event, it was printed in the *Hudson Daily Star:*

Raise our country's tri-hued emblem,
Let its blendings proudly fly,
'Twas its like that led our fathers
When the battle tide was high.

'Twas bequeathed us; and to keep it
We will fight like royal sons
Who have never learned to tremble
At the boom of rebel guns.

But John Van Ness's mother, Catherine Douw, widowed at thirty-two, knew death as more than a schoolboy's abstraction. She was the mother of three sons in a nation about to make war upon itself. Such displays of patriotism were lost on her. Not even the sight of John Van Ness several weeks later with his glorious sword, the embodiment of the community's wholehearted support, cheered her up one bit. On June 4 she entered only two lines in her diary: "The Cuyler sails today, and my dear Van Ness is gone. May the Lord bless him and keep him as in the Hollow of his Hand."

JULY 1861

William Henry returned to Washington after having taken sick on the battlefield. John Van Ness was cruising off the Florida coast near Tampa. The hayfields at Talavera rippled with gold, and Hoffman began the yearly haying. Not even the impressive new mower, which John Van Ness had purchased for $120 a few years earlier, made the job any easier for Hoffman to supervise alone, and much of the farm's income depended upon a successful harvest of hay. Catherine Douw wrote to William Henry that all was well at Talavera. Pippins and Baldwins were turning red-gold on the trees. They should have a good crop of cider. Meanwhile, deep in the apple wood, next year's crop of fruit buds was growing and setting with each day of hot July sun. Even so, she believed that "Hoffman has entirely too much for one person." She awoke several times at night and, upon hearing the wheels of a carriage, rushed downstairs, thinking that it was her dear William Henry returning home. Each time the sound of wheels turned into the barnyard, and she knew he had not come. The relative calm, both at home and with her sons, seemed to allow her to express her frustration at the war in general and at a neighbor named Mercer in particular: "I feel so provoked at those southerners for forcing us to all this expense and trouble. Mercer is the greatest secessionist you ever saw. he talks like a fool. he would have rejoiced if they had taken Washington. I tell you he gets it hot and heavy if he talks secession over here—"

The summer continued uneventfully for John Van Ness. The *Cuyler* had some rough cruising off Cuba, but for the most part, he wrote, he was bored and beginning to worry about affairs at Talavera because Hoffman had not written. He complained to William Henry, but in a typically protective manner: "So anxious I was to hear everything about the farms, the horses, cows and the milk business. . . . It was duty to write to me. It is inexcusable. Of course he will say he is very busy, but I know it is only his intolerable habit of laziness and procrastination. Don't say anything to him about it."

Of equal concern to John Van Ness was the way in which Laura's southern cousins began to slight her because of her northern alliance. In a rare burst of anger he cursed them soundly when he next wrote William Henry: "I don't care about what they say of me, but for them to treat Laura with neglect. Confound their rebellious skins. It will be a long time before I forgive them. Poor Laura."

DECEMBER 1861

By winter John Van Ness was even more worried about affairs at Talavera and wanted Hoffman to find a man to help him with the farm at Talavera. Near the Ship Islands he wrote Hoffman a letter wishing him a Merry Christmas, then gave him detailed instructions about the place:

I hope you will get a good man to work the place on thirds. Then for mercy sakes, sell some of those horses. What will you do with Bill? I think upon the whole, the Raspbury's herd better go. You can't attend to them and situated as you are they will only be a bother and an expense. Make a nice patch at the bottom of the garden below that grape arbor where we have corn and potatoes for family use and let the rest go.

. . . Make a good bargain with whoever rents the farm and make him understand that he is to be responsible to Laura and pay the money regularly to her. I can scarcely afford to let the whole thing lie idle another year. If I can make anything out of the Navy, I will of course use it for the good of the family, but I want Laura to have the benefit of whatever comes from Talavera.

104

As for news of the war, he mentioned that 570 houses in Charleston had been burned. "Confound their rebellious skins."

JANUARY 1862

By the end of the month Tom had been seriously wounded, a minié rifle ball cut out of his upper thigh by the ship's surgeon after a skirmish with the *J. W. Wilder* of Handsboro, Mississippi. The *Cuyler* had come upon the schooner in the morning, fifteen miles east of Mobile Bar, at anchor after having slipped the blockade by flying the British flag. When they steamed toward it, the *Wilder* attempted to flee. They saw it slip, make sail and steer toward the beach, where it grounded almost immediately on a sandbar. The crew and captain quickly fled, disappearing onto the shore, and the *Cuyler* went on with the business of securing its prize undisturbed by enemy fire. A small boat was put over the side, and Lieutenant John Van Ness led a boarding party, armed with pistols and cutlasses in case the *Wilder*'s crew should return.

By two o'clock in the afternoon they had managed to make the *Wilder* fast by securing their largest hawser to its foremast. John Van Ness ordered the men to load into the small boats and return to the *Cuyler*. It was then that the enemy decided to attack, opening fire from hiding places in the sandhills. John Van Ness managed to make it back to the *Cuyler* unhurt, but Tom, who seemed to have insisted upon accompanying his master as part of the boarding party, was wounded.

John Van Ness wrote to William Henry about the skirmish five days later: "I am almost afraid to write to Laura and tell her the whole truth, but the ship has anchored now. It was no trifling matter (to secure the schooner) But I returned to the ship without accident. Our boat is riddled with ball and the schooner galley and foucsle is filled with holes. It looks like a pepper box."

As usual, he included mention of Tom in his reports to the family. And as usual Tom was seen through the lens of the idea of the faithful slave whose every action was motivated by service to the master.

When I left in the same boat in the morning, Tom
came down the side ladder with a large box of ammunition buckled around his waist and a musket with
a huge bayonet on the side. Said I, "Where are you
going?" "I want to go with you sir. I want to go
where ever you go."
    . . . You can imagine my feelings when the boat
came alongside to see Tom lying among the
wounded, stretched out on the bottom of the boat.
They were covered with blood and as we hoisted
them out I could not prevent the tears running down
rather freely because I knew that it was only the poor
fellow's devotion to me that led him to volunteer. I
had him carefully carried to the guardroom and to my

great relief the surgeon soon examined him and found him shot in the thigh. The ball had gone up ten inches and he made a counter incision below his ribs extracted a large Minié rifle ball which I have in my possession. He is doing very well and is in no danger whatever. It is only a flesh wound but the surgeon says there is no other portion of his body where a ball could have gone that distance without touching some mortal part.

Four days after the incident, John Van Ness wrote to his brother William Henry, asking him to inquire about the possibility of a pension for Tom, given his wound. He kept the conical-shaped bullet with him and brought it with him to Talavera when he returned. I was pretty sure that Tom's bullet was still in the house, for in the dining room curio cabinet, nestled in its own cloth bag, was a Civil War bullet. And if that was Tom's minié ball, enshrined like a talisman next to Mohican arrowheads, bits of Roman tile and a rock from Pompeii, it was further proof that to John Van Ness and the family, Tom was not seen as an independent person but an extension of them all.

Once Tom and the two seamen and one other landsman who had also been wounded in the skirmish had been cared for and ordered restored to the *Cuyler,* the crew had time to search the *Wilder.* In the ship's hull they discovered valuable medicines, a Confederate flag "ingeniously secreted in a bag of coffee" and, to everyone's delight, a huge cache of Havana cigars. "She was the J. W. Wilder bound from Havannah to Mobile loaded with coffee, cigars, medicines and a thousand other little things which we know our citizens are much in want of. There were many loose boxes drifting around in the cabin and among the baggage, which was apprehended. . . . I will send home by the Connecticut about 4,000 or 5,000 of the *very best Havanna's* worth $800. I will tell Laura to send you as many as you want."

William Henry, a heavy smoker, much to his mother's disapproval, delighted in the expectation of Havana cigars. He received the letter in Washington, where finally restored to health, he was contemplating which army regiment to join. He must have written to his brother for advice, for at the end of his letter John Van Ness encouraged him to consider joining General John Grubb Parke: "I am anxious to hear your decision about Gen'l Parke. I think it would be a good thing and it certainly would be a good position for you. It seems almost as if I would accept as I think we will all have to fight before this confounded war is over. I am only thinking of poor ma. It will pain her so much . . ."

While John Van Ness described his skirmish with the *Wilder* with great detail and excitement when writing William Henry, the last few months had clearly sobered his thoughts about the war. When he wrote to Martin Hoffman three days later, still off Mobile, it was to urge him again to find a man to run Talavera.

My Dear Brother,

I was really very glad to receive your letter. I think you are getting to be quite a respectable decent sort of a white man. After you once get fairly started you do pretty well. I am glad that you are getting along so well and to hear also that you will be able to make all your payments and expenses. I think that will do very well. I hope you will secure a good man for Talavera. It is too much for our man to do justice to, and besides I hope to have something from Talavera although I don't know whether I will get more than enough to pay the interest.

He went on to ask about the horses. He was clearly trying to be positive about Hoffman's general lack of communication, but it irked him that he had recently learned from Tom, who received word in a letter from Bill, another servant at Talavera, about a recent transaction of horses. Apparently the workhorse, Old Squire, had died, and Hoffman had traded the horse, Tom, for a black horse called Dandy. "You do not speak of it. You must have had a busy fall and I would have liked to have been there to have helped you. I think that was a good operation selling hay and buying stalks. Don't go it too strong. Keep within bounds. You know there is such a thing as running any business into the ground."

His main point, however, in writing to his youngest brother, was to insist that he not consider also enlisting: "William Henry talks of 'pitching in' and as I am already 'pitching in' I think you had better content yourself with pitching hay and corn stalks."

APRIL 1862

This time spring came on slowly, the cold hanging in a dreary progression of rainy days. The news from down south was equally chilly. On April 4 General George McClellan had shipped 121,500 troops and 14,592 horses south to Fortress Monroe in preparation for his campaign to capture Richmond, the Confederate capital, by way of Yorktown. William Henry and Willi had boarded one of the army steamers shipping troops south for this Peninsula campaign. Catherine Douw sat at her little round table by the library window and could think of nothing but the war. When she wrote to William Henry, she penned in large dark letters across the small envelope "Colonel William Henry, c/o General Franklin, near Yorktown" and prayed that the letter would reach him.

My dear son,
Where you are and how you are, I do not know. I feel almost as if I am writing to the wind. Still I think of you so much, that it is some comfort to write you.
I have not heard from Van Ness, I saw in the Herald last evening that the Cuyler had taken another prize in Cuba. I hope he will be home soon. I am watching the papers daily. I do dread the Yorktown

battle. It is life and death with the rebels now and they will not have any thing undone.

As the letter progressed, she did her best to report on events at home and even to amuse him by relating an anecdote of Tom's recovery aboard the *Cuyler:* "Van Ness says that Tom is well again and getting quite hardy. He said one day that Van Ness said, 'Tom, why is it that you are not down with sea sickness?' 'Oh, Tom says, Sir, it does no good to be sick for every little swell.'"

Only in her closing did she again reveal her anxiety, urging him to pay close attention to his duties to God: "My dear son, May god bless you and keep you in the hollow of his hand is my ever constant prayer. Commit your way unto the lord so as not to neglect your duty to God. May he keep you from every ill and give you faith, fervent and abiding—write as often as possible, good bye your affectionate mother, Catherine D. Philip."

By mid-April General McClellan had still not begun his attack. Fooled by the Confederates, who marched the same regiment in and out of cover, around and around, so that it seemed as if their army were much larger than it was, McClellan sent word to Washington that he faced an army of 120,000 strong, and he requested more reserves. He was beginning to earn his nickname, the Virginia Creeper. Meanwhile, between the rain and the heat and the unfamiliar terrain, Union troops were falling sick to waves of pestilence and disease. Soldiers had a one in sixty-five chance of being killed in battle, but one out of every thirteen died of sickness and disease: cholera, dysentery, malaria, measles, smallpox and yellow fever.

Catherine Douw no longer had the heart to describe events at Talavera when she wrote to William Henry. She was so beside herself with worry that even her Christian imagery became infused with her motherly instinct to hide her son. She closed her letter, "May the lord bless you and protect you and hide you under the shadow of his wings."

Again, she beseeched him: "PS—Do not let anything draw you aside from your duty to God whatever else you omit or neglect."

In contrast, Martin Hoffman, the son who stayed behind, wrote three weeks later to tell William Henry how much he had enjoyed his brother's descriptions of sleeping within range of Rebel guns near Yorktown. They received little real news from the papers, Hoffman complained. But apparently there had been much talk: "What seems to be the opine of intelligent men. The idea is gaining ground here that it will be the greatest battle ever fought in the world."

In typical Philip family fashion, he went on to inquire about William Henry's horse: "How does poor Willi stand the racket? I am afraid it will be the last of him. I wish you could have had old Bill. He would had endured the hardship well and if you ever got in a tight place and meant to run away he could have brought you out one mile or twenty, it would be all the same to him. Or if you just ever wanted to catch a flying rebel. . . ."

A few weeks later he wrote again to say how much he would have liked to witness the battlefield. "How I would like to look upon such a scene. It must be an awful thing to listen while there is such a battle proceeding. The country is looking splendidly now on account of a fine rain. Goodbye. God bless you and keep you is my constant prayer."

MAY 1862

The apples were in full bloom when Catherine Douw sent her next letter to William Henry, addressing it to Franklin's Division, Army of the Potomac, near Yorktown. She clearly tried to cheer him up with news of events at home but was too worried to mask her fears. The Battle of Shiloh with its horrific casualties had sobered the entire nation, and the irony of the battle's name would not have been lost on her. A fervent student of the Bible, Catherine Douw would have known that Shiloh in Hebrew means "place of peace": "Hoffman laying out a great many trees, intends to set out more. I am setting out flowers. I have very little ambition this spring, but I must keep doing to keep my mind occupied for it is too much to think of you and Van Ness both being away. I have no news. Nothing seems of any importance nowadays but War—War and unknowns of war."

Her concern was no longer with the progress of the war, but with her sense of its spiritual corruption. Before closing her letter, she warned William Henry about alcohol and tobacco: "This war is so demoralizing, it stains everyone, to beware, 'he that thinketh he stands, to take head, lest he fall.'"

JUNE 1862

After eleven months at sea, John Van Ness finally returned home for six weeks of leave, while the *Cuyler* docked in the Boston Naval Yard to undergo repairs. On the fourteenth he wrote to William Henry, still south near Yorktown, sending news of home and of Hoffman's first child, Catherine, who was born earlier that year.

> The country here is looking beautifully. I never saw anything like it. It is almost impossible to realize it. I have not seen a blade of green grass since I left. You can imagine how I am luxuriating in these green fields. I am also laying back on green peas, asparagus, lettuce *and strawberries* by the bushel. Poor soldier think of that and think of a fellow after a year keeping on beans and salt horse. What a quantity he is naturally consuming.
>
> . . . I found ma in a pretty good stew. Somewhat excited but I have cheered her up. Baby is great.

The next time he wrote to William Henry, on the twenty-fourth, it was to send news of Tom, who, recovered, was fully enjoying life back on land: "The country is look-ing very lovely and Talavera is in all her glory. It is like draw-ing teeth to leave again. Tom arrives home on Sunday having lost all of his money $120.64. It is too bad. He is always so careful of my things that it never occurred to me that he could lose his money. Hoffman seems to be getting along very well but you must certainly send him the money for those notes. The baby is certainly the most engaging little thing I ever saw."

JULY 1862

Catherine Douw wrote to him on the Fourth of July dur-ing a quiet moment when John Van Ness, Laura and Hoff-man and his wife, Sarah, had all gone into Hudson, where John Van Ness was to give a patriotic speech.

My dear son,
My eyes have been so very weak and inflamed of late
that I have not written at all, or read any thing. They
are better now. I will write a few lines to you today
and then finish tomorrow. I am all *alone* in the house
today, everybody is gone to Hudson to spend the 4th.
I feel extremely anxious about you today my dear
dear son *where* and how you are. I cannot think of
anything else—various unknowns are afloat—one,
that our army has been replenished—next, that Mc-
Clellan is in Richmond, then that he has retreated. I
do not believe them but still it makes me *hold my
breath*. I hope and trust in the lord.

The next morning, still inspired by the tremendous ap-plause that he received the night before at the Hudson City Hall, John Van Ness also wrote William Henry. By now even those as far north as Talavera had heard news of the recent skirmish at Yorktown. Newspapers had termed it the Seven Days Battle because it began on June 24 and ended exactly one week later. John Van Ness shared his mother's concern. "My Dear Brother, We are filled with the most painful anxiety and suspense for the last week in fact the whole country has been in a most terrible state."

Three days later Catherine Douw wrote again, echoing these sentiments: "Words cannot express the anxiety that we all feel about you my dear dear son." Later that month the family at Talavera heard that William Henry was dead and waited anxiously for a telegram. But it turned out to be a rumor. William Henry had again become ill, probably with a recurrence of undiagnosed malaria. He was sent back to Washington, D.C., where this time his health prevented him from returning to the battlefield for almost a year.

SEPTEMBER 1, 1862

On August 30 the family received a telegram informing them that Lieutenant John Van Ness Philip was aboard the *Florence Nightingale*, a hospital ship stationed in New York Harbor. The *Cuyler* had been taking prize after prize off the Florida coast when somewhere near Tampa a mosquito carrying yellow fever found its way on board. By August 26 the captain of the *Cuyler*, Francis Winslow, had died and John Van Ness as well as the ship's surgeon were also sick. Despite his weak condition, John Van Ness took command, steaming the ship north to New York as fast as he could. But within three days the ship's surgeon also died and John Van Ness fell into a raging fever.

As soon as they heard the news that John Van Ness had been transferred to a hospital ship near Staten Island, Martin Hoffman and Laura rushed down to New York City. On a stormy night they made it across the harbor to board the *Florence Nightingale*. The next morning Martin Hoffman sent word to William Henry. The doctor had informed him that John Van Ness probably would not live long: "the doctor filled him with brandy and champagne hoping that he would hold out to see some of us as that seemed his *great burden,* for

he longed to see some homeface before the struggle came. . . .
Of course he was much changed but still his voice was clear
and while he was able to talk spoke only of home and all the
loved ones there. He seemed so grateful to see me and said
he knew that some of us would break through and come to
him."

Laura spent that night at her dying husband's side. The
next morning, at age thirty-nine, Lieutenant John Van Ness
Philip, second-in-command of the USS *Cuyler,* was reported
dead.

CHAPTER TEN

Talavera, 1866

Once again April had arrived, bringing with it the welcome spread of green at Talavera. On the twenty-fourth, Laura Johnson Philip, by then an official war widow and receiving the standard thirty dollars a month, sent a hasty letter to William Henry, congratulating him on the birth of his first child, a son. The news brought great renewal to everyone at Talavera, for they had had a long, sad winter. In early January, Catherine Douw had died. She had anchored the family for so long and through so many changes it was hard for any of them to know how to proceed. "And now it is all over. We have lost her and shall now hear her good words of counsel and motherly advice no more. Yet our loss is her gain, and this must be our great consolation," wrote William Henry to his wife Eliza after arriving home at Talavera.

Two years earlier William Henry had written to his mother to announce his engagement to the "sweetest, best and nicest girl in the world," Eliza Worthington. He had made sure to note to his mother that his fiancée, whom he called Lilah, was educated in Europe and could speak several languages, then closed his letter mischievously: "The only objection is her rather advanced years, she is actually over twenty one, although I am happy to say she is not quite twenty two. Still, one can't have everything you know." As soon as Laura heard the news, she had made a package of the family's lace shards to send to the young bride and in great excitement had traveled to Baltimore with several trunks filled with her own finery so as to be on hand to help with preparations for the wedding.

Now Laura wrote to send her thoughts to dear Lilah, whom she was glad had "come through the ordeal safely." Laura noted how moved she was to hear the baby's name: "Like you I cannot help thinking of one who would have rejoiced so much at his birth."

The baby was not to be named after his father as was the custom, but after his father's brother. Christened John Van Ness Philip, he bore the name of the family's fallen hero and grew up to become my grandfather.

116

Three years later William Henry, now the father of two more boys and well established as a successful lawyer in Washington, purchased Talavera and the farm from Laura. She soon remarried and moved north to the town of Ghent. By 1871 Martin Hoffman and his family had moved to Titusville, Pennsylvania, where he became a partner in an engineering firm that produced engines and steam boilers. No doubt he was glad to leave agriculture and finally be allowed independence from the family.

Tom disappeared. For a time after John Van Ness's death, family letters mentioned concerns about him. He had traveled to Boston with a woman whom the family believed was no good. Martin Hoffman tried to find him but failed. In the 1865 census, three adult black servants were listed along with family members. Two of them were from Virginia, bringing up the question of whether they had been other freed slaves, but Tom was not mentioned, so it seemed he was gone.

The horse Willi, by then retired to Talavera on a special diet of grain and hay, had a luxurious box stall near where the cows had once been stationed. When the new farm manager, Leroy Van Hoesen, wrote to William Henry about "the place," he did not fail to mention Willi, the dark horse that, like Lieutenant John Van Ness, had left Talavera and traveled south to participate in the Civil War. For two years, Willi had carried Colonel William Henry on and off southern battlefields.

CHAPTER ELEVEN

Household Accounts

When I open the slim Chinese red journal, three parched sheets of paper fall out: an 1873 bill from a Paris dressmaker, an 1874 receipt for children's clothes from the Lilliputian Warehouse on Regent Street in London and a bill for $93.84 from a shipping company in New York City, dated February 15, 1882. The bills interest me, for they are addressed to Mrs. William Henry Philip, my great-grandmother, but not as much as the volume in my hands. I push them aside and look inside the cover. There I find what I am looking for, a familiar spidery hand that reads "Eliza W. Philip, Accounts at Talavera 1869." In my hands, light as an old-fashioned paperback, rests the journal that my great-grandmother began the year she and my great-grandfather bought Talavera from Lieutenant John Van Ness's widow.

I close the cover for a moment to read the spine. Along its half-inch width large gold letters spell CASH. I flip quickly to the back and see that the last page is dated 1896, a mixed entry describing my grandfather's emerging role in politics, his younger brother Gaston's first job as a geologist and engineer and seasonal work done on the land: "Gaston went to the Adirondacks on a US. Geological Topological Survey Tour. Left early June from Washington. John Van Ness sent as a delegate to a democratic conference in Chicago, also as Representative to a Democratic Reform Convention in Indiana. Mrs. Folger set out for me heliotrope, verbena, balm and scarlet geraniums, featherfew, cypress, marble petunias, hydrangea and passion vine."

Twenty-seven years of entries on the family's visits to Talavera and the time they spent there. I can't believe my luck. When the journal begins, my grandfather John Van Ness is three years old. By the time it ends he is a young man, almost thirty. The journal in my hands, along with the four others kept by Eliza Worthington while mistress of Talavera, open a window onto life at Talavera for my grandfather, his two brothers, Gaston and Hoffman, and their sister, Elizabeth—the generation that lived at Talavera after Catherine Douw and her three sons.

As soon as I begin reading, however, I am caught by another surprise, one so clear and ironic that before I can stop myself, I have laughed out loud, a startling sound in the dimly lit library of the New-York Historical Society. The reference assistant, whose job it is to protect the archives against possible manhandling by researchers like me, gives me a sharp warning glance. I smile at her, a "don't worry, everything's fine" kind of smile and turn away from her gaze, but I can still feel the beam of her watching eyes. I try to ignore it. I know she is only trying to do her job. Each year the archives in the New-York Historical Society suffer from theft. As the director kindly explained to me one day, the staff believes that some of the worst culprits are researchers whose own families' pasts are housed there. In other words, as soon as the assistant reads the name Leila Stott Philip on the call form for the Philip–Van Ness papers, I am a prime suspect.

I try to behave so as not to alarm the assistant, but the

more I read, the more I want to hoot. I can't help it. Eliza Worthington's journal could be the wall above my desk at home, plastered with yellow Post-It notes about meetings, and research leads, the name of the antibiotic and the date it was given to my son for bronchitis, a taped-up coupon for orange juice, the phone number of the art shipper who will be picking up some of my husband's work. Everything I need to remember and can't gets taped to the wall. My generation calls it multitasking; my great-grandmother called it household accounts.

Eliza Worthington ordered her journal carefully, however, and that is not at all like my haphazard bulletin board of a wall. The first pages list an index for entries in specific areas: "Butter, Eggs, Chickens, Raspberries, Vegetables when sown, Wages to Servants, Flowers." When I turn to those pages, I find seasonal and yearly accounts for the market garden, poultry output and butter production at Talavera, areas of the farm that she seemed to have managed in addition to supervising the care of the house and grounds, tending the children's needs and managing their busy social lives. Her journals record seating plans for dinner parties for twelve and a constant flow of visitors.

Under wages for servants she records whom she has engaged to cook, clean the house, keep the gardens and nurse the children. Flowers were her great joy and extravagance. She might only give fifty cents to the tea peddler and do so grudgingly, but when it came to her ordering flowers, the list blooms. Geraniums, pansies, pink masses of them, feather-few and summer and fall blooming roses, sweet alyssum in a variegated flock, lemon verbena and heliotrope, her list goes on. Individual orders for flowers to set in the gardens or cut flowers for the house could run as much as ten dollars, as much money as four barrels of Seckel pears could bring when shipped downriver to the New York City market.

But the body of Eliza's journal, like the three others with it, reminds me of the mosaic of Post-Its on my wall; the range of her duties and concerns is dizzying. She kept chronological entries for purchases "$1.75 for bronze candlesticks" (they still sit on the library mantel), "$2 for boots for John Van Ness." She noted the seasonal comings and goings of family and friends from Talavera—"Arrived June 5th and found the house in order"—and kept a running list of whom she visited and when—"visit to Livingston Manor, up to Ghent to visit Laura H." (John Van Ness's widow, now married to a Mr. Harrison). She jotted brief notes about adventures with the children: "lovely picnic to lake Chalotte, took boys fishing on the back farm, little Johnny caught five fish." She kept notes on the house and grounds: "Contents of linen closet, winter 1876" and "elms doing well, but grow slowly, set out nine white pines measuring the ridge between the house and barns, afterwards twelve more." She suffered from headaches and also made careful note of them. "I was taken with one of my bad headaches on that Sunday before Easter, directly after Church and was obliged to go to bed and remained there until the following Saturday when I sat up for a brief time."

There was the occasional recipe. One recipe for oyster stew has been carefully backdated December 6, 1864. Eliza was a bride that year, and given the family penchant for oysters, the recipe probably came from her new mother-in-law, Catherine Douw, then still alive and living at Talavera. I don't particularly like oysters, but I make a note to try it: "Oyster Stew—2 quarts oysters, 1 quart milk, ½ lb. butter, spoonful of flower, mace, salt and pepper to taste."

At times Eliza Worthington would paste in newspaper articles, mainly beauty tips and housekeeping ideas:

> **Sleep's Time**—Sleep obtained two hours before midnight, when the negative forces are in operation is the rest which most recuperate the system, giving brightness o the eye and a glow to the cheek.

> **The Uses of Borax**—The washerwomen of Holland and Belgium so proverbially

clean, and who get up their linen so beautifully white, use refined borax as a washing
powder instead of soda, in the proportion
of a large handful of pulverized borax to
about ten gallons of water.

Or she would write notes on watercoloring techniques.
Occasionally, half-finished sketches of people and places appear. But mainly, braided into her collection of daily and
weekly notes, is an ongoing record of the children's heights
and weights, their accidents—"Hoffman fell from the banis-
ter about the fourth step from the bottom and broke his collar bone . . . two weeks in bed was prescribed"—and their
childhood illnesses. The dates of scarlet fever, measles and
whooping cough are all carefully recorded. In an unusually
reflective entry in 1874, Eliza records the birth of her fourth
child and the family's first girl, an infant she will name Elizabeth Worthington Philip after herself, but the family will always call Bessie. "Bessie was supposed to weigh 12 pounds
when first born but the old nurse Aunt Martha, thinking it
unlucky to weigh her, it was not done accordingly. A number of bouquets were showered on the young lady during
the first week of her existence and many little encum-
brances, socks, blankets. Everybody seems so glad that it
should be a dear little girl. For her own sake she is most precious to us, but so wedded have we been to boys that it feels
a measure as if I had been disloyal to them."

Before the journal comes to an end, Eliza Worthington
will lose three children: her handsome eight-year-old,
Charles Worthington; then sunny William Henry, born at
Talavera, and finally the baby, William Houston. In one entry she proudly described this last baby, who was also born at
Talavera only to succumb to illness there fourteen months
later: "Houston weighed thirty five pounds when one year
old—had also both upper and lower front teeth and several
back. Up until this time he has never taken a dose of medi-

cine. Fresh cow's milk from one cow was his only food until a year old—then a baked potato and slice of bread in milk was given him at four o'clock in the afternoon."

Several pages later she records scarlet fever moving throughout the nursery, beginning with Hoffman, and pens her stark, final entry for William Houston: "Precious Houston taken sick on Thursday afternoon at half past five."

In 1881 antibiotics had not yet been discovered. The baby probably died from the same illness that made his older brothers and sister ill but from which they recovered. Eliza Worthington will not mention him again, either in letters or in her journal. I had discovered his place in my grandfather's family only by accident, the day I was browsing through the family Bible and found his date of birth and death carefully recorded. His name had given me a shock, for the only family person named William Churchill Houston Philip that I knew about then was my older brother Bill. But it wouldn't be the first time that I would discover that names in my family were like revolving doors. One generation had them; then the next generation took them over.

Kept with Eliza's journals are some odd papers, including a long elegy to a lost child titled "Poem for My Brother Charles." The poem was dated 1875, and I wondered if Eliza had written it herself as an antidote to her grief. The other likely candidate for authorship, my grandfather, would have been only nine years old at the time, and while he was already pretty good in Latin and geography, the five stanzas of metered verse could not have been his. Eliza had clearly grieved deeply when she lost her first child. That year her mother had sent her a palm-sized volume titled *Consolation for Those Who Mourn*. She kept a marker on page three: "Not my will, but thine, be done" (Luke, 22:42). I would find that small green volume among scores of other books on theology and Christianity that had been carefully packed in wooden trunks and stored in one of the barn lofts. Almost all the books were signed "Eliza W. Philip." Like her mother-in-law, Catherine Douw, Eliza was a devout Christian who read avidly. She was catholic in her taste, reading meditations and lectures from a wide range of scholars and preachers, including those of the evangelist preacher Dwight L. Moody, whose seminary later became the Northfield Mount Hermon boarding school where I had finished high school.

"Multitasking," "household accounts." The range of Eliza's duties, concerns and responsibilities was impressive, but I can't help being disappointed at first by the brevity of her entries. After a while, however, I begin to realize that their short length, like the way they jump from notes on watercoloring to a record of the December pork killing, tells me something important about her. She wasn't a writer, for one thing. Unlike her mother-in-law, Catherine Douw, whose ability to turn a Christian image on the page made words leap, Eliza Worthington wrote in a sparse, matter-of-fact style. Even the elegiac poem to her lost child, while touching, was formulaic and predictable. For her, keeping a journal must have seemed like yet another of her many pressing duties. Probably the few daily lines that she did write were an exercise in self-discipline, especially as her life would become busier, more complicated and increasingly filled with financial worries.

In the first years of her marriage to my great-grandfather William Henry, Eliza spent only summers at Talavera, enjoying city life the rest of the time, but as the number of children multiplied, her journal described increasingly long stays at Talavera. They would leave for Washington as late as December and return while there was still snow. William Henry was often detained by his law practice in Washington, and she would travel on alone with the children and the servants. She did not seem to mind the arrangement, especially as it was not long before her parents were coming to stay at Talavera on extended visits as well. Slipped between journal pages for the year 1872 is a Western Union telegram sent by William Henry from Baltimore on February 21. "Will not return until tomorrow," he wrote, "detained here." Eliza and the family were at Talavera that season, a good two weeks before even the robins and red-winged blackbirds had returned from warmer climes.

It was not unusual that Eliza, as mistress of Talavera, managed the market garden and estate grounds as well as the house, but as time went on, she seemed to take an increasingly active role in overseeing the work on the larger farm as well. When William's brother, Martin Hoffman, decided to leave Talavera and seek his fortune in the manufacturing business in Pennsylvania, William Henry had decided to sell most of the dairy herd and find a farm manager to run the land as crops and hay, which until the turn of the century and the advent of motorcars would bring a good price. That January a Claverack neighbor wrote to recommend a man for the job. "Col. Philip, My Dear Sir," began the letter's author, a Mr. J. Philip, "I think I have found a first class farmer for you. His name is Leroy Van Hoesen. I knew him personally some years ago as an excellent man."

Leroy Van Hoesen and his wife and child soon were living in the tenant house just up from the barns. While he ran the crops, oversaw the haying and tended the small but profitable apple and pear orchard just down from the garden, his wife took over milking the remaining cows, making butter and caring for the poultry. For the next eight years Van Hoesen ran the farm, writing regularly during the winter months of events on the place, usually including mention of Willi, William Henry's mount during the Civil War: "Everything is right about the Place. We are having nice wintry weather not much snow. I will send you a box of poultry so you can have them by Christmas. Old Willi is fine, I think he will winter. The children are all having the Hooping coff."

Some years earlier the house had been broken into, but nothing had been taken. When he went to look for the robbers, Van Hoesen found a pair of demijohns that someone had left on the floor. "Your haus is all right and everything is well. As soon as I sell the corn and hay I will deposit your portion in the bank." He and my great-grandfather were apparently sharing portions of the land and school taxes on the farm, for in that letter, dated January 15, 1873, he informs my great-grandfather that his share of the bill will be $95.65 in land tax, and $7.50 due for the school tax.

Tucked in with Eliza's journals and papers are also several handwritten sheets of directions for work to be done on the place that my great-grandfather had clearly given her, not Van Hoesen, to oversee. For October 1879 the list contained twenty-five items, including "paint waggon and buggy, continue stone wall in back lots, dig out and lay foundation for stone gate posts, straighten farm road and cut down the edge of the woods, draw manure regularly from rear of stable to bring for compost, make a keg of cider." That spring Eliza was busy overseeing a few remaining items on the list. Most of her letters to her husband during the 1870s are full of cheerful descriptions of their life at Talavera and a wish that he rejoin them soon, but on March 27, 1879, she has a bone to pick with him. She begins with news of the place. The peacocks that a Mr. Miller has set aside for them will be coming soon, and a man has come by trying to sell Eliza a large milk goat. "He asked me to come see a goat that he has for sale, half deer he says. I fear it will be too large and expensive, but I will see it tomorrow." She is following her husband's instructions and has two men busy putting in the new cistern while a man named Stickles is at work on the orchard trees. What concerns her is her belief that Van Hoesen may be taking liberties. She chides her husband for not making his arrangements with the farm manager clear. "Van Hoesen wants to keep three pigs. He took off a load of undivided hay to Bristol to sell. Was that right? You ought to have been clear with him before you left."

Apparently, the carting off of the undivided hay was not quite right, for within four days Van Hoesen has been released as the farm manager of Talavera. On April 1 a new lease has been drawn up for a local farmer named Andrew Stickles, probably the man who had been working on the trees. Stickles will get a half share of the potatoes, grain, hay and corn grown at Talavera, including the land planted in potatoes last year by Van Hoesen. In the terms of the lease, which runs for two years, he has been given an area to plant as his own garden and use of the hogpens and hogyard. He and his family will live in the tenant house.

While I would learn to surmise something of Catherine Douw's emotional state by her use of Christian metaphors and imagery, "May God Bless you and keep you as in the hollow of his hand," reflecting quite a different mood from "May God Bless you and keep you as in the hollow of his hand . . . and hide you in the shadow of his wings," I could find nothing similar in Eliza's journal until I began to read more carefully her pages of the poultry and vegetable accounts. I saw a dramatic shift in the 1881 entries.

In 1880 she records proudly that she sold $58.69 in vegetables and seems happy with this sum. She does not bother to break down this income into categories but merely comments, "Aside from this, fresh vegetables enough to bountifully supply our table for a large family." One year later, however, she is working the garden with much more ambition, almost doubling her profits to the sum of $113.80, carefully noting that this was accomplished by the addition of turnips, cabbages, carrots and two barrels of pears, which brought $2.25 each. The next year she increases her profits to $162.46, raising her take by sending apples downriver: two barrels of Baldwins at $6, two barrels of Greenings at $4.50 and two barrels of unnamed apples for $4 each. She also sends corn. Her accounting for the sale of eggs and butter becomes similarly more meticulous: "Eggs, spring 1882, 96 dozen, butter 43 lbs." She begins to keep a notepad on which she records which hens are setting and the number of their eggs: "Hens Setting—Game hen 13 eggs, Spanish hen 13 eggs, Dominique 14 eggs, Brahman 14 eggs." She also records the amounts of poultry meat sold: in 1882, eighty-nine pounds at fifteen cents a pound and eight pounds of turkey. The sales figures are small, yet so carefully noted. Was this the same woman who only nine years before had confidently ordered the latest of Paris fashions?

The spring of 1881 had come on early, a rush of light across the valley, setting the fields ablaze with green. The river opened quickly, flooding its banks. Only a few years earlier they had resilled all the barns, but still the runoff from a sudden snowmelt was terrible. By the first week in May, the perfection potatoes that Eliza had planted on April 26 had sent up feathery green shoots. You could stand by the hawthorn hedges in the center of the garden, look down over the terraced slopes and the fields and grow dizzy from the many levels and hues of green. Just east of the gardens, the hundred apple trees set out in 1866 were wild with bloom. Already the two hired men who helped Stickles were out with the teams, plowing and planting the back fields.

Eliza had journeyed north to Talavera as early as she could that year. My grandfather was enrolled in Claverack College, better known as the Hudson River Institute, and was bringing home perfect marks in Latin and English, Declamation, Astronomy, Arithmetic and Military Drill. William Henry had left Washington several days earlier with a cough, not unusual for him. His bouts of malaria during the Civil War had left him prone to illness. He was a tall, thin man, and when he was not well, his hollow cheeks and deepset eyes gave him a Lincolnesque gauntness. By the time William Henry had reached New York City, his cough had become runaway pneumonia. On May 7, still waylaid in a New York City hotel room, he suddenly and unexpectedly took his last breath.

For Eliza Worthington and for her children, nothing at Talavera would be the same again. She would never stop missing William Henry, but more immediately she had become a widow with four children and a large estate to maintain on an insufficient income.

ೂ

By the time I reach the last pages of Eliza's journals, I am sorry to put the slim volumes away; so much life is compacted in those hastily written five-by-seven pages. But it is almost closing time in the Historical Society's library, so I close the red and black account books and take a quick look at the receipts that I had set aside earlier.

On October 31, 1874, Eliza ordered clothes for the children. I have only to glance to see that neither my grandfather nor his brothers or sister wore the equivalent of Old Navy. At the top of the ornate stationery for the Lilliputian Dress Factory is printed the proud disclaimer "Manufacturers and warehousemen to Her Majesty the Queen of Great Britain and Ireland, the Prince and Princess of Wales, Grand Duchess of Russia, Princess Frederick Charles of Germany, Queen of Denmark and the leading families of Europe, Asia, Africa and America."

My grandfather, John Van Ness, was eight by then; his younger brother, Hoffman, just six. Bessie and Gaston and William Houston were not yet born, and Charles Worthington and William Henry had not yet died. For the children, Eliza Worthington ordered Irish balbriggan stockings, British wool socks, Segovia wool undervests and dogskin gloves and gants de suede.

The next receipt is from a Paris dressmaker to whom she sends $240 for two dresses, two sets of gloves and a matching bonnet, the equivalent of two years of monthly wages for her servant girl, Lucie.

The final receipt is a receipt for transport from New York to Washington. I see train fare for "remains and self," ferry tickets, then the cost of reboxing and disinfectant. Tucked into her red journal, Eliza had saved the undertaker's bill for transporting my great-grandfather's body from New York City to Washington D.C., where it was interred in the Van Ness mausoleum. The bill is dated February 15, 1882. For Eliza Worthington, used to dressing her boys in the garb of princes and herself in clothes of equal finery, the hard times have begun. No more $240 bills from Paris dressmakers, no more gants de suede for the children.

The extra income she could earn from vegetables, dairy and butter helped cover Talavera's bills, but soon their previ-

129

ous lifestyle is beyond her means. By 1887 her account in the Farmer's National Bank of Hudson is only $457.99. Eliza Worthington makes a critical decision: They will spend summers at Talavera, but during the rest of the year they will live in Europe to save money. My grandfather had already graduated from St. Paul's Academy in Long Island by that time and Hoffman was almost finished with his studies at St. Lawrence Academy in Lawrenceville. No one quite knows exactly where they lived and when, but letters and a trail of dressmaker and pharmacy receipts seem to indicate that aside from frequent travels throughout France and Italy, Eliza Worthington based the family in Dresden until 1894.

Eliza's headaches apparently returned. Even back in the happy times at Talavera her journal records her taking to her bed for as long as five days to recover—migraines in the days before Imitrex. She has trouble sleeping and begins to travel to various spas. When she is not taking a cure, she is often traveling to churches and cathedrals. Like her mother-in-law, Catherine Douw, she fears Catholicism and is careful not to visit cathedrals on the Sabbath for fear of angering what she believes is the one true God. But she collects a great quantity of prints, etchings and lithographs as souvenirs: *Capella del Principe di Sansevero*, *La Madone de Saint Sixtei* and an enormous engraving of *Cardinal Guido Bentivoglio*.

Still a young girl when they leave for Europe, Bessie learns to be unusually independent. In an undated letter from their early years in Europe, Eliza Worthington writes to her daughter from somewhere in France, where she is convalescing. "Darling Bessie, Your postals have given me a great deal of pleasure and have conveyed a great deal of news in the short space. Only I beg of you, eat no more *candy+cakes* as you will *surely* be ill." Eliza is staying in a hotel taking a cure. She mentions that her sleeping is getting better, but that her doctor wants her to stay another week. She is not sure if she will do this but explains that if she does stay, she will write for Bessie to come. The plan is for her to send a servant girl named Marie to go fetch Bessie, then bring her back home so that

Bessie won't miss school. As in her opening, Eliza closes with motherly concern: "Lock the house up when you leave and put some water on the ferns. Your devoted Mother. E.W.P"

By the time Bessie is fifteen, she and her mother seem quite settled in Dresden. They have just celebrated Christmas when Bessie sends the following letter to my grandfather. "Dear Van Ness.—It was awfully kind of you to send me that beautiful little brooch. It was just what I wanted and have seen nothing like it over here. We go to the opera quite often and I enjoy it very much, it's rather nice having it so early for then it doesn't prevent me from getting up early and going to school the next morning. . . ."

My grandfather, who had graduated from Princeton three years earlier and then gone on to study law at Georgetown, has begun studying at the École de Droit in Paris. Hoffman has come to visit for the holidays, as has Gaston, their younger brother. Just seventeen that year and busy studying at the University of Heidelberg, Gaston Pearson has already demonstrated the kind of original, creative thinking that often marks the second and third born. He is studying geography and engineering because he plans to explore the South American jungle and bring home emeralds.

Gaston was one of those children in whom the faces of both parents are so perfectly blended it made you gasp. He had inherited something of his father's gaunt solemnity, but overlaid with the sparkling, slightly imperious beauty of his mother. His face was a gravity of angles—the strong forward nose, the decisive chin, cheekbones that soared—but this was offset by his unruly, dark, almost black hair and his unforgivably rakish eyes. It was as if his face contained opposite forces, both duty and abandon, but held in perfect sway. Women found him irresistible.

Bessie adored and idolized her older brother, but Gaston was in trouble again, spending too much time with the pretty fräuleins of Heidelberg. Already he is showing the penchant for good times, beautiful women and liquor that will end in tragedy.

131

In her letter to my grandfather, Bessie, cheerfully rambles on, talking about her drawing lessons as if her aptitude for art was already well known in the family. "I draw four hours a day twice a week. I think my master is a very good one. Gaston arrived on the 23. (late at night as usual). Dresden has the most dismal damp and foggy atmosphere of any place I was ever in. The skating promises to be pretty good if it stops thawing every other day." Bessie had begun to show talent and a determined interest in sketching and drawing. Probably she had been encouraged by her mother, a lady watercolorist of no particular talent but considerable interest. Reading along in one of Eliza Worthington's account books from her travels in Europe, I often come across half-finished sketches of people and places. Tucked away with her miscellaneous papers—calling cards, dinner invitations and party lists, bills and articles from *Harper's* and *McClure's*—are several sheafs of delicate, accomplished watercolors, all landscapes, deftly touched with washes of green and yellow and cerise, pale blue.

By 1894 mother and daughter are corresponding about which Paris art school Bessie should attend. Just eighteen, Bessie of course wants to study art in Paris. In 1894 the lure of Paris for young aspiring painters was like nothing that had come before. With its prestigious government art school, the École de Beaux-Arts, its spring salons and many private academies, Paris had become a mecca for young artists from around the world. Bessie can't study at the government École because women are not allowed, but she can enter one of the many private academies, which had admitted women since 1870. She has two of the most famous ones in mind: "As for the studio, of course it would be splendid if I could get into Duran's but I have rather counted on going to Julien's. Every one says that the first thing to consider is the distance of one's studio from one's home because they are generally too fearfully far away, and as one has to be there at 8 o'clock in the morning, distance has to be considered. I have heard of two different branches of Julien's, one on the Rue Vivienne and another at Rue de Berri. Both are said to be very good.

With love to Hoffman. Ever your loving daughter, Bessie W. Philip"

While the atelier of Charles-Emile-Auguste Duran, a popular painter of society portraits, had gained notoriety for the presence of rising stars such as John Singer Sargent, who studied there for two years, Julian's was the most popular, distinctive and successful of the private art schools. At the Académie Julian, students learned that correct draftsmanship was fundamental. Before being allowed to draw from real life, students had to first master drawing from engravings, then from casts. Each week a subject for composition was given to students to work up in their own studios, and once they had progressed to drawing from real life, they drew and painted from the model.

Within this strict progression, however, Julian's stressed innovation and fostered an atmosphere of fierce competition among students. For Rudolphe Julian, who had founded the school in 1868, an artist's success depended upon dedication, the study of appropriate masters and the forging of an emotional toughness that would allow an artist to persevere in the face of adversity and criticism.

In following her desire to pursue a career in painting, Bessie was probably inspired by early women painters like Mary Cassatt, who had arrived in the 1870s and become a sensation, in part because her family's support of her talent was unbelievably unusual. But the wave of women studying in Paris would have peaked by the time Bessie arrived. And studying at an *académie* did not mean that women received equal treatment. Bessie may have chosen Julian's for reasons other than its many locations. Its admission policy did not discriminate against women, and while it continued the Parisian custom of having women pay more tuition than men (at Julian's a man paid twenty-five francs a month for one half day of instruction, while a woman paid sixty), this was still much less of an inequity than at Duran's, where women paid one hundred francs instead of the thirty required for men.

That Bessie was considering the branch of Julian's located on the rue Vivienne was also interesting, for this studio had been created in 1877 only for women. Whatever location of Julian's that she eventually chose, however, and it seems likely that she ended up there rather than at the studio of Carolus-Duran (Charles Duran), Bessie would have enjoyed what became a renowned camaraderie among the large group of Americans studying there in the 1880s and 1890s.

Pharmacy and dress receipts from Paris for 1895 indicate that by that time Bessie's mother had joined her there. But the following spring, when, as usual, they return to Talavera for the summer, Eliza stays on through the fall. She is not well. On October 28, at the age of fifty-four, she dies in her sleep. The next day the *Hudson Gazette* prints the following obituary: "The sudden death of Eliza Worthington Philip which occurred last evening at her summer residence near Claverack has overwhelmed her friends with sorrow and filled them with sympathy for those dear ones to whom she was so devoted." Interestingly, within a few paragraphs, the obituary focuses upon memorializing her as a wife and a mother and as the mistress of Talavera. Her years of travel in Europe are not mentioned. "Mrs. Philips was entitled by birth to a high position in society and through her many graces she was widely known and much admired. While the social side of her nature was marked still she especially shone in her home life. She was devoted as a wife and bore with patience and submission the bereavements that came to her in the death of her husband and children and to those who are left she has been a loving and devoted mother. Her house reflected her beautiful, enthusiastic and lovely nature. It was full of cheerfulness and comfort and in it she dispensed a gracious and generous hospitality."

The glowing mention of Talavera I found particularly interesting, for only seven years earlier, F. H. Webb, in his local history titled *Claverack, Clover-reach,* had described the long, illustrious history of the Philips and Van Nesses at Talavera, then made a delicate allusion to Eliza's difficult financial state by noting that the house was "at present in a state of neglect."

After her death, my grandfather gathered up his mother's collection of religious prints and, unwilling to throw them out, but unwilling also to have them hanging in the house, carried them up into the cathedral heights of Talavera's upper attic. There the large sheets, including the enormous engraving of *Cardinal Guido Bentivoglio,* flopped down like great white leaves and rested, gathering dust and darkness.

For my grandfather and his brothers and sister, a new era has begun. Bessie makes her way back to Paris, where out of grief or rebellion or simply giddy with her new freedom, she throws herself into the life of a Paris bohemian and moves to the Left Bank. Within two years she has begun to study painting with the bad boy of the Paris art world James Abbott McNeill Whistler.

Exactly how and even if Bessie ever studied very closely with Whistler is not clear, but when she recounted those years in interviews later, she emphasized that he had been her teacher. At least one of the paintings done by her that remains could be said to be Whistlerian, for it is a sparsely painted beach scene with a spare composition and an emphasis upon tonality rather than detail. And Whistler had returned to Paris in 1898, to found an art school, which he named the Académie Rossi, after his model Carmen Rossi, who ended up running the school, but which was popularly called the Académie Whistler.

Twenty years earlier Whistler had gotten into a bitter fight with the art theorist and critic John Ruskin, and his reputation had for a long time flagged, something he blamed on Ruskin and every other figure of the art establishment. Whistler had reacted to Victorian painting and its moral agendas by rejecting narrative and refusing to paint in a detailed, finished manner. In his portraits and seascapes, he was interested in what he called harmonious totalities rather than adherence to realistic details. Ruskin had accused him of throwing paint on his canvases. But for students wanting something progressive, Whistler was an icon, a James Dean–like figure of rebellion. He argued with critics, squabbled in public and was known for his hot temper.

In 1898 Whistler's career was on the rise again after years of bitter nonattention, and he was in Paris, but he rarely took on students. It is possible that Bessie studied at the Whistler Académie and caught his eye. It is also possible that she had minimal actual contact with him but chose to identify with him as the primary influence of her Paris days. By twenty, when she would have studied with him, she was already demonstrating what would become her lifelong trajectory of rebellion against Talavera and her family background.

Yet perhaps she really did study with Whistler, and he had recognized her talent and tough original spirit and encouraged her. Among the few scattered papers about Bessie that I could find was an interview that she gave to the *Florida Times-Union* in 1964. About her studies with Whistler in Paris, she said, "He was a strange little man who wore a little black velvet bow in his hair. He was very angry most of the time and very sarcastic. He wrote a book called 'The Gentle Art of Making Enemies' and I daresay he was good at it. He was such a fine painter; I remember his portrait of Thomas Carlyle, one of the finest things he ever did. Roman style, very classical. And I remember he permitted me to study with him only after he learned that I had won a gold medal for my work in Washington at the Corcoran Gallery."

After their mother's death, my grandfather took an almost fatherly concern and interest in Bessie, something she clearly did not appreciate. If he had known the details of her Paris studies, I doubt that he would have approved. But as luck would have it, as far as Bessie was concerned, he was conveniently busy in Cuba and then the Philippines. That same year both my grandfather and Hoffman signed up for the Cuba campaign. Hoffman was soon accepted into Roosevelt's elite New York troop, the Rough Riders. Bessie continued living on the Left Bank without either of her older brothers there to tell her what she could and could not do.

Soon Gaston leaves Europe as well, accepting a job on the Isthmus of Panama Canal. The letter, which comes directly from the secretary of the Canal Commission in the Department of State, is strangely worded for a job offer. Gaston will receive ninety dollars a month and expenses, but the letter goes on to set out strict terms for his conduct: "If your services prove satisfactory, your return passage from Darien will be paid when the commission no longer needs them; but bad or unsatisfactory conduct on your part would result in your discharge without payment of passage home." It seems likely that either my grandfather or Hoffman had pulled strings to get their brother the job but had warned the commission of Gaston's need for discipline. He does not seem to mind, for at last he is headed for South America.

Bessie continues on in Paris. Then, in the winter of 1900, my grandfather receives word that she is dangerously ill with typhoid fever. Still stationed in the Philippines, he contacts Hoffman, who has just accepted his first diplomatic position, deputy consul to the embassy in Tangier. Hoffman rushes to Paris and takes Bessie to Tangier, where he believes the warm sun will help her convalesce. She seems to make a speedy recovery, for within months she is photographed riding Pedro, one of the two Barb stallions that Hoffman had purchased from a village headsman so that he could play polo with the Tangier Tent Club and, in keeping with the local sport, chase wild boars through the brush with long spears, a pastime called pigsticking.

Aunt Bessie would not have been allowed to join the bloody sport, even if she had wanted to. But in keeping with the tradition of turn-of-the-century lady adventurers in the Arab world, she is dressed like an "honorary male" in men's pants and blousy man's shirt. She sits forward in the saddle, a style of riding still considered unladylike in England, where for women, riding sidesaddle was preferred. In the photograph, her face has almost disappeared beneath her huge grin. She and Hoffman spend several months together in Tangier before Bessie makes another bold move, one that supports the idea that she really has studied with Whistler. She leaves for Tokyo to study wood-block printing.

Forty years earlier it had been Japanese wood-block prints, considered valueless in Japan and thus shipped to Europe as wrapping for ceramics, that had caught the eye of French artists, who began to collect them. Among painters of his time, Whistler had been one of the first to be influenced by these prints and evolve a distinctly Japanese style. From 1900 through 1902 Bessie would reside in Tokyo, studying traditional wood-block printmaking and living an expatriate life about which little is known.

CHAPTER TWELVE

Hardly a Hasty Word

By May 1903 my grandfather, Bessie and Gaston all had returned to Talavera. In a slim journal that he titled "Farm Diary, Talavera," my grandfather recorded five busy months when they lived there together, in apparent harmony, although they had come home for different reasons. Gaston seemed broke. He had apparently behaved well enough in Colombia to remain at work for the U.S. government on the isthmus canal for some time, but by 1902 his brothers were worried about him again. That October, Hoffman, still happily posted in Tangier, wrote my grandfather about Gaston's unsettled ways, which more and more often involved various women. "I hope you let me know your first news of Gaston. I hope he does not go and get married on that $100. If he could find the right sort of girl. I believe it would be a capital thing for him in many ways." Soon Hoffman was commenting that he supposed low finances had brought Gaston to Claverack. My grandfather responded with discouraging news: "It is very disheartening to feel that Gaston has an idea apparently but to spend what money he can get his hands on but I believe that is the worst he would do."

Perhaps Gaston had already gotten into his infamous "trouble." One family story recounts that he got into a fight with a man over a woman and shot the man. The man died, and Gaston was sent out of the country for a while until the affair settled down. He was also known for keeping company with the illustrious architect and notorious woman chaser Stanford White and was with White one night in a New York City club when the architect supposedly shot a man. The family didn't want Gaston called as a witness and so had him conveniently sent abroad for some time. It is impossible to track down which, if either, of these stories is true, but what is clear is that just as their father, William Henry, and his brother Lieutenant John Van Ness had spent years sorting out the screwball finances of their younger brother Martin Hoffman, so they cared for the handsome ne'er-do-well of their generation, Gaston Pearson.

140

Bessie was delighted that Gaston was returning home. She was also returning for unclear reasons, probably some of them financial. In November 1902, she wrote my grandfather from Tokyo: "I have at last really decided to leave Japan, but I can't resist the temptation of going home via India and Tangier. Train from Calcutta to Bombay. I will send a cable from Calcutta." That February Hoffman traveled to meet her in Gibraltar. He and my grandfather were still trying to convince her to settle down to a respectable life in Washington, D.C., where I imagine they hoped she would have some chance of finding a husband and getting married. But Bessie would have none of it. She promptly informed Hoffman that she planned to journey on to southern Spain. Half apologizing for his failure to influence her, Hoffman wrote my grandfather that he had heard Bessie had been quite a *hit* in India, then explained: "She has done all this *by* herself and I suppose it is wonderful that *nothing* has happened. . . . I can say that I seem to have no weight with her."

By early spring of that year Bessie was writing to my

grandfather from England, where she was staying with a Lady Cecil of Stockton Hall. She was thrilled with the horses, which she described as "perfect marvels of endurance" and had been enjoying the attentions of a young man who had offered her the pick of his stable so that she could follow the hounds. She proudly described how she was also being provided with horses by a renowned horse dealer in Leicestershire who had no doubt drummed up some business for himself by telling her that "the bold and determined way I ride over the country necessitates the very best."

No doubt my grandfather would receive the bill. He had returned home to take over managing the farm and sort out the family's affairs. Hoffman, my grandfather, Bessie and Gaston all had agreed that it was time for them to create independent finances. Up until that point, whenever Bessie or Gaston needed funds, they would write my grandfather, who would forward the bills to an agency called Fishers, which handled whatever funds they had inherited from their mother as well as their jointly owned property in Washington, D.C.

In October 1902 Hoffman wrote from Tangier, where he was still deputy consul to approve my grandfather's decision to introduce beef cattle. Money was apparently tight all around. "I think your action in buying the cattle for us was good business—especially considering the poor quality of hay this year. The price you paid not too high. I see old Snyder still draws his advanced wages. I sincerely hope that an extra man's wages will not be added for the care of the cattle through the winter. Has Peyton S. paid his pasture bill?"

By the summer of 1903 my grandfather had quit his position as chief of the War Department's Bureau of Insular Affairs, the plum he had received after returning home from active service in Cuba and the Philippines. From that point on, everything he did was shaped by the volatile economics of agriculture in the valley, by the sprawling yellow house and by his role as eldest son and caretaker of the family. When I finally put the pieces of my grandfather's life together, it was amazing to me to consider how much his decision mirrored the path of the family's dead war hero, Lieutenant John Van Ness, after whom he had been named. Like his uncle, my grandfather had ascended rapidly in a military career, then in his thirties, while enjoying that success, had abruptly left it behind to live at Talavera.

In 1902 my grandfather headed home a confirmed bachelor, not the delighted husband of a beautiful heiress, as Lieutenant John Van Ness had been. But like his uncle, he showed a great love for the land at Talavera and became interested in the larger social and political aspects of agriculture.

In many ways, my grandfather was more of an eccentric in his decision than his uncle had been. In 1902 agriculture in the valley was not booming the way it had been in the years leading up to the Civil War, and the romantic era model of the gentleman farmer, with its moral and political agendas, held little popular appeal.

Still, my grandfather headed home, stubbornly, or nostalgically, or out of a sense of family duty, right back into history, back to tradition, back to Talavera, back to the land. For several years he had been serving long distance as the vice president of the Columbia County Agriculture and Horticultural Association, that vestige of scientific agriculture founded by his uncle. Now he entered politics, running as Columbia County's Democratic nominee for the state assembly. He lost the election and the money he had spent financing his campaign, but in the photograph of him taken for his 1903 campaign poster, he looked out with vision and optimism, his blue eyes keenly focused on an unseen target, his entire then-youthful face, with its strong eyebrows and long, slim nose, a study in classical symmetry and pose.

When I opened the small black book that recorded his months at Talavera from that time, I saw his evident pride in his Dutch heritage, for pasted inside the cover was a black-and-white image of the Van Ness coat of arms, with its silly knight's helmet, three stars and the words *Pro Deo Et Nobilissima Patria Batavorum*. The first pages recorded the names of people he was then employing to work on the farm: Fred Snyder as "head man and farmer," Sidney Kells as "second man and laborer," John Schram as "laborer—no rent, farmhouse" and William May as "ditcher for 1.25 per day plus board." The advanced wages that Hoffman complained about for Mr. Snyder totaled thirty dollars a month with house and garden and board for one cow and one hog. Mr. Snyder's wife cared for the chickens, did the milking, made butter and could earn an extra ten dollars a month by boarding workmen. The second man earned twenty dollars a month with room and board.

Then my grandfather described the busy, varied and cheerful life he enjoyed as the twentieth-century version of the gentleman farmer, as busy with the landscaping of Talavera's grounds as he was with overseeing the planting of young trees and crops on the farm. His journal began:

MAY— Weather cold and season backward. Planting began

MAY 16 Set hedge of honey locust in West side of garden—2 men and 3 horses

MAY 26 Finish planting young orchard

MAY 29 Leave Talavera at 7:00, arrive Copake Flats 9:00 (a distance of 21 miles) trout fish on Roleff Jansen kill

In addition to introducing beef cattle, my grandfather was expanding the orchards. To the one hundred trees planted near the gardens that his mother noted in her journal to be "doing nicely" in 1888, he added a new orchard, which he called block eight: "Baldwins, Newtown Pippins, Bellflowers, Seek No Furthers, Crabapples and Greenings." Next to the volumes on agriculture and landscaping collected by his uncle, my grandfather carefully collected the latest reports from the Department of Agriculture as well as important new works such as S. A. Beach et al.'s encyclopedic *The Apples of New York* and Jesse Buel's *The Farmer's Companion*.

As important to my grandfather as his records of the growing number of apple trees, the types of sheep, cattle, hogs and poultry kept at any given time and the progress of various crops were his notes about his riding horses, Freeship and Hari Kari, and his two white pointers, Lady and Jumbo, which he kept to hunt partridge and woodcock. The journal records his many trips to visit friends, to fish for trout and to attend meetings. He might ride to Hudson to board the *Ontario* and steam downriver to New York City to shop for a new hat, then, given the sartorial standards passed on to him by his mother, complain about it soundly: "Could not find but one hat at all smart in the whole town and that I found at Brooks. We are about two years behind the English styles that we try to copy." He might oversee the planting of corn one day, then leave for Washington, D.C., by train to visit President Roosevelt at the White House and travel back to New York with Mrs. Roosevelt, journeying back up the Hudson by boat.

On June 3 he delivered a lecture titled "Farming in the Philippines, the Moro Tribe, etc." for the Claverack Grange. That week brought on a typical burst of June heat in the valley, and he noted: "Heat more oppressive than in Cuba or Philippines." Bessie and Gaston were soon off in the runabout, heading the two driving horses, Toma and Talavera, toward the cool shade of the Catskill Mountains. My grandfather, ready for any excuse to go fly fishing, used the rationale of the terrible heat to hitch Hari Kari to the rubber-wheeled wagon and, once the cool of the afternoon began, set out with his fly pole for the Copake Flats or the Greene River. On June 10, heat or no, he drove twenty miles north to Chatham to attend a reunion of the Grand Army of the Republic and Spanish War Veterans.

A heat wave in early June is not uncommon in the Hudson Valley, and that year it must have been followed by just enough rain, for by July 16 my grandfather recorded thirty-one loads of hay brought into the barns, along with six loads of rye and four loads of potatoes. Two days later he rode to Hudson to pick up twelve hundred cabbage plants and had three men set them out along a ditch. Soon good news surfaced on the family front as well: Gaston had received a telegram from the U.S. Panama Canal Commission asking if he could be ready to leave for Panama in a week. He had been offered a position as one of the assistant engineers for the Panama Canal.

On August 2, Bessie and Gaston left Talavera in the morning. Bessie was to accompany Gaston to New York City and see him off. My grandfather was clearly very proud of Gaston and probably relieved: "Gaston will be one of the Assistant Engineers on the Panama Canal—the largest artificial waterway ever undertaken by man." He added: "We have lived together for a year here without hardly a hasty word between us."

In another month my grandfather was busy with harvest preparations for second crops of hay and rye and corn, for plums, cabbage, apples and pears. On September 7 he took a break to ride to Lenox and participate in a gymkhana there. On Hari Kari, he won first place in "slicing three lemons in succession cut with a sabre at a full gallop." Then he rode home to oversee the planting of twenty-six bushels of rye in the nine-acre "Pine Tree Lot," where a spreading Carolina hemlock, planted by his uncle forty-six years before, still punctuated the view, rising as an emblem of that once-wild American land.

My grandfather's interest in agriculture and commitment to farming Talavera did not seem to waver even throughout those years of agricultural slump in the Hudson Valley, but by 1909 things had begun to look up. Hay was no longer profitable, since cars and trucks, tractors and streetcars were replacing horses in the city and country alike, but again cities like New York and Boston needed food.

Many of the valley's farms had gone belly up in the wake

of the agricultural depression that followed the Civil War, but now cities had grown to the point at which once more population had outpaced food production, and prices were good for those farmers who had managed to hang on. Apples shipped to New York City from Talavera began bringing twenty-two cents a pound on the barrel, and that year Talavera apples were of high enough quality to be shipped via the FK Fisher company to London, England. Prices for sheep were also rising, for the journal recorded Talavera sheep bringing forty cents a pound per head in the nearby town of Philmont.

By 1909 my grandfather had expanded his farming operation to include six hundred acres in the Old Forge area, his favorite trout-fishing ground. He had purchased five farms there on which he ran sheep. That year, from a herd of 227 ewes, 185 lambs were born. He had also added sheep at Talavera, for his farm journals from that time noted the transfer of ewes and lambs between the two locations. Soon, in complete faith with the rustic tradition of English landscaping, when you stood on the front porches at Talavera, you could look out across the lawns to front meadows dotted white with the bushy, woolly shapes of Shropshire ewes. My grandfather continued planting and shaping the grounds at Talavera throughout his life there, but in 1909 he set out a record number of ornamental trees, on April 12 alone, a hundred European larches, a hundred catalpa speciosas and a thousand honey locusts. In May he set thirteen arborvitaes along the farm drive and planted two magnolias, one by the house and one down by the recently constructed tennis court. A small berm rose up on the far side of the court, so identical to one landscaped at nearby Olana that several horticultural historians believe the berm at Talavera to have been influenced by Frederic Church's design. On the house side of the berm, my grandfather planted another stand of pine, creating a green wave of trees.

It would never occur to me when I was growing up that someone had deliberately planned out, then planted the many nooks and crannies, sudden glens and secret sheltered places that we ran through and hid in as part of our games. But all these improvements took money, and how my grandfather acquired such lavish amounts of it, I am not certain, but spend he did. By 1909 he and Hoffman had taken over full ownership of Talavera. Although Bessie and Gaston continued living at Talavera, they had relinquished their share of it years earlier for one dollar, the equivalent of the British peppercorn. An act of self-sacrifice, necessary to keep the family homestead intact, or an act of relief? From that point Gaston and Bessie were free of any financial responsibility toward Talavera. Only Hoffman, whose diplomatic career did not bring him back to the United States to live until 1950, remained on the deed of Talavera as a long-distance partner. For the next five years he helped finance the orchards.

Presumably Gaston was still working in Panama in 1905, the year the deed was signed, for a Washington lawyer signed on his behalf. Soon after, my grandfather deeded to Gaston and Bessie Pierce Place, a thirty-acre piece of land that bordered Talavera to the north. The property came with a lovely white house and magnificent horse barns, and Bessie seemed happy with the arrangement. No doubt, after traveling the world on her own, she was not about to keep house for her brother, especially not a house like Talavera, which had become the vocation of many women in the family before her.

The years 1910 to 1914 came to be called the golden age of agriculture in the Hudson Valley, and a large part of what contributed to the return of good times for farms there was the newly discovered cash crop fruit. For some time apples grown in the valley had held a reputation for exceptional flavor. As Hudson Valley fruit growers would have it, the popular expression *okay* evolved from the Old Kinderhook fruit stamp *O. K.* that labeled boxes of apples grown just north of Claverack in the Dutch settlement of Old Kinderhook. Buyers reached for the fruit boxes marked "OK," and the expression became synonymous with anything that was good.

By 1914 hundreds of farms were raising apples and pears up and down the temperate Hudson Valley.

My grandfather clearly believed in the future of this trend, for by 1909 he recorded planting 1,864 apple and pear trees. On July 5, 1910, he sent Hoffman a detailed list of the trees he put in—"Yellow transparent, Greening, Northern Spy, Pewaukee, Baldwin, Clapps Favorite and Kieffer selected"—and a bill for Hoffman's share of the cost of tree purchase and planting, which came to $389.33. My grandfather outlined his plan to begin producing a new apple that he believed would do well: "The McIntosh Red is an apple of excellent flavor and color and sells extremely well, but is hard to grow from the stock obtained in nurseries; therefore it is better to graft it upon a thrifty growing variety like the above." My grandfather was convinced of the economic viability of fruit and clearly wanted his brother and business partner to be convinced as well: "If the trees are brought into proper bearing conditions and bear, the return from them will be many times greater than anything else that can be put on the land; and therefore everything should be done to further the interest of the trees."

It seems that Hoffman was easily convinced, for my grandfather moved ahead on his systematic plan to transform Talavera's farm from cattle and crops to fruit. These first orchards were interplanted with alfalfa, buckwheat, yellow flint corn, turnips and beans, but gradually, as the number of trees increased, he planted only ground cover crops like clover and buckwheat, Japanese millet and rye that were plowed back with the Clark cutaway harrow to condition the soil. The next spring my grandfather had three men clearing land of rocks and stumps with 40 percent Red Cross dynamite in order to plant 760 more trees, creating two more orchard blocks. This pattern continued until the entire farm, save for two small hayfields and the designated twenty-five acres of "park" around the house, was planted in apples and pears, with scattered blocks of peaches, cherries and plums.

CHAPTER THIRTEEN

Talavera, 1913

T he fall of 1913 promised to be a good harvest at Van Ness Orchards. The older trees were bearing well, and the one- and two-year-old plantings, benefiting from the hot summer and my grandfather's insistence upon regular watering, had grown beautifully. The younger trees had been hard hit during July by a typical midsummer flare-up of mites, but my grandfather had gotten them under control through regular applications of pesticide, usually one gallon of lime and sulfur concentrate, mixed with one pint of black leaf and a hefty five pounds of lead arsenate.

But there was trouble on the family front. Bessie had decided that she was sick of living in the Hudson Valley. She was also, it seemed, sick of Talavera, sick of her brothers and sick of being a Philip. She held a public auction to sell off her share of family possessions, which, because she was the only girl, meant most of the silver, crystal, furniture and even some of the family portraits. Later, in a slim memoir, she wrote how she "despised the Hudson Valley Aristocracy." By then she had a plan that she knew she should keep secret from her brothers.

Appalled and outraged by what they considered an act of family treason, my grandfather and Hoffman bought as much as they could of the family things which Bessie put up for sale. On my wall is taped a Western Union telegram that Hoffman, then the secretary of the embassy in Constantinople, sent to my grandfather: "Must have sideboard." The same summer that he sent the cable, Hoffman was busy helping save lives in the midst of the growing human tragedy around him. He had already been awarded the Red Cross Balkan War Medal for his work bringing relief to victims of cholera and Turkish aggression. Still, while engaged in humanitarian efforts across the globe, well aware that that part of the world was about to erupt into further violence, Hoffman felt keenly the need to preserve the family place, with everything just as it had been at Talavera.

My grandfather managed to buy most of the Dutch silver, the portraits, the dining room set and the sideboard that Hoffman wanted. Then, on September 7, Bessie initiated stage one of her larger plan. She hired a young German couple to help her and prepared to drive south to Florida, where she intended to buy some property and move. She loaded up her seven horses and three dogs and set out in a reconditioned school bus.

My grandfather was soon busy, not only with the upcoming farm harvest but with his decision to run a second time for the state assembly. However, after his recent expenditure of funds to buy back the family things from Bessie, he did not have enough money to finance his campaign and took a four-thousand-dollar loan from a friend along the river who accepted his portrait of his great-uncle General John P. Van Ness as collateral. The portrait, a handsome rendering done by Gilbert Stuart, was a family heirloom, but my grandfather clearly assumed that he would be able to pay the loan back shortly, for the two friends did not bother to draw up papers. The deal was completed with a handshake.

Then October arrived with multiple shocks. Gaston, perhaps floundering without the company and watch of his

younger sister, became sick and died. The stated cause was
pneumonia. The unstated cause was alcoholism. Gaston had
begun to exhibit a family intolerance for alcohol that later
surfaced in my father. There was speculation that my grandfather too had begun a habit of drinking, for eventually we
found mountains of glass whiskey bottles hidden under the
outhouse.

One month after Gaston's sudden death Bessie sent my
grandfather a letter from Haycross, Georgia. "Dear Van Ness,
I forgot to tell you in my last letter that I became Mrs. J. Peter Stark. . . ." She had eloped with Jacob Peter Stark, the
man who had been taking care of her horses at Talavera. Unknown to my grandfather or Hoffman, he had traveled south
to meet up with her. They planned to buy land in Florida
and build a winter resort there for people who liked riding
and fishing.

Uncle Jack, as he came to be called by my father and his
brother, seems to have been accepted by my grandfather.
Perhaps he and Hoffman were simply glad to see their sister
married at last. They may also have known Jack Stark for
years. One of the names in their mother's journal under the
list of Talavera servants was one Louisa Stark, probably Jack
Stark's mother, if not another close relative.

My grandfather was soon distracted by another problem.
He lost the election and could not pay back the four-
thousand-dollar loan, especially as Hoffman had decided that
he would like to withdraw from partnership in the farm.
Busier than ever in Constantinople, where a cholera epidemic was leaving thousands dying in the streets, Hoffman
did not demand half the value of the farm and estate, which
technically, as half owner, he was entitled to. Still, my grandfather was hard pressed to find the five thousand dollars that
they agreed upon.

The winter of 1914 my grandfather closed the south
wing of the house and lived on the north side to save money.
He rearranged the portraits in the dining room, removing
Marcia Burns, General John P. Van Ness's widow, so that she

would not stare across at the shamefully empty space where the portrait of her husband had hung. To fill in the gaps on the walls, he brought in the elegant Ammi Phillips portraits of his grandmother and grandfather and shifted the more elderly rendition of Catherine Douw and her three sons a little to the left along the walls.

The kitchen was still in the cellar, but my grandfather had a dumbwaiter put in so that he could live there with minimal help from servants. Before the cracking of green in early spring, it was not uncommon for at least one ice storm to thrash against the house. By the time the storm was over, such a thick coating of ice coated the trees that when even the gentlest of winds blew, the drooping fronds of pine and hemlock that surrounded the house tinkled like bells. Alone at Talavera, how could my grandfather avoid thinking about the wasteful, sad demise of his younger brother, the infuriating flight of his younger sister? Meanwhile, after an ice storm, the young apple and pear trees became icicles, their fragile fruit buds, already swollen, waiting for spring, next year's crop safe in their ice cocoons.

It was six years before my grandfather married the daughter of the wealthy Stott family just up the road. The winter of 1914 the lovely Helen Stott was still far from Columbia County, traveling through Egypt, where she was photographed in great style on the back of a large camel.

152

CHAPTER FOURTEEN

The Lives of Aunts

*T*he wild aunt, the radical aunt, the aunt who had been forgotten altogether. My family didn't talk about these women, so of course I was keenly interested in the shadowed, slightly forbidden topic of their lives. I knew their names: Aunt Bessie, Aunt Leila Stott, Aunt Lee. But what I learned about them I often discovered by accident, coming upon a campaign poster, or a gold-tipped riding crop, or a newspaper article, or a photograph, or, while sorting the linen closet one day, a beautifully embroidered tablecloth from Vienna. These aunts all had lived at Talavera and had left their mark there: a random possession now enshrined, or a photo, or a favorite chair, so that they became part of my childhood there, part of what I would discover as I explored the old house and barns or overheard while taking in fragments of adult conversation in the formal dining room. But these were just fragments of whole lives, lives that, for the most part, had been lived off the record.

Aunt Bessie was the only girl in the family and as such pretty much did as she pleased. Fate had granted her tremendous independence and a definite lack of guidance. Her misbehavior and lack of reverence for family connection made her an appealing role model in my mind, as did her freedom and general boldness. When I was nine, ten, eleven, I was most in awe of her because she was famous for fox hunting sidesaddle. I could just see her astride one of the large dark warm bloods with which she was often photographed in full riding habit, her gold-tipped riding crop held nonchalantly at her side. When the powerful horse rose up and over the fence, her long black dress swept out behind. Then they were down and galloping after the hounds, racing and roiling just ahead. Later I would go to live in Japan, just as she had done.

While my grandfather, as the eldest son, fashioned a life with Talavera as its center, taking over responsibility for the house and actively farming the land, Aunt Bessie seemed to spend her life fleeing it, a kind of heiress on the run. Only the problem was, even then the family finances were limited. She would write to my grandfather from Calcutta, from Tokyo, from Tangier, from Paris, ignoring his pleas that she return to Washington. Usually these letters, filled with her plucky descriptions of people and places, ended with an address where—could he please send her a line of credit? She seemed to be running low.

While Aunt Bessie seemed to fall in love with her expatriate notoriety, her maid, Isabella, was rightly mortified. In her slim self-published memoir of her travels, *Around the World in Three Years,* Bessie proudly describes how a policeman had to be called to break up the crowds that had come to watch them cross the street. No doubt the Japanese stared agape at Isabella with her black skin and Bessie with her red hair. Isabella soon returned to the United States, but Bessie stayed on, living in a traditional Japanese house with her bug-eyed Japanese spaniel. Clearly, she had loved reinventing herself in foreign terrain. Even when I had gone to Japan during the 1980s, people there had stared at my blond hair and blue eyes. Sometimes on the train I would feel a hand stroking the fine blond hairs on my arm. I had only to open my mouth and speak fluent Japanese to astonish. I felt I understood something about Aunt Bessie's reluctance to go home.

I never got a chance to meet my aunt Bessie because she died when I was eight, but my oldest brother and my oldest cousin had. In the photographs of their trip to visit her in Florida, she is keeping company with a fine-boned collie. Her once-red hair swirls around her face in a white flame. She died on the edge of a trailer park in a tiny house. By then she was a devout vegetarian—living on a diet that consisted mainly of nuts and grains—impoverished but seemingly unperturbed.

Although I grew up worshiping the idea of my aunt Bessie and her exploits as a kind of childhood hero, she was a distant figure to me, someone whom I felt I should not imitate, even though I wanted to. In contrast, my other aunts, especially the radical aunt, the political one, my aunt Lee, came to represent a kind of role model, a possibility, even an obligation for a way to be. This feeling was no doubt accentuated by the fact that we both were named Leila. I assumed that I was named after her.

Actually, as I would discover, this was only partly true. I had been named more directly for another Leila in the family, Leila Stott, my father's little sister, who had died from meningitis when she was three. Apparently my grandmother, a superstitious person, had not wanted me to be given this name, but when I was born on April 18, my grandfather's birthday, she had decided that the coincidence was auspicious. I suspect that for my grandmother, the sight of three-year-old me tumbling on the lawn must have been a poignant déjà vu. But she never mentioned that Leila when I was growing up, nor did she keep a photograph of her in the library, where we always gathered.

I found out about Leila Stott in high school when one day I noticed for the first time the black-and-white portrait of a little girl resting on the bookshelf in the far sitting room. I asked my mother who she was, and I don't remember feeling any surprise when my mother told me that my father had

155

had a little sister named Leila Stott who had died. Such silence toward the past was typical of my family, and I never
thought to question it.

In the photograph, Leila Stott is looking down at a white
ball resting by her feet. She is dressed like a princess in a
white frock, white bonnet, white stockings and white shoes.
Her face a hazy study of three-year-old glee. When I look at
the photograph now, I think not so much about her as about
my father. He had been seven when his little sister died, and
in the flurry of letters from that time, uncles and aunts express concern at his enormous grief: "How is young Johnny
doing with the terrible shock? It must seem to you all, just
too much to bear."

Leila Stott had been much beloved, but she was of the
past and had been deliberately left there, so that she did not
seem part of the family's history. The aunt whom I thought
about the most from high school on was my aunt Lee, Leila
Vanderbilt Stott. She floated in the background of my
emerging sense of who I was so strongly that once I had begun my quest into the past, she was one of the family members that I most wanted to find out about. So far with little
success.

My childhood memories of her clustered like stars, but as
with all the aunts and even my grandmother, the rest was
dark space. She remained as much of an enigma as my
debonair grandfather, perhaps more. I had tantalizing bits of
information about her. I knew that she had studied in Vienna
at the turn of the century when it was still Europe's intellec-
tual hotbed, that she had been an early suffragette, that she
had run for political office in the American Labor party, that
she had been a union organizer and a teacher and that she
had helped found a school in New York City. I knew that she
had never married. But I had no details about any of it.

My mother remembered that two boxes of my aunt Lee's
personal papers had been kept in the downstairs bedroom at
Talavera, but during the property division in 1973, these papers along with her campaign poster had disappeared. I had

searched everywhere, especially through family papers housed in the New-York Historical Society, but could find nothing. In some ways I was not surprised. Aside from short diaries, shopping receipts and correspondence, little remained to document the lives of any of the women in the family. While my grandfather was a stranger to me because I had never known him, I could look up the facts of his early military years in the Spanish-American War and World War I, his political life in various Roosevelt ministries in Washington and his involvement with the farm at Talavera by reading through the boxes of his papers.

In contrast, nothing was on file about my great-aunt. Was it because the family felt her work had been insignificant, or had there been a conscious or unconscious effort not to preserve her active, somewhat radical past? I couldn't say, but I wanted to know more, especially after I found in the library closet a deed in which she lent my grandfather and grandmother thirty-six thousand dollars. The deed was dated 1936. Times were bad for the farm, agriculture in the valley having peaked, then busted during the Depression. But Aunt Lee had thirty-six thousand dollars to lend my grandfather, money that kept the farm at Talavera solvent. I am pretty sure that she was never repaid, for in the letters between her and her sister, there is no mention of the loan, nor is there a receipt of repayment.

Both my great-aunt Lee and my grandmother dressed in similar versions of fine cotton dresses with soft floral prints, always in colors of purple and blue. By the time I was six they were old and frail. Betty made them soft-boiled eggs and toast for breakfast, and when I think of them, I can see still the bits of dried yellow egg that would often remain at the corners of their mouths, the white Kleenex tumbling out from the edges of their sleeves, the white paper skin of their hands. Both wore glasses, the pointed kind with shimmering rhinestones in the corners. But my grandmother often took hers off, and I remember the startling Caribbean blue of her eyes, which even later, when her speech had become a tangle of guttural sounds and the blue clouded with cataracts, continued to send out waves of interest and love as if she were marooned in her failing body, shipwrecked, but still hopeful, her eyes beaming out signals, a steady, hopeful SOS: "Here I am, here I am."

Unlike my grandmother, whom I remember mostly sitting in the library, Aunt Lee liked to sit and read on the south porch. She was a fixture of our summer days, an accepting and benign presence that seemed to welcome our constant interruptions. My mother remembers her patience with me one summer, when too young to go to school yet, I pestered her to teach me how to read. I recall her large old-lady shoes crossed at the ankles, the book on her lap, her eyeglasses hanging from a chain around her neck. She would sit there, steeped in sun, framed by splashes of red and purple and white, the geraniums and petunias that always filled the long window boxes along the edges of the porch. When I was very little, I would pick berry boxes full of yucca pods down in the garden, then walk carefully back to the porch and carry my pretend cucumbers up to sell to her. How the long white fingers would struggle with the clasp of her black purse, eventually fishing out a dime. Then how eagerly the thin arms would reach out and grasp me, a hug so faint I felt enclosed in a circle of air.

In the horse stables I would catch sight of her campaign poster, which had been tacked on the wall by the crossties. Since I was always down there doing one thing or another with the horses, I saw it often. In the black-and-white photo, she looks much younger than when I knew her, a vigorous, confident-looking woman who stares ahead as if to say, "Here I am, take it or leave it." But what I really liked was the caption underneath, the large black Roman letters that proclaimed "Vote for Leila V. Stott." When I bent over to pick stones out of a hoof or to stab at piles of the pungent sweet manure with my pitchfork, I could feel the power of those words and her unknown story. She had been a teacher and a spinster, her loves and desires kept secret from her family to the end. Had her role model been her forebear on the Livingston side Elizabeth Cady Stanton? Stanton had shown the possibilities of resisting, yet making good use of the landed patriarchy into which she had been born.

I once tried to ask my father about my aunt Lee. I was seventeen at the time and feisty with my newfound awareness of feminism. When I asked him why he thought my great-aunt had never married, he answered that she had been beautiful and that several men had wanted to marry her. He didn't talk about her political activism or her dedication to her work. He wanted to impress upon me that she had not been a spinster by default, that she could have married if she had wanted to.

The blank spaces. These erasures of personal history that time and my family had wrought upon these women's lives was in such stark contrast with the detailed way the lives of the family's men had been recorded that I wanted to recover these women, my aunts, my past.

159

It was my mother who suggested that I call Janet Chester to see if she had known my grandmother or great-aunt Lee. Mrs. Chester had belonged to the Ladies Democratic Club of Columbia County at the same time that my grandmother and aunt had been members.

"Sure I knew your grandmother," Mrs. Chester said easily when I called her on the phone. I could hear her take a breath before she began. "Your grandmother, now she was something. What a charming, adorable lady. And I knew your great-aunt Lee as well. The sixties was our time. Yes, it was. I would pick your grandmother up and drive her to the meetings. Dinner was at six; then there was a lecture. Every month we would go. Sometimes Lee was with her. She was something, they both were, those Stott girls. Oh, the times we had . . ." Mrs. Chester's voice trailed off for a moment, then came back. "And you're Julia's daughter? Isn't that something. I knew your father too, what a wonderful man. I love to talk about old times, I really do—"

I quickly interrupt and ask when I can interview her. She can meet me the next week, if I will come to her house. She and her husband have sold their place in Taghkanic and live on upper Warren Street in Hudson.

JULY 20, 1999

By the time I arrive, the main street is glazed with sun. Kids in shorts and tank tops mill about stoops and entryways or wander, rubber-thonged, aimless in the heat. Hudson, a sprawling river town, once so depressed that it seemed to be folding in upon itself, was undergoing a revival as an antiques center. Lines of antique shops faced out along the street.

At the stoop of a large town house, I adjust my bag, checking that my tape recorder and list of questions are in place, then reach for the doorbell. There is none. I try the door handle, and it turns, the door opening into a narrow foyer and a curtained inner door. Again, I look around for a doorbell and find none. Then I notice that the inner door has been left ajar. I push it open slowly, calling out, "Hello. Mrs. Chester? Hello?"

My words are soon swallowed in a flood of wind and sound, the slurring roar of a fan on high. No one answers. I call again, louder this time to be heard over the roar of the fan. Only then does a loud, clear voice answer. "I'm in here."

I turn to the left, following the voice and the noise, and find myself in a sunny front room crammed with bookshelves and dark furniture. A large woman in a casual but carefully pressed white blouse and light slacks sits facing me. Mrs. Chester. Although two red armchairs and a couch are arranged nearby, she sits on a hard wooden chair, bolt upright. At her feet I notice a half-empty glass of iced tea. By one of the red armchairs, I see another glass of iced tea still full. Beads of cold sweat jewel the glass. She has been waiting for me. As soon as I step in, she stares at me intently, her arms extended sphinx style along the sides of her chair. She does not get up but leans forward slightly and begins to speak. Her voice is muffled by the roar of the fan, but still I hear each word clearly.

"There are things that I know that I am *not* going to tell you." She says this not unkindly but very firmly, emphasizing each word as if she has been pondering this decision for a long time but is still uncertain if she has made the right decision. The fan whips her brown curls forward around her ears. I stop in front of her and stand still while her large brown eyes focus on me so intently I think I can see her eyes beginning to bulge.

"You see," she begins, her voice softening, putting her hands in her lap, "there are things about the past that are"— she stops for a moment to choose her next words carefully— "things that are personal."

I stare at the large woman seated like Hitchcock himself in an opening scene.

Personal? Things she is not going to tell me? Perhaps it is the heat, my having rushed so as to be on time, the melodrama of her words, but for a few seconds I struggle against an impulse to giggle.

Then she breaks the silence, waving me in with a friendly wave of her arm. "Come on in, sit down, anywhere," she begins, her voice loosening from its previous resolve. She gives me an easy, generous smile and points around the room. "Look at this mess, such a clutter. We had to move everything in here from our old house. We've been giving furniture to our children, but there's still so much to move, but really, this heat is terrible, just terrible."

I glance briefly around the room crowded with dark furniture, bookshelves and books, then concentrate upon introducing myself and asking her permission to tape and use my conversation with her. When she nods yes, I quickly flick on the small tape recorder and sit on a nearby chair. I don't want to lose a word of this conversation. She has snared my interest, as I suspect she knew she would.

"Are you writing a book?" she asks me directly. When I say yes and explain that it is about my family and the land at Talavera, she nods approvingly. Now it is my turn to lean forward and to try to capture her attention with my gaze. For some reason I suspect that this secret she has declared but withheld has little to do with my grandmother or my great-aunt. Perhaps she knows something about my debonair, enigmatic grandfather.

But I ignore her opening statement, at least for now, and begin by asking her to tell me what she remembers about the Ladies Democratic Club and about my great-aunt Lee and my grandmother. Mrs. Chester smiles. Her beaver-bright hair shines in the light. She begins to speak, again choosing her words carefully but without hesitation.

"She was very involved with, well . . . the past. I met her when we were trying to get new members for the Ladies Democratic Club. We had a wonderful organization. Absolutely wonderful. It was a social gathering, but everyone was interested in politics. Politics was fun then; it was social. Not like today. Anyway, I would pick your grandmother up, and we would go to the meeting, and we would visit all the way there and all the way back. I always drove. She could drive herself, but I always drove her to the meetings. Then when we drove back I would visit with her, you know, before saying good night. She would tell me lots of things about her husband, about the property, all down and around. They had lots of acreage. I don't even know if they even thought about where the boundaries were. She'd just say, 'Way out there, you know, all the way to Lake Taghkanic.'"

Mrs. Chester pauses for a moment and laughs, a fond, sentimental laugh. "That's it. And she would talk about her boys. Your father, she called him Van Ness and then Nicholas. She would say, 'Van Ness is coming this weekend with the children,' well—" Mrs. Chester laughs and looks at me "—that must have been you she meant. I know she loved it when the grandchildren were there. Do you have lots of brothers and sisters?" She waits a minute for me to nod, then returns to her memories. "Your grandmother would tell me about her mother and father, how they had owned the Stottville mills, and I remember that she told me about being involved in women's suffrage. That was very important to her."

I interrupt her reverie, to ask her again what she remembers about my grandmother. She replies easily. "She was a wonderful, wonderful lady. She was adorable, really she was. She always wore lace collars and had handkerchiefs, small leather pocketbooks. Blue dresses. I think she liked everything she did, but women's suffrage, that was big for her. You know I picked your grandmother up one night, and it was stormy. Your grandmother said, 'You know, my sister and I went out on a night like this. There was a women's suffrage meeting across the river in Athens, and we went, unknown to our parents. We got over there and had a wonderful, successful meeting, but then, when we went to come back, the river was freezing over. And oh, my, there we were in a rowboat, rowing through the ice.'"

I hear again the family stories of how my grandmother and great-aunt would sneak out at night to attend suffrage meetings. How they would tiptoe past the rooms of their sleeping parents and the servants, then step over the lolling dogs to slip out of the house. How one night they crossed the river as usual in a rowboat to get to a meeting in Athens, but when they headed back across, they discovered that the dark, flowing river was beginning to crust with ice.

I imagine my grandmother and her older sister in their long close-waisted dresses, tiny buttons up and down the front. My grandmother's blond wavy hair was coiffed and piled upon her head, a gentle confusion of rolled hair and tortoiseshell combs. But my great-aunt had already begun to keep her curly blond hair short. Glasses rested on her short nose, making her square chin seem even more pronounced. They had loved crossing the river at night, the miles of dark, flowing water, an endless freedom. But on the way home the ominous crunch of the oars breaking the dark ice had scared them. The hard row back across the channel, a one-mile width, seemed much longer heading home. Even traveling together in Egypt, they had been more chaperoned than now. By the time they finally made it back to the shore, their feet in thin leather boots were soaked and freezing, and they still had a long walk back up the hill from the landing. All across Stottville the lawns were shadowed with blue predawn light, the night dew having frozen into a sparkling sheet of white. As soon as they crossed their own lawn, they quickly called the dogs to keep them from barking. My grandmother's white bull terriers would have leapt at her in delight. But perhaps the family's St. Bernards, tongues lolling, were still asleep on the carpets inside, too lazy to be roused by the rustle of their skirts across the porch, the click of the latch on the front door. Those Stott girls. But once again they had made it home.

My grandmother seemed to have let her political activism for women's rights cool after her marriage to my grandfather in 1921, but Lee went on to organize union strikes at the Stottville mills, at times donating large sums of money to the millworkers' cause. She and my grandmother both had traveled to Italy to study with Maria Montessori, but while my grandmother used that knowledge for her family, home schooling both my father and uncle until they were ten and seven, Lee carved out a career as an educator in New York City, helping Caroline Pratt found the progressive Play School, later renamed the City & Country School in the hope of attracting more students. Later she returned to politics, running for state assembly in Columbia County on the Democratic and Labor party tickets, a campaign she lost.

Mrs. Chester clearly enjoys talking about the times she met my great-aunt, but her memories only confirm my sense that my great-aunt was an earnest, forceful and somewhat distant figure. "Lee was different," Mrs. Chester continues. "Your grandmother was a homebody, you know. She loved her home. But Lee was different . . . and she loved to travel. I am sure that your grandmother wanted her sister to come live with her at Talavera, but Lee would have none of it."

No matter how persistently I try to tease out of Mrs. Chester her secret, the mysterious story that she knows but has decided not to tell me, she holds firm to her initial resolve. I decide to shift my approach and begin asking her to tell me what she remembers of Talavera.

"Oh, the house was beautiful. Not crowded, you know, but kept. It was like Olana or the Roosevelt home in Hyde Park. It was nice, but it was old. It felt like an old home. In those days I don't think they replaced things. If something was broken, they didn't go buy a new one; they covered it. If there was a hole in the drapes or something. I can't explain . . . You just didn't go out and buy new things like today. Things were tasteful, sometimes severe, the chairs and things.

Olana, Frederic Church's gorgeous house and carefully landscaped estate. Hyde Park, the extensive Vanderbilt and Roosevelt mansions. As Mrs. Chester speaks, I find myself stunned by her comparisons. The Talavera I remembered has always been just home, maybe even a bit threadbare. But the house that Mrs. Chester remembers belonged to a golden era of wealth and taste in the Hudson Valley. I find myself leaping to embrace her vision, even though I suspect she is exaggerating.

"I remember one Sunday afternoon your grandmother was going to have several of the officers of the Ladies Democratic Club over for tea. Your grandmother had asked me to come over on a Saturday to go over little things with her about the cookies and where to set up the tea service and so forth. She was telling me about the wallpaper. She wanted to do something about it. She was upset about it, it was kind of like ready to come off, but I said, 'Oh, don't change it, don't ever do anything to it, it's tradition. And I like it just the way it is, and that's all that counts, you know.'"

Mrs. Chester laughs a little, thinking back. I can just see

165

the wallpaper that she is mentioning. The year after my grandmother died, a huge section had fallen off the curving back wall of the dining room. My father had climbed up a twenty-foot ladder to nail the thick sheets back on, but not before my mother had cut out a foot-square swatch and separated the layers, discovering eight layers of paper underneath. No matter how faded and torn it became, everyone hated the thought of taking the old paper down. On all sides of the elliptical dining room, ornate flowers and vines twisted up tall blue poles. The twilight colors of the room—the muted reds and purples of the flowers, the dusky greens of the vines and the soft gray tones of the background—made it seem as if you were not in a room at all but, rather, sheltered in some primitive forest. Even though the room looked glorious when it was finally repapered, we all felt so sad to see the old wallpaper gone that my mother framed a section and hung it in the sitting room.

"So then Joe Resnick was going to run for Congress." Startled, I realize that Mrs. Chester has been talking all this time, and I have been hardly listening. I glance down at the tape recorder, relieved to see the steady spin of the tiny tape wheels.

"We were talking about doing something, and your grandmother said, 'Well, I could do something on the lawn,' and I said that would be absolutely lovely. And it was. Before I knew it, I was going there, and we were doing it. We had a wonderful gathering. Lots of important people came from Albany and New York City."

Once again, Mrs. Chester's memories collide with mine. I remembered that gathering vividly because during it I had learned how to ride a two-wheeler. The morning of the event, enormous white tents had mushroomed up across the lawns. By late afternoon the meadows gleamed with chrome, cars parked bumper to bumper. Big people, big tables, big chairs, trays of food, endless white teacups. The lawn had become a maze that we kids had to weave through to find our parents. I was mad because I had to wear a dress that itched terribly all around the neck, where it was stiff with smocking. I soon gave up tasting the doll-size sandwiches and ran down to the garage. No one was around. It was my chance to pull out my older brother's small red bicycle.

My plan was simple. I would start on the drive behind the back steps to the kitchen and ride the slight incline down to the barns. At some point between my hauling out the bicycle and actually trying to ride it, a tall man with a graying beard appeared from the cedar walk and was beside me. I don't remember any conversation, I don't, even now, remember his name, although when I recounted this memory to my mother she believed he must have been my uncle Bill Whitney. Soon he was patiently keeping the bike steady while I got on, holding it for a few steps while I pedaled, then letting it go. I'd waver for a few pedal turns, then fall over, pick the bicycle up and bring it back to where the man stood, ready to help me get started again. Finally, one time, his large hands pushed me off down the drive, and I didn't fall right over, miraculously, the wheels kept turning, my feet kept pedaling, and in a wavery line, I made it all the way down to the barns before crashing into the packinghouse doors.

"Your grandmother was a dear. I enjoyed every minute that I spent with her. She had a lot of get-up-and-go. There were so many times, so many, many times." Mrs. Chester continues to talk, again clasping her hands. "Your grandmother would talk about Lake Taghkanic. She told me about that, and it was called Lake Charlotte or Charlotte's lake, after an Indian person or something. She always talked about acreage. Franklin Roosevelt was running for office, and he knew your grandfather, and he would visit. So would Clifford Miller, he was another landowner."

I interrupt to ask if Mrs. Chester thinks Talavera was much bigger then.

"Oh, yes, well, of course," she says, looking at me with some astonishment, as if to say, "Don't you know that?" "Talavera was just the beginning. They owned all the way down to the

167

Old Forge. A lot of those people over there were just share-croppers really, the Coons, the Orsteds, they were people from Denmark. Then"—Mrs. Chester pauses for a split second—"eventually they became the owners of the land."

Mrs. Chester's voice carries on gaily, but then she falls silent. She knows that I have heard it, that glimmer of hesitation. She isn't certain anymore of what she wants to say. She purses her red lips as she thinks of how to proceed. *Things that are personal. Things that I know that I am not going to tell you.* I had heard stories about the Old Forge as the place that my grandfather had apparently loved to go to fish for trout. Had he owned much more land and lost it?

"I have always wondered about my grandfather." I probe, deciding that it is time for me to work more actively to flush out her secret. "My father didn't talk about him very much at all. I mean, I wonder what he was really like."

Mrs. Chester's voice leaps to life again, quicksilver, a trout flashing. "That's why I don't want to talk about it. I don't want to say anything about it. I don't want to be the one. It isn't something that was awful. It's something wonderful. I was surprised that so many people knew, not just the old generation, people like my daddy. And it's nothing bad. It was, well, just not so wonderful for your grandmother."

She looks at me quickly as if to register the impact of her words. "I heard he was just wonderful, this young, handsome guy and in his riding boots, and on his horse he was just great. And your father, he was such a nice man, he really was, a wonderful guy."

Mrs. Chester's voice trails off. She is pulling away again.

"I don't know that much about who my grandfather was." I continue, pushing harder. "My sense is that he was perhaps distant from his family."

"That's because he had interests other than home interests." Mrs. Chester says firmly. "So he would be out and about. You know, there are lots of people like that. You can't find fault with it."

"Do you mean out and about for work or socializing?"

"Well, it was that," says Mrs. Chester evasively, "but I think he had interests in his farms and I think he had interests in the people *of* the farm. You know . . . They said he was great. My daddy lived in Taghkanic; he remembered him riding through."

I listen quietly, but I am no longer buoyed by the initial hilarity of our meeting, no longer flushed with the chase. Clearly, she is trying to tell me that my grandfather had an affair, or affairs, perhaps even while he was married to my grandmother. I can see the photograph of my grandfather that sits in the library, dressed as always in beautifully tailored clothes. Waves of shock flood through me. Was this the dark wing of a dream that I have always felt flying over Talavera, the mystery that surrounded my grandfather and propelled my father to believe even more fervently in those old values of honor and family and land? A bone from the past has been flung my way, and suddenly I am not sure that I want it.

"People knew that he was very interested in his acreage," Mrs. Chester continues. "He was always around and about. What do you call a farmer who is always out there and has all these people under him?"

"A manor lord?"

"Yes, that's what it was in those days. He was interested in his farms and in the people on his farms. There are photographs of him on his horse. That's the way it was. That's how people lived."

Mrs. Chester continues to look directly at me, but with these words she announces that she has closed up shop. At least for now she doesn't want to talk anymore, and her cheeks go slack with relief when I finally give up prodding her into further conversation and begin to thank her for her time and gather my things to leave.

"I don't care what you say," she tells me as I am walking out. "Those were wonderful days. I look back and think over all the times with those people in the twenties and thirties. I've read Edith Wharton. I love her books. I do. She'd sell something and pack her trunks and live for two years in Europe on two thousand dollars. Can you imagine? How wonderful. Money was different then. It takes people like you and me to keep those things alive. To say, 'Oh, I remember,' and to write them down."

Her voice gathers under her, racing forward. "I love the past. So many people are going forward, but I'm not like that. I love it, the past, the nostalgia. Do you know I have never forgotten anything?" I decide not to interrupt, to give her room to tell me what she knows when she decides she can. There is nothing else I can do. It is when I have packed up my tape recorder and am half out the door that she throws me another clue. "If you could get some pictures of your grandfather," she says coyly, then pauses. "Sometime we'll take a drive to the Old Forge. If I could only show you how he looked on his horse, how dashing he was, and we could drive to the old places. . . . Then I could tell you." She clasps her hands. "Oh, if you could see it, there is someone in the county who looks so much like your father. If you could just meet this person, I know you'd see it. Then—"

My face must be giving away some of the shock that I feel, for Mrs. Chester breaks off in midsentence and shakes her head vigorously. I watch the brown curls of her hair fly around her head like meadow grass in a storm. "No, no," she says, retreating to her previous position. "If you don't know, I'm not going to tell you."

But she has told me. She believes that my grandfather had an affair and that the relationship produced a child, a man now living in Columbia County who resembles my father. But how can Mrs. Chester be sure of all this, unless— I am struck by an even more uncomfortable thought: Mrs. Chester is related to this person. Could he be her husband? That would explain how she had seen photographs of my grandfather. But then why not just tell me, why the melodrama? No. I decide that as compelling as this story is, Mrs. Chester must be making it up. The question I need to answer is why.

I stagger back out into the heat, wondering what I have

begun. That night I dig out a picture of my grandfather on Hari Kari, the champion steeplechaser that his brother Hoffman had bought and that he had raced in the Maryland Steeplechase in 1902. Many horses had fallen during the race, some had broken their legs, but Hari Kari had come in the winner, taking home the enormous silver punch bowl that each May we filled with punch or pea soup (depending on the weather), then loaded onto the flat wooden trailer. Surrounding the punch would be food for seventy, the usual number of guests who came to my mother's annual apple blossom picnic.

In the photograph Hari Kari shines in the sun, his muscled haunches ready to leap the heights for which he was famed. My grandfather wears a bowler hat and, in the style of the day, sports a curled black mustache. To me the mustache looks like a thick black caterpillar, and Hari Kari decidedly more dashing than my grandfather, but I decide that the photo will have to do. I put it in my bag to take to Mrs. Chester. But when I call her the next morning, no one answers the phone. It rings and rings until I hang up. Throughout the day I keep trying. Still no answer and no machine to say that they cannot come to the phone. Days go by, then weeks. I call at all hours to see if I can reach her but have no luck. Mrs. Chester begins to seem like a mirage, appearing, then transpiring.

What did I know of my grandfather anyway? I knew his saddles. I knew the elaborate lines of riding boots and bridles that filled the tack room in the barn. I had seen his VN 49 plates for the Packard and letters written to him from President Roosevelt filed among the pedigrees of his purebred hunting dogs. I had found the letters that he had written back and one note asking if Johnny, my father, then a student at the St. Albans School in Washington, be allowed to research an article for the school newspaper in the White House library. One afternoon, while rooting through the tack room, I had pulled a crumpled newspaper out of my grandfather's Chilean riding boots and found a newspaper article dated 1903 describing his run for the state assembly.

I knew what he looked like from the photographs of him on horseback appearing stern and accomplished, or handsome in evening clothes, his eyes flint blue, staring ahead with a steady, unwavering confidence. But I also knew my own father's reluctance to say much when I sometimes asked him about his father. "Your grandfather was very outgoing and accomplished. People liked him a great deal" was the kind of answer he would give me. In the white silence of what was unsaid, I understood that my grandfather had remained a distant figure to my father and his younger brother.

A slender thread from the past had come unraveled. I kept calling Mrs. Chester. Each time I listened, disappointed as the phone rang and rang and was not answered. Then one day, eight months later, a familiar voice answers the phone.

"Well, yes, hello. I saw your mother last week at a meeting of the Fortnightly Club. Your mother is so nice, she really is, then doing all those apples, I mean, really, she is something." Mrs. Chester and her husband had been away, first to Georgia, then to North Carolina. "We're back now," she explains, "and you know, I'm glad you called, I've been thinking, *Oh, I should call her,* but I didn't. I have something to tell you." We arrange to meet for lunch in Hudson in two weeks.

❧

"I am going to tell you everything," says Mrs. Chester brightly as we sit down to lunch at a restaurant across the street from her house, "because there comes a time." I lean forward, straining to hear over the clatter of dishes and conversation in the busy restaurant. "But first, tell me, how is Mother? Are the apples okay?"

"She's fine," I say. "Getting ready for the blossom."

That morning my mother and I had driven through the orchards to check bud stage. In the young trees damage from deer was terrible. Throughout the winter she had seen their tracks, and now we saw where they had grazed on the tree buds, a sweet carbo-load for them and death for many of the year-old trees. As usual, they had ignored the bars of soap, the bags of human hair and lines of cassette tape that were supposed to scare them away. Recently it had been mentioned that the thing to keep deer away was lion dung. Nobody had any answers to the deer problem, except for fifteen-foot-high deer fencing, which costs over a thousand dollars an acre to install.

The sap was rising quickly, though, and my mother was sure that green tip would come on early. Sure enough, on our way back we had watched a flock of small black birds descend on the meadow, the telltale glints of red on their wings. The red-winged blackbirds had returned. Deep in the woods, the skunk cabbage would soon unfurl, along with pussy willows, bloodroot and yellow marsh marigolds, purple hepatica. Spring was on its way.

We order quickly, coffee and cake, and then I wait for Mrs. Chester to begin talking about my grandfather. Instead, she begins to describe the land and a road that leads east just five miles south of Claverack, the old Churchtown-Taghkanic road.

"Now," she says when the waitress leaves, "you follow that road, and you know those red barns when you turn at the corner? Yes, that's right, the Merrifields; of course, they grew apples, so your mother probably knows them. Well, there's a woman in her sixties, Sarah Orsted, and she has a cousin, Anna, who is in her eighties. The Orsteds were a family from Denmark. . . . I don't know how they came to live there. But Mr. Philip would ride all over. The Orsteds had a daughter; she's Anna's mother; I don't know her name. . . ."

As she speaks, I strain forward to hear and write notes as fast as I can. She clearly thinks it important to describe each farm along the road.

"Then, over the hill, you pass a beautiful old colonial and another house. Then you get to the Posts' farm. Now, Mr.

Post worked on the railroad. He had five boys. They bought a farm there and had a family, you know." I nod, but I don't know. I have no idea what she is talking about, and already I am confused by the litany of names, people and their farms, the farms and their people, so mixed together that they seem to blend. But I keep writing as fast as I can. I don't want to interrupt the way she chooses to tell me her story. Gradually Mrs. Chester describes the road as it passes through the modern townships of Churchtown, West Taghkanic, East Taghkanic and Ancram, the area local people call the Old Forge. Taghkanic had been one of the original seven towns that made up Livingston Manor, and the first lord of the manor, Robert Livingston, had built two iron forges along the Taghkanic Creek, some of the first industry in the county.

Geologists refer to this area ten miles east of the Hudson River as the High Taconics, a series of landslides that slid off the Berkshires during the creation of that range 460 million years ago. A natural division between High and Low Taconics left a perfect situation for the formation of waterfalls. Over time, creeks broke through the faulted rock, cascading down. Farmers had little use for the area's rocky scenic beauty. They mainly knew it as hardscrabble farmland, thin-soiled and dank, good for grazing and sheep, but too rugged to crop out, completely different from the rich, loamy soil that made up vast stretches of land closer to the river. Still, acres and acres of this land, which stretched east toward Massachusetts, were originally attached to the Livingston Manor as tenant farms.

As Mrs. Chester continues to describe this countryside, she begins to weave in this early colonial history, when most of the valley stretched up and down the river as a system of manors run by lords who had been granted many of the same lordship privileges as lords back in England: jurisdiction over the tenants and the right to determine and collect taxes. Not surprisingly, the lords accumulated great wealth, while the tenants lived in subsistence conditions, impoverished by

174

high rents and poor land. Rents paid not in cash but in chickens and wheat and labor.

"Back then Lake Taghkanic was called Lake Chalotte," she explained. "Your family's property went all back there, acres and acres back to the Old Forge. Your grandfather would ride back there. Miles and miles. Everywhere on his fine horse. It was nothing to him. People said he was a sight. I bet he was."

Mrs. Chester stops for a moment and leans across the table so that her face is even closer to mine. I stop taking notes for a moment and bob my head vigorously, anything to keep her from getting off the track of her story now. She seems encouraged by my interest and continues.

"He rode by to see the land, to check on things; he had people working for him, you know, sharecroppers really. There was one family that had come from Denmark. Their name was Orsted, and they worked on his land in the Old Forge. The family had a beautiful daughter. She was seventeen, eighteen. Your grandfather would ride by, his horse prancing, the sun glancing off of his beautiful boots." Mrs. Chester slows her voice, building the suspense. "He was dashing. She was beautiful. He became smitten with her. I mean, why wouldn't he? They had an affair. She became pregnant, and they had a baby. She was named Anna."

175

Mrs. Chester looks at me now to see how I am taking this news. I stare back at her openmouthed. "You mean the same Anna that you mentioned earlier?" My ears are ringing slightly as I flip back through my notes to find the names I had jotted down.

Mrs. Chester ignores my question. "Her mother and father were probably proud of the baby," she says, "and they got the farm."

"Here," I say, squinting down at my notebook to read my penciled notes, "you mean, Anna Post?"

"Yes, that's right. And she grew up and was beautiful. She must be eighty-seven now, but she lives right there on the farm that was given to her because of who her father was. Right there in the Old Forge. If you could just see how much she looks like your father."

"Anna Post." I repeat the name. "You mean, she would be my aunt then, right? A half aunt?"

"Exactly. And the thing is I bet she knows who her father was. I mean, come on, she got this farm that had belonged to the Philips—your family."

I continue to stare at her in some confusion. I had gotten used to the idea that I might have an uncle out there somewhere, someone who looked like my father. I had it all worked out to ask her if this man was her husband. But of course a woman could look like my father. I had just made the wrong assumption. Still, I feel thrown into darkness all over again. I had wanted to talk to Mrs. Chester to find out more about my grandmother and elusive great-aunt Lee. I knew that my great-aunt's story was only half told by what the family chose to remember or record, and I was eager to be surprised, even shocked, by what I might find out about her. But I hadn't been prepared for this, the discovery of an aunt whose life had been left out of the family history altogether.

"An aunt," I say again, as if to get used to the idea by saying the words.

"Oh, I can just see it," Mrs. Chester continues. She clasps her hands so that her bracelets jingle. She loves the romance of the story she is weaving. "How dashing he was. How he fell in love with that beautiful girl. The family was given a farm, to take care of the baby. That's the way things were done then. Look in the courthouse, you'll see it on the deeds. I'm sure it's there."

I still don't know what to say. According to Mrs. Chester, my father had an older sister, whom I have never met. That she is only a half sister does not make her seem any less important. Not only is she still alive, but if what Mrs. Chester has been telling me is true, a vast class divide has kept her a secret, even now. But not a secret to everybody.

"How did you know this?"

Again, Mrs. Chester answers me easily. "Oh, lots of people knew, at least in Taghkanic they did." This time, when she leans toward me, she lays one hand on the table and beats a light rhythm to emphasize her words. "Anna had class; there's just no other way to describe it. You could see it right away, oh, the way she looked, the way she moved, her face. She carried herself with such poise. That's something in the blood, I don't care what you say. She had a sister because her mother married Mr. Thorpe and had another daughter, but that sister looked completely different. Anna was so beautiful. She was, well, just aristocratic, that's what she was. Breeding, you know, the family you're from . . . everything is in breeding."

Mrs. Chester looks me dead in the eye. I suddenly feel uncomfortable, wondering what she sees in me, but I return her gaze, all the while thinking that I have somehow fallen into a Charles Dickens novel. More unsettling yet, Mrs. Chester's words confirm so much of what I had lived and grown up with that I know she speaks a truth that is rarely discussed. Class lines do exist, and in Columbia County, as in most of rural America, they have always been based upon the ownership of land.

Even though my family, as early Dutch New Yorkers, were never as rich as the original Livingston Manor lords that Mrs. Chester describes, so that their actual wealth, like that of all those in the middle ground, has been unstable over time, prone to dips and rises, they did own land, land that was further signified by its houses and farms, Talavera and the farm there, farms in Taghkanic, the old Van Ness mansion in Washington, D.C. Talavera was not just an agricultural enterprise; it was a country seat, the homestead and rural retreat of men who spent winters in cities like Washington, D.C., and New York. Geographically, Talavera was only ten miles from East Taghkanic, but socially it was as far from that community of small, once tenant-owned farms as Mars. I think of the child Anna, my aunt perhaps, growing up ten miles from her father, from her stepbrothers and from their growing families, but kept apart, so that none of us could benefit from what the other might have to offer. The lines of class appear for what they are, a harsh, superficial grid.

The coffee and the lemon cake that we have ordered arrive. We drink and eat without talking for a few minutes. Then I am bothered by a new question. "How old were you when you first heard about this Anna?"

As before, Mrs. Chester answers me easily, almost cheerfully, clearly relieved to have gotten this secret off her chest. "I was probably seventeen. It was a family gathering of some sort, and I said something about Norman Post's wife being so beautiful. Then I said something about how she didn't look anything like her sister. That's when my mother said, 'That's because she had a different father. It's a long story, but she is the daughter of the landowner Mr. Philip.'"

"Do you remember what you thought about it at the time?" I ask.

"Never gave it a thought. Never. Never."

So Mrs. Chester knew this story, the people of East Taghkanic knew, but my own family did not. Or did they? Was it possible that my father suspected that he had a half sister but never talked about it? I ask Mrs. Chester if she will help me find Anna and try to contact her. Mrs. Chester says that she will try. I will have to wait, but she will make some calls. Her uncle is Anna's husband's brother. She will ask him some questions. Before we leave I ask Mrs. Chester again if she thinks Anna knows who her father is.

"Oh, I think so. I mean, there's the farm. Come on. The land, that tells it all." Then she leans toward me conspiratorially and adds, "Anna had a daughter, and what do you think she named her? Valerie. Think about that name, Valerie, Val. What does that sound like? Talavera. I think she named her after Talavera. I think she must have known about her father and named her daughter after the family place. Yes, I do."

"Do you think she will agree to meet me?"

"I don't know," says Mrs. Chester. "It must have been hard. But I think she would. I really do. I think she knows who her father was, and I think she would be really happy that you wanted to meet her. Go look in the courthouse. I'll check also. Then you and I will take a drive to the Old Forge so you can see everything."

A daughter named after Talavera. Family land deeded to an illegitimate child. The plot seems to be racing forward ahead of me, and still I have no idea how much of it is true. As soon as I can, I search the courthouse for any deeds of land transfer between my grandfather and a family named Orsted. Since Anna is by Mrs. Chester's reckoning about eighty-five, five years older than my father would be if he were alive, I look for the years 1915, 1916. Eagerly I flip open the heavy deed book and scan the page. The only land transfers for my grandfather, however, are for lands trans- ferred between him and a woman named Alice Rockefeller, and they are not for lands located in the old Forge. If any- thing, her name only adds another complication to the story. I had found an accounting for the farms on the Old Forge property and at Talavera typed up and signed by Alice Rock- efeller, who had presumably been working in a secretarial ca- pacity for my grandfather. Either that, or they had been business partners. But Alice Rockefeller was not a secretarial type. In high school I had hung in my room a photograph of another Alice that my grandfather had known. She intrigued me with her Chekhovian air of studied elegance. Years later, when I read "The Lady with the Pet Dog," I would imagine the protagonist to look like the woman in that photograph with her plumed hat, the dark fur lining her coat as glossy as her dark, distracted eyes. The photograph had been signed "Alice Roosevelt." Had my grandfather kept close company with beautiful women at both ends of the social spectrum?

I knew that my grandfather had indeed owned land in the Old Forge area, for I had found the farm logs that recorded sheep pastured there. By 1915 he was planting orchards there as well and had set out thousands of fir and pine trees and a handful of ornamental trees that showed he was interested in landscaping those farms as well as Talavera.

One faded blue map had clearly penciled boundaries: Scism Place, Cronk Place, Shaugnessy Place, Banner Place—a total of six hundred acres along with houses and outbuildings. Finding out what had happened to that land had been on my list of things to do. Perhaps now I had a partial answer, but if acreage had been given to Anna's family to provide for the baby, why is there no record in the courthouse? As often has happened in the course of my research on my family and its land, I have made progress only to hit a dead end. So many riddles in the past. Pandora's box, letting loose confusion. I would have to wait until a way forward opened.

᜝

"All I do is live in the past. Isn't that awful?" says Mrs. Chester when I phone her the next month to arrange a time for us to drive through the Old Forge. "But I grew up in a wonderful home with wonderful parents. I remember when my father got the first hay-loader. It was the first in the area. All the other farmers came to watch. It was great, and after that everybody bought one. Everything was just a few hundred dollars back then." She is surprised to hear that I can't find the deeds but admits that she hasn't had a chance to look herself.

One week later, we are driving east along the Churchtown-Taghkanic Road, past Churchtown, past West Taghkanic, then across the parkway, east toward the border with Massachusetts. Within minutes, rolling farmland gives way to woods and hills, dark green stands of conifer. Here and there the woodlands and fields give way to a farmhouse, newly renovated and landscaped. Most of the farmhouses along the road have left their history as struggling tenant farms long behind. Now they shine with fresh paint, firm-timbered, beautifully landscaped. Some have swimming pools, gardens, riding horses—the old farms transformed into weekend retreats. Mrs. Chester, whose family still owns several hundred acres in East Taghkanic, seems to know each one.

"I'm going to take you there via the Old Forge road," says

Mrs. Chester, "because then you can see everything. Where he used to go, where Anna's mother lived, everything. But first, tell me, how is Mother?"

"Fine," I answer, "busy."

"Oh, yes," says Mrs. Chester, "What she manages, that house and all the apples, I can't believe it, really. Did you get that terrible frost?"

"No, we were lucky, no frost."

"Oh, good," says Mrs. Chester, and sighs loudly, relief. "Honestly, I just don't know what these farmers are going to do. They can't make any money. They just can't. Now with this freeze, I tell you, it's tough."

I nod. The bloom had come a good two weeks early this year, and several days ago, right when the flowers were in peak bloom, temperatures along the river had dropped as low as twenty-eight degrees. Most orchards had suffered big losses, especially in pears, but for the second year in a row we have been spared. My mother and I had driven out to look over the blossoms and found only scattered brown ones. Petal damage had occurred in some low-lying blocks of apples, but my mother was pretty sure that the pollen was still good and that the bees would find it, for only about half the white petals had withered. The next day a sudden wave of heat had sent the damaged petals stretching. The day before, we had held our annual apple blossom picnic, but it was so hot we had picnicked along the garden's outer edge, enjoying the cool of the cedar walk. When I had left this morning, the orchards were a haze of pink, each tree buzzing with five or six bees just as they should be.

"I had always heard that my grandfather loved the Old Forge," I muse. "I think he would go there to trout-fish."

"Exactly," says Mrs. Chester. "You see, there was nothing here before, just property. It's amazing really, to think about it, all that land and no houses. This was all rural. There was nothing here. Not a thing. I remember this road. It was all dirt."

I look out at the landscape, surprised to see how many of

the trees are still tightfisted, the ground a winterish brown. All along the road leading out from Claverack, the trees are budding out, the land sloughing off its winter colors and beginning to shine green. We must have driven into higher elevation. I comment that riding from Claverack to Copake was quite a ride for my grandfather, but Mrs. Chester shakes her head.

"Oh, no. When you're riding in the country, hill and dale, miles and miles seem like nothing. He would have ridden across the fields anyway, and this was all property owned by the Philips. The Livingstons originally, but then somehow they had married or whatever, and people got some here and there." She sighs. "He must have had a good life . . . really."

We begin to pass farms and old houses. Mrs. Chester seems to know each one.

"There, see that farm." Mrs. Chester points to a complex of tumbledown barns on a hillside, a family-owned farm that has clearly not yet changed hands. Fanning out in all directions are lines of old stone walls, sheep fence. The weathered barns look flung against the hill, like driftwood. One has caved in completely, and the front porch of the small house slants so severely it seems to be falling off.

"Oh, that was a beautiful old farm." Mrs. Chester continues. "Again sheep. My father used to tell me the name of the people, but I've forgotten now. What a shame. Here, now we are coming to the next place; that's the farm that the Posts bought. Mr. Post worked for the railroad. Anna married one of the Post boys, Norman."

Soon woods begin to spill down closer and closer to the road until we drive through a forested canopy.

"Here, now we're coming to it. See that up there. That is the road your grandfather would have ridden down; we will turn down there." She points to a narrower road leading off to the right. I turn the car, and we are soon driving deeper into woodland. "Yes, this is it. Back then it would have been a dirt path."

I can imagine the joy of riding along such a road, the sun dappling the leaves, the cool forest air and the steady, spirited clop of the horses' hooves on the cool packed dirt all conspiring to make one feel as if it were a perfect moment. I try to imagine this new grandfather, the one who would have been riding through a green field of joy, each leaf buzzing with desire as he rode toward his Anna, a woman he must have known he would never marry. How long had they been involved?

"Now, this was all open property, okay. Nothing here. Now up ahead we're going to come to the Old Forge Road. This would have been Van Ness Philip property, all of it."

What we have driven through is more like a thousand acres rather than six hundred, but I have come to see that for Mrs. Chester, the story of my grandfather meeting Anna's mother is a romance without bounds.

"And this is where—" Mrs. Chester interrupts herself to crane up through the woods on the left. "Interesting. People have bought this property and built. Look up there. I tell you, really." We both look at the modern house peeking through the trees.

"You see, it's never been settled. It's always been kind of wild like this. Now this was all covered with heavy forest, lots of pine trees and oak trees. You have to imagine that. It was all trees, trees, trees. And up in the hills were the bushwhackers. Those were the people who whacked the bushes and made baskets. In the spring they would come out and buy everything they needed and sell all their baskets and live for another year."

I drive on slowly, listening as Mrs. Chester continues. "What history, what incredible history lies here. I mean, this was really, really backwoods property. And this is where your grandfather used to ride. It's wonderful, isn't it? He would ride up here to the lake. Come on, he would spend the whole day, riding along, going up to the lake—"

Abruptly Mrs. Chester stops talking and peers ahead.

When she sees a turn, she gestures with great excitement at a narrow dirt road leading off to the right. "There, there is the road. Turn right there."

As soon as we make the turn, it feels as if we were driving back in time. We pass a farmhouse, but it has clearly not yet changed hands. The next farmhouse is the same. House walls need paint; barn roofs sag. Then we come over a hill, and tucked into the side of the hill stands a newly built beige house. Across the road from it is a complex of three barns.

"This is it," says Mrs. Chester suddenly. "This is the place that your grandfather gave to them." I look at the modern house in some confusion, but Mrs. Chester explains, "The original was old; it was a lovely old colonial, set back a little more. This was the Orsted home. Mr. Thorpe used to have his horseshoeing business in the barn. But nobody is home. They are in Florida."

I point to the drive, where a car is parked, but Mrs. Chester only says, "Yes, isn't that amazing," and keeps driving.

I want to stop the car. I want to get out and knock on the door, at least to walk around the place that links Anna to my family, but it is clear that Mrs. Chester feels we must not stop, at least not today. I remind myself that we haven't made contact with Anna yet.

"No," says Mrs. Chester, as if reading my thoughts. "Today we are going to go all the way through. I want to show you everything here. All where he used to go. This was all property. All of it. All of it was Van Ness property."

Within minutes we are back in conifer stands. Beside the road a creek rushes by, and soon I am guiding the car slowly across a single-span pony truss bridge. Underneath, the creek, called a kill, follows the Taconic fault line, plunging down, the water falling 100 feet in less than 250 yards. Waterfalls. Waterpower. A small green state sign on the other side names it the Old Maryburgh Iron Forge at Ancram, founded in 1772 by Robert Livingston and kept in operation until after the Revolution.

When I see the sign, I can't help thinking it ironic that the

Livingstons, like the Philips and the Stotts, all families to whom I am related, helped found the iron, carpet and textile mills that by the middle of the nineteenth century were transforming the purely rural landscape of Columbia County into an industrial one. While my great-grandfather on my grandfather's side, William Henry, had headed south to fight in the Civil War, my grandmother's family had been busy up north, overseeing the Stottville mills that were prospering under Union army contracts for woolen clothing.

Columbia County's transformation from a rural to industrial landscape, a process that gathered warp speed after the Civil War, was heralded by most as great social progress. Of course fortunes were made along the way. But my own family's involvement in the building of iron forges and carpet and wool mills could seem ironic, at least when I considered our current status as agricultural preservationists, struggling to keep a farm intact and one small spot of land free from development.

185

"Look at those waterfalls, isn't that something?" says Mrs. Chester. "You know, whatever you want to write about, it is here."

"Have *you* ever thought of writing a book?" I ask.

"No," she says emphatically. "No, no. As much as I love history and everything, no." We drive along, saying nothing for a while, the silence comfortable. We have shared something now: this drive, the story of Anna and our interest in opening up the past.

"When did you last see Anna?" I ask casually.

"Thanksgiving. I saw her at the Merrifields getting pies. Don't you think I thought, *Oh, if I could just tell her?* She carries herself so nicely, the way she speaks, her face. You know, every time I'd see your dad at the train station going back to the city I'd think, *Oh, they do look alike, they do,* but . . ." Mrs. Chester looks out the window and falls quiet.

I think of my father then and how he and Anna could never meet and feel a wave of sadness and fatigue. Now that I have seen her house, the land in the Old Forge, it seems impossible that the story of Anna might not be true. But even if I get to meet her, what then?

"What made you pull back last summer from telling me about Anna?" I ask Mrs. Chester.

"Well," Mrs. Chester begins, still looking out the window, "I thought, as much as people know, maybe I shouldn't say anything. I can be very closemouthed anyway, you know. It's just something. I don't know. But I wonder if your daddy ever knew. You know. Those are things you wonder."

"I wonder that too," I say. "Were you surprised when I called you last summer?"

"Yes," says Mrs. Chester, "yes, I was."

We both fall silent for the remaining miles. When I let her off at her house, she sits in the car for a moment before getting out. She says philosophically, "Well, I am glad that we had this time together and saw these things." She gets out of the car slowly, as if something were still on her mind. Then she turns to me and flashes a mischievous grin, her red lips glowing. "Wouldn't it be great if we find out all about it, then discover that everyone knew anyway?" She waves gaily and shuts the car door with a slam. I drive off, down the long center street where in a few blocks I turn back up through side streets to Route 23 then Route 9H, the Old Post Road, where today the land stretches out on either side, a great shout of green.

✤

Mrs. Chester's plan is to ask her friend Sarah, Anna's cousin, to call Anna and find out if Anna will speak to me, or at the very least to get Anna's address from her so that I can write her. But she has to wait until Sarah comes back from Florida, where she goes each winter, and to find a way to have that conversation. She can't just call Sarah up; she has to find the right moment. But first she has to run into Sarah. It all takes time. Days, then weeks go by. Each time I call Mrs. Chester, she says, "I haven't seen her yet." Then, one week in early June, when I phone, Mrs. Chester has news.

"I found out everything," she says, "We were at the beauty parlor and heading back out. I said that I had always admired her cousin, that she had so much character, so much poise, and Sarah said, 'That's the Philips.' And Sarah should know. She is a very busy person, and she knows everything and everybody, and she is going to call Anna up, how about that?"

Mrs. Chester is going to call Sarah to set up a time for me to meet her so that I can get Anna's address from her. Then I will write to Anna myself. Mrs. Chester lays this sequence of events out for me, then coaches me on what I should say when I write Anna. "You will have to say, 'I've been writing this book, and I would like to ask you some questions about things I've been reading about. I really would love to meet you. . . .' You'll know what to say."

Two weeks later, when I call Mrs. Chester for an update, I discover great news. "I called Sarah," Mrs. Chester says excitedly, "and do you know what she said? She said that Anna would enjoy it much more if she could meet you. Isn't that perfect? She wants to meet you, and she knows. All these years I wanted to tell Anna, but I didn't want to embarrass her. But she would have wanted it. I have her phone number. You tell me when you want to come over, and I'll call her and we'll set something up."

While I wait to hear from Mrs. Chester, I consider talking to my family about what I have learned but decide to wait. Even though I had begun to believe that Anna was my aunt, it was still possible that much of this story, like the six hundred acres of family land that had grown into thousands, was not true. I had found nothing about her in family papers or in the county deed books. If the story was true, this was a family skeleton that had been skillfully hidden. I knew that I could count on my mother's being gracious, and upon my oldest brother to be interested and warm, but I wasn't sure about how everyone else would feel. I decided to wait until I met her.

When the day comes, a Sunday in June, the heat begins early. I dress carefully, an indigo blue shirt, a dark cotton skirt with a pattern of small flowers and a blue cotton blazer. I don't want to appear too stylish, but I want her to know I have made an effort. It is too hot for stockings, but I wear my best slip-on shoes. I realize that I am nervous. What if she doesn't like me? What if I don't like her? As I glance in the mirror, wetting my short, unruly hair, it occurs to me that when I meet Anna, I will be representing my whole family. I rub in some hair gel to paste down any loose ends.

By the time we drive up, she is leaning out over the rails of the porch. The first thing I notice is that like my father, she is tall. But I can't tell if she looks like him because all I seem to notice is her dress, not the design, which is simple and elegant, but the colors of the floral pattern—turquoise, teal, violet and navy—a spectrum of blues, the same old-lady colors that my grandmother and great-aunt had always worn, a field of blue that pulls me from the car.

When I step out, I leave my notepad and tape recorder behind. There she is, my would-be aunt, leaning out toward me with such expectation, such openness. I am on the porch and see her strand of white beads, her shiny white hair, her wide smile. The strongly .defined nose that, yes, could remind me of my father. Hello, we both say, and then she clasps my hand between both of her own and holds it tight, a clasp that seems to say everything. She sees me as a niece she has never met and she knows this and she is so glad that I am here. As I look at her, I feel my doubts dissolve. I stand looking at a generation that I had thought, with the death of my father, was gone. But here she is, my father's half sister, and our meeting, only now, but still not too late, has stunned us both. I have so many questions to ask her. But first this moment, when I feel that the past has opened its door. We keep holding hands. I had not realized how worried I had been that I would discover an aunt who was bitter about the past, but if anything, Anna seems to shine with joy.

As soon as we have finished our greeting, Mrs. Chester,

who has come with me, walks into the house with Anna to meet her husband. They are just back from church, Anna explains. I fetch my notepad and tape recorder, take a deep breath and walk in. As soon as I enter the sunny living room, I hear Anna saying, "My mother never lived it down, she never did." Anna is talking to Mrs. Chester. I shake hands with her husband, who has seated himself in a nearby chair, and ask Anna if I can tape our conversation and include her story in my book. She nods.

"I think it is time that things were out in the open and talked about," she begins matter-of-factly, her voice surprisingly soft. "It's time." She looks at me for a minute and laughs. "You know, I always felt I must never bother them. Mother said that she had promised that she wouldn't ever bother. I felt that even though I had never made any such promise. Oh, I was curious, but I tried to put it out of my mind. They don't want to be bothered with me, I thought. They don't want to know about me."

189

Never bother them. Writing this now, I think back on that moment and wish that I had followed my impulse to get up and hug her, responding to the wound that was rising beneath those softly spoken words, a lifetime of grief at being forgotten, of knowing that her father and his family were living ten miles away but, as far as she could tell, wanted nothing to do with her.

Instead of getting up, I sit very still. Was it to respect her dignity or protect myself? I don't know what to say, but I must say something.

"That must have felt just rotten," I murmur.

Anna laughs, but not unkindly, and looks at me. "I was christened Anna Van Ness Philip," she says, her voice tinged with pride, " but later my mother changed my last name to Orsted like her."

As Anna speaks, the story unfolds. At each turn of events, I keep reminding myself this is true. I would have to write a novel to begin to understand the complex knot of duty and desire, human passion and frailty that set Anna's life on its trajectory. But at least I can sketch out the facts as they were related to me. Anna's mother, also named Anna, had apparently worked at Talavera.

"Well, she was the maid, I suppose," explains Anna, after a pause. "She took care of the house. My uncle Floyd had worked there, he was the chauffeur, and I guess she started working there too." Anna doesn't know how many years her mother worked there before 1916, the year Anna was born, but she thinks it was several. As she talks, I am wondering if her mother had begun working at Talavera that long winter of 1914, after Gaston had died and Bessie had moved away. If so, might not Anna Orsted, with her clear, laughing features, have seemed to my grandfather, alone at Talavera, nursing his losses and defeats, an angel who had walked in just in time?

The brother and sister must have lived for periods of time at Talavera, for it was too far to commute by wagon each day. And there was a large family at home. Anna's grandparents had come from Anslat in Denmark and been married in the Copake Church. Many children were born, and many died, including twins. When it was clear that Anna's mother was pregnant, my grandfather arranged for her to go to Albany to have the baby. Nobody knew. Not her parents. Not her brother. Not even her best friend Lizzie.

"My mother would tell me the story. How she told everyone that she was going to Albany to study to be a milliner," explained Anna. "Then one day, oh, about nine months later, Lizzie saw her go by in the wagon, a tiny baby in her arms." Anna laughs. "She never sounded upset about it."

Anna also remembers her mother telling her stories of my grandfather's taking her to dinner at Keeler's, the Albany restaurant where still today people dine to be seen, of visiting friends with him and taking a trip to Massachusetts. According to Anna, my grandfather had wanted Anna's mother, then twenty-six, to go to college, but she had refused.

"I was supposed to be educated too," Anna says, "but I was too scared to go. My mother said, 'You are supposed to go to college,' but I just refused. And I had met Norman by then, and we were very much in love." She looks over at Norman and smiles. He nods but remains quiet, his silence protective. He seems happy that I am there but clearly does not want Anna hurt. They have been married for sixty-four years.

"I met Norman when I was nineteen," continues Anna, "and we were married when I was twenty-one."

Again she laughs, a soft, gentle sound that waves across the room, strikingly free of bitterness or regret. "When I was little, I used to like to draw pictures. I guess I began to show that I was good at it, and my mother used to say that there had been someone in the family who had been a painter. I forget who it was now."

"My grandfather's sister painted," I say quickly. "Did she ever mention meeting a Bessie?"

"Yes, that was it." Anna's eyes flare open in surprise. "Yes, a sister, she must have meant her. My mother talked about all the people she met at the house. A sister who was very accomplished and a brother who got into some trouble, I think. The Roosevelts would come to visit. Dinner parties and things. My mother was probably serving them."

"Do you have any of your paintings?" I ask.

Anna gives a little laugh. "Oh, some watercolors and things. Most of them got burned up in the fire. Our house burned up three years ago, everything. But my daughter, Valerie, brought these back."

She points to several framed watercolors on the opposite wall. I get up to take a look. The watercolors are all landscapes and barns, country roads, snow scenes, nothing like what my outrageous aunt Bessie would have painted, but still, the coincidence seems fantastic. Each one is lovely. When I look at them closely, I see that most of them are studies of her house, the barns, the wooded road that leads here. The colors are serene; the brushstrokes, so precise yet tender, show her great love for this place, her home.

"Did you ever study art?" I ask, sitting back down.

"No. Oh, no, I just did it as a hobby. And I haven't painted now in a long time. I can't see well enough anymore."

I ask her if she remembers my grandfather, and she says no, but that he must have visited for a while because he brought her a silver cup, a silver knife and fork and a pearl-handled rattle with silver bells, all from the best stores in Washington, D.C. He also brought her a pink dress, which Anna remembers well.

"Oh, I remember that dress!" Anna exclaims. "I loved it because it was so beautiful. It was pink and had all smocking on the front, you know. But one day I cut holes in it. I remember my mother was so upset."

"Did you cut the holes on purpose, do you think?" I ask, thinking about the kinds of things my own toddler would do if he was mad, but Anna shakes her head.

"Oh, no, I think I was just cutting paper dolls or something. I think I was,"—she laughs a bit, embarrassed—"I think I was sitting on the potty at the time. My mother was so upset."

According to Anna, my grandfather also brought her mother gifts. "Mother had an elegant locket with pearls on it and a gold watch pin with her initials engraved on it. She had dresses and suits that he must have bought her."

But by 1917, when Anna was just beginning to toddle across the room, her light brown hair flying, he stopped visiting. Then the money he was sending became infrequent.

"There are letters about it somewhere. Norman had put them in a tin box along with the deed to the property, so when the fire was out, we dug through the ashes and found them. Nothing romantic, just how was the baby doing, you know. Then my mother sued him for money in 1920. I don't know how much money she got, but she did get money from him, but I don't think she heard from him after that. They were just living here after that. Then, when Mother remarried, she asked him to sell her the farm so that she could have the title in her name."

"She bought the farm from him?"

"Yes, she wanted everything clear."

I feel my heart sink. Not only had my grandfather abandoned his baby daughter, but he had not provided for her the way Mrs. Chester had thought.

"You know I looked for deeds in the courthouse," I say to Anna. I am sure that my voice reflects my confusion. "I wonder why I couldn't find anything."

For the first time Anna's husband chimes in. "He didn't want nobody to know about it. Someone else's name is on the deed."

I look at him startled. So much intrigue. That was why there were no deeds in the courthouse. He had transferred the property to Anna's mother through a third party.

"Do you have them?" I ask.

"Yes." He nods. They were saved from the fire. "I can find them; they're here somewhere."

Again I think to myself Why? Was my grandfather just a scoundrel? Had he fallen on hard times? I recall the thick files of letters between my grandfather and his sister and brother; letters posted from my grandfather around that time came from Claverack, Washington and then France. Where had he gone in 1917? Was he running from the grief of a love he had decided was not possible or trying to disentangle himself from an affair that he felt had gone further than he intended? By 1921 he was back at Talavera and about to marry my grandmother, Helen Stott of Stottville, just up the road.

"We'll find the deeds," Anna says. "You can make copies of them if you want. My mother always said to me, if we hadn't sued him, maybe we might have seen more of him. I heard that his mother had someone picked out for him to marry and that he eventually did."

When Anna says this, her voice sounds sad. She clearly blames her uncle for forcing her mother to hire a lawyer to pursue my grandfather. But I point out that her mother must have needed money, she had a baby to support. Anna nods and remembers that yes, they were very poor. Her uncle was supporting them, and then he became ill. "She thought the world of him," says Anna suddenly, and again I hear the sadness in her voice. "I know that. Even before she died, she said he was the love of her life."

"How long do you think they were involved?"

"I don't know," Anna answers, "long enough for him to take her on trips, I know that. And he took care of her in Albany, of course. But Valerie knows more about it than I do. Mother loved to talk about him and the things they did, but I guess she knew it upset me, so she didn't talk about him much around me. I just wanted to get on with my life. I tried not to think about things, I guess."

Again, I make a mental note to try to find out where my grandfather was from 1917 to 1920. I hate the grandfather who seemed to have turned away from his baby daughter. Even when I remind myself that I know too little about what happened to judge, instinctively I take the woman's side.

When I ask Anna what her mother would say when Anna asked who her father was, she answers thoughtfully, "My mother told me what my father's name was, but she also told me, 'Never tell anybody.' Sometimes she'd say Mr. Philip, sometimes she'd say captain. Mostly Mr. Philip, never by his first name. She'd say, 'If anyone asks you who your father is, say you don't know.' So I learned to lie when I was a little kid. I didn't like the sound of 'I don't know.' So I'd say, 'He was here, but now he isn't, so I don't see him anymore.'"

Anna laughs, thinking back on those days. I continue to be amazed by her lack of any evident bitterness.

"Kids would tease me terribly at school," she continues. "I was always crying, coming home crying. Then one day, a little boy who was always getting picked on terribly said to me, 'You mustn't let them make you cry, you mustn't. You don't see me crying, do you?'"

"He was trying to help you out."

"Yes," says Anna, "yes, he was. I will never forget that."

Anna leans back on the couch and looks at me. Even at eighty-five, she is poised and gracious with me and my questions. She is clearly shy and making a great effort to tell me everything she can remember. She wants me to know her story, to be sitting right where I am, listening.

"You see, back in those days, my mother had the idea that she had sinned. She'd say, 'I have sinned.' You see, my grandmother had been rather preachy. And Uncle Floyd, he was always throwing the Bible at you."

"That must have made you feel even worse," I say.

"Well, yes, I suppose it did," says Anna, "One time my mother and I were looking through a catalog, and there was this red dress that I wanted. But later I overheard my mother say to my uncle, 'Well, not for her anyway.' I remember feeling that I mustn't stand out in any way. Sometimes when people came over I would hide under the table, I felt so inferior."

A heavy silence fills the room. I do not want to dismiss the gravity of what Anna is saying by small talk. But as I sit there, I can't help thinking that my own father would have wanted to know her. And as Anna talks, I begin to see another grandfather, one who could be heartless. No doubt he told himself he was acting out of a sense of honor. But honor to whom? What a paradoxical, contradictory thing that sense of honor was and how it had wounded someone he probably never meant to wound.

195

Mrs. Chester breaks the silence, speaking hurriedly. "And the thing is, today it would be no big deal. Everything has changed. But he must have cared for her a great deal. I think that. Otherwise why bother? She was such a beautiful girl. Don't you have a picture somewhere of your mother?"

At Mrs. Chester's insistence, Anna gets out a photo album, compiled of pictures that Valerie had been keeping and so were saved from the fire that burned their house to the ground three years earlier. I look at the small photographs of her mother and see that even in the grainy prints Anna Orsted is radiant.

"Mother always said that he was the love of her life," repeats Anna, "even right up until the end. She was never angry, even up until she died. She died in 1987. She tried not to talk to me about him much because she knew that it upset me, but I gathered from her that he felt he couldn't marry her because he would be marrying beneath his station. You know . . ." Anna pauses here, then chuckles, "I remembered once overhearing people say that here in the United States there aren't any social classes." For the first time since she has begun talking, Anna's voice becomes heated. "But sure there are. There's the lower class and the upper class. I always felt that there was."

I glance over at Anna and realize that her large figure has begun to slump down into the cushions of the couch. She is growing tired. "Would you like to see the photographs that I brought?" I say quickly.

Anna nods her head eagerly and leans forward in anticipation. When I turn over a photograph of my grandfather, taken about the time she was born, she looks and looks. "Oh, my," she says.

"Does he look the way you imagined?"

"Yes," she says slowly, but I hear a long "but" in her voice, "sort of."

I wonder if she is disappointed in what she sees. But then I pull out a copy of his obituary, and Anna brings the clipping with its photograph up close to her face and studies it for a long time.

"Have you seen that before?" I ask.

"Yes, Mother sent it to me, I think. I can't remember. Mother was very upset, of course, very upset. But I guess it was then that—" Anna looks down and is quiet for a moment, collecting her words. "Well, I had my own life and everything, but that was when I knew that I would never meet him." Anna wipes a tear from her left eye, and I am reminded that for her, this is all she will ever have of her father.

"Did your mother have any photographs of him?"

"Well, Mother had a photograph of him on a horse, I think, and there was a silhouette, but they all burned in the fire. We lost everything except a few letters and the silver cup and spoon. We found those in the ashes. Valerie has them. But you know, one day—it was quite a few years ago now—

I opened the paper, and there was a picture of someone from your family, could it have been your brother? And I looked at it and I said to myself. 'I look like him. That's who I look like.'"

We work back through the years, and I realize that the photograph that she must be referring to was a publicity shot of my eldest brother, blond and handsome, taken during his acting days, when he had achieved local notoriety for his roles on television soaps and in the Merchant-Ivory film *The Bostonians*. Probably she had noticed the photograph because of the name under it, John Van Ness Philip, my grandfather's name. She had carefully cut the picture out of the paper and saved it.

"Would you like to see a picture of Talavera?" I ask, and when Anna nods yes, I pull out a large black-and-white glossy print.

Anna pulls it toward her quickly. Her eyes travel up and down the white pillars. Then she sighs. "Oh, my," she says, then puts it carefully down.

"Have you ever seen the house before?"

"Well, Valerie drove me by there once. She has done some research. And once there was an open house, the local historical society or something, and I thought of going, but then I just felt too awkward."

"Would you like to see it in person, to visit?"

"Oh, yes," she says quickly, "I would like that very much."

I glance over at Mrs. Chester and suddenly remember her speculation that Anna's daughter had been named after Talavera. As I begin to gather my things, I ask her how she chose the name Valerie for her daughter.

"Oh." Anna laughs. "Valerie was a girl in my school. I always thought she was so beautiful. So I chose that name."

I click off the tape recorder, and we begin our good-byes. Anna says that she will have Norman find the box of letters and deeds, and I promise to make Anna copies of pictures that I brought of her father. We agree to meet in Hudson soon.

It is clear that Anna wants to meet my family, that for her, walking into Talavera would be like walking into a fairy-tale version of her life. I walk out thinking about how to make that happen. This time, when I leave, I give her the hug that I had wanted to give her earlier. As I come forward, her smile opens like a bird's wings. I feel her large arms folding around my back, protective, hopeful. Anna Van Ness Philip. She is the lost aunt. Found.

CHAPTER FIFTEEN

Anna

*T*hat night I told my mother about Anna Post. We were sitting on the south porch after dinner, enjoying the cool night. When I looked up at the tops of the fluted Corinthian columns, I could just make out the shadowed patterns of palmettes and acanthus leaves. The moon was still low and hazy. My mother responded with a shocked silence at first, then wanted to know everything I had found out about this would-be aunt. She was sure that my father never knew that he had a half sister because if he had known about her, my mother was sure he would have tried to find her. I asked her if she would be the one to tell my brothers and sister that they had an aunt they never knew about, and she said yes. Then she said she had to think about how to contact Anna.

One month later, when the busy harvest weekends were winding down, my mother called Anna Post and introduced herself. She invited Anna to Talavera that Saturday so that they could meet. My oldest brother, whose picture Anna cut from the newspaper and saved for many years, was up that weekend, helping with the harvest, and so he met her too.

They had tea in the dining room, sipping hot tea out of my grandmother's Dresden china, stirring with the little silver spoons that belonged to General John P. Van Ness. All around Anna, the family portraits bore down, but she was not alarmed. She was delighted by everything she saw: the candles lit at noon, the fire sparkling in the grate, the curio cabinets packed with souvenirs from generations of grand tours, the mahogany table where on many occasions her mother must have served my grandfather and the Roosevelts, perhaps even Gaston and Bessie, their own cups of hot steaming tea.

A few weeks after her visit Anna told me about it on the phone. "I was overwhelmed. It's so large and . . . but your mother was so nice, and your brother. I kept thinking I should write you. For a long time I've wanted to tell you how much this has meant to me. That you wanted to meet me, that was what was important. It's like this huge weight has been lifted. . . . A few weeks ago my granddaughter called me. She had decided to look up her birth parents— she's adopted, you know—and finally she had met them. She said to me, 'Grandmother, now you know how I feel. I feel complete.'"

Anna had laughed, another of her gentle, unassuming laughs, which by then I knew conveyed much more than she could say. I was glad then, for her, for me, for everyone.

What I discovered when reading through the deeds and letters was also surprising. The Old Forge property—a house, three barns and five and a half acres—was indeed transferred to Anna Orsted via a third party in 1926. Across the top of the deed was written in pencil *not for publication*. Even that transfer was not recorded in the courthouse. In 1926 my father was four, and my uncle just two. My grandfather was clearly trying to hide any connection to Anna Orsted and his illegitimate daughter by her. But Mrs. Chester was right about the farm's being given by my grandfather, for he handed it over for one dollar, a token amount to make the gift a legal sale.

When I looked through the papers and deeds that Anna saved, I saw that although by 1920 he had paid in full, initially he had had great trouble coming up with the five thousand dollars that he had promised Anna's mother in 1917. Letters to Anna's mother from the Hudson lawyer she hired to represent her case, however, urged her to be patient. At one point the lawyer relayed to her a letter that my grandfather, whom he referred to as Major, had sent him. My grandfather wrote: "These notes are alright and perfectly good. I am only too anxious to pay them in full and will do so at the earliest opportunity. Is there any distress at this time that has to be relieved? I am just at that point where everything practically is outgo, but this condition will shortly change to the reverse."

The letter was dated August 5, 1917. My grandfather wrote from France, where he was still on active duty as an officer in the Fourth Division of the U.S. Army. That July the Germans initiated their last major offensive of the war, and the Fourth Division had been ordered to attack the German main line of resistance between Rivière de Cligon and Ruisseau d'Alland. By August 6, when the offensive ended, the Fourth Division had lost 53 officers and 1,357 enlisted men. Another 179 officers and 5,296 enlisted men had been wounded. Despite heavy bombardment, the Fourth Division established and held the first bridgehead across the Vesle River.

As I discovered, my grandfather's involvement in World War I started as early as 1915, when he began helping with the Plattsburgh training plan, becoming a sergeant major in the First Provisional Plattsburgh Regiment. He remained in France some months after the end of active fighting.

While he was away, Alice Rockefeller was handling the farm accounts for the Old Forge properties and Talavera. In November 1917 she typed up an inventory of the Scism House, the farmhouse next door, which was almost identical to the one in which one-year-old Anna and her mother were living. The list held twenty-seven entries and described a life stripped down to the essentials:

Bread box
Water pail and dipper
Kerosene can
New broom
4 oat meal dishes
3 cups and saucers
5 soup plates
5 plates
salt and pepper shaker
water pitcher and 5 glasses
Lantern
Tea kettle, dish pan, tea pot, kettle and cover, 2 frying
  pans

In 1939 my grandfather began selling his Old Forge lands to finance the college educations of his two sons. That year my father was at the top of his class at the St. Albans School in Washington and about to enter Princeton, where a few years later his younger brother followed.

CHAPTER SIXTEEN

Another War

*I*n 1941 Germany invaded Russia, and Italy and Germany invaded Egypt. In the death camp of Auschwitz-Birkenau, the mass executions of Jews were soon to begin.

By winter my grandfather had sold most of his Old Forge lands. My father was busy in his second year at Princeton. With his blond hair and gray-blue eyes, his tall good looks, my father looked like a Scott Fitzgerald version of a Princeton boy. He was already passionately devoted to orange and black, the Gothic buildings and walkways tumbling with ivy, the cheerful lines of shops along Nassau Street. On a letterhead headed "8A Holder Hall," he wrote to my grandfather that he was trying to get on the staff at the *Daily Princetonian*. He was on break but working as hard as he could to collect enough interviews to get an editorship. Every day he rushed out with his pad and pen, then typed like mad. He thought the interviews were going well and that he had a shot, but the best news of all was that out of the blue, Mrs. Roosevelt had called him up personally to invite him to dinner at the White House.

My father figured that he could justify the trip to Washington, D.C., since he could conduct more interviews there. Written after the event, his letter brimmed with excitement: "Dear Daddy, The President was there, Mrs. Knudson, the secretary of the Navy, Harry Hopkins and Justice Douglas— and we sat through jokes, discussions, and stories about everything inside and outside the New Deal, the defense program, the war—not for publication of course, but quite an experience for me." My grandfather would not have been surprised. Only a month earlier he had written the president directly: "Van Ness jr. is trying for the Princetonian and has to get certain interviews . . . It occurred to me you might see him for a minute or two . . ."

By that point the family sleigh that had belonged to my great-great-great-grandfather Martinus Hoffman was on display at Roosevelt's Hudson River estate in Hyde Park as part of an exhibit of the early Dutch culture of the valley. It seems that after dinner, that night in the White House, the president took my father upstairs and showed him the presidential library.

My father made it onto the staff of the *Daily Princetonian.* Within a year he worked his way up to the position of managing news editor. He decided to major in the School of Public and International Affairs, in large part because my grandfather envisioned a career for him in politics or government service. But already my father had other ideas: He wanted to be a journalist and in that way to travel the world.

On December 7 all that would change, but not for the reasons anyone might have expected. On that day the Japanese bombed Pearl Harbor. Within twenty-four hours the United States joined the Allied powers in declaring war on Japan. Then Germany and Italy declared war on the United States. Another war. Like his father before him, my father would graduate from Princeton and go directly into the military.

There seemed to be no question that my father would enlist as soon as possible. His first choice was the marines, but he applied too late and was told that the quota had been filled. In a letter to my grandfather, he railed: "If I had just acted a month ago (and realized the necessity) I could be in the Marines now, and could just kick myself for not doing so. . . ."

In the same letter he asked his father if he should give up his first choice and join the navy, something he clearly did not want to do, but a move that would get him into action sooner. He added that in any event, he needed my grandfather to send his birth certificate and a letter stating that his parents were permitting him to enlist. That April my father turned twenty. In May the quota was increased, and he entered the Marine Corps as part of the Reserve Officers' Training Corps. From that point on, his studies at Princeton became a funnel, channeling him toward the war. He took five classes a semester to complete requirements in three years instead of the usual four. He and his fellow editors on the *Daily Princetonian* worked around the clock, filing the latest news briefs on the war. In addition to these university commitments, he began courses in officers' training.

When I read over the mimeograph of his academic transcript, I saw that, not surprisingly, his grades soon crashed. But he completed his senior thesis on time, and it must have been considered better than adequate, for he graduated with honors. I had found a black-bound copy in the barn loft, and read the title with surprise: "A Study of the Price Mechanism of the New York Apple Market." Had my father even then been preparing himself to take over the farm? His thesis in the almost two-hundred-page economic history was that the Hudson Valley apple industry was headed for trouble because of its poor marketing practices. His conclusion, although vague, was prophetic: "A long period of hard times will probably be required before producers and dealers are induced to take decisive action in making necessary improvements." I heard the same sorts of comments fifty-five years later at meetings of the Columbia County Fruit Growers Association delivered by Cornell University professors brought in to try to help the troubled fruit industry. While they spoke, the audience glared.

In a photograph of the commencement services of 1943, more than half the graduating class was wearing khaki, my father included. Two months later he began active duty training and spent thirteen weeks in Camp Lejeune and twenty-four weeks at Quantico. At that point he was considered ready to ship out. A photograph was taken of him then: First Lieutenant John Van Ness Philip 039636/0302 USMCR. In the picture his face looked butter soft, so full of hope it made you wince. He had inherited nothing of his father's cool detachment. The eyes that looked toward the camera were so earnestly looking forward, trying so hard to hold their gaze steady, that you could tell right away he was shy. When I looked at the photograph, I saw another one, a picture of my father aged five, playing with his toy farm by the smokehouse at Talavera. In his recruiting photo he was twenty years old but looked like a boy. He *was* a boy, and he was about to go to war.

Ten months later his division was preparing for a special assignment. On the Hawaiian Islands they practiced beach landings. As soon as the amphibs reached the shore, they ran like hell in choreographed patterns to trick the enemy. They learned how to camouflage themselves with sand and seaweed, how to fight from "spider holes," basic foxholes with camouflaged lids, how to attack heavily fortified positions and how to streak across beaches riddled with minefields. They didn't know it yet, but they were headed for Iwo Jima, considered the most heavily defended island in the Japanese archipelago. Twenty-two thousand Japanese, commanded by Tadamichi Kuribayashi, were waiting for them. While the marines trained, the Japanese dug thirteen thousand yards of underground tunnels and fortified the hospital and four-story gallery they built within Mount Suribachi, a volcanic crater that dominated the island's tip. By D-Day the sides of Suribachi had become an invisible grid of pillboxes, one thousand of them, some with concrete walls five feet thick, and the rest of the island was similarly fortified. The Japanese soldiers on Iwo had been told that the marines soon to land on their island were murderers, lunatics and felons, freed from institutions on the condition that they fight.

As the Fifth Division Marines trained for Iwo, they knew that they were headed for a terrible situation. Newly revised navy standards on journalism allowed an unprecedented amount of coverage in the weeks building up to the attack. Some of this news filtered to the waiting marines, so that well before D-Day they knew that Iwo's defenses were lethal. They also knew that 40 percent casualties were predicted. Iwo was to be a classic amphibious assault: men put ashore to kill or capture anyone who stood in their way. The marines, playing cards, swabbing the deck, studying again and again their rubber maps of Island X, looked at one another and knew how to figure the odds. For every three of them who dropped down into the landing boats, only two would come out alive.

Not surprisingly, the mood in the transport ships as they headed for Iwo was tense. The marine chaplain reported outbreaks of ghoulish black humor. Periodically, one marine would play taps at dinnertime. For the umpteenth time, the units were drilled on their assignments, but once Island X was identified as Iwo, the regimental surgeon reported an outbreak of diarrhea. One seasoned reporter, who traveled with them, commented: "The marines bound for Iwo spoke more flatly . . . of the expectation of death than any assault troops I had ever been with before."

After I had read about the situation for the marines heading for Iwo, I was confused when I sat down to read through my father's letters from that time. In all of them, my father never mentions Iwo or his fears about going into action. Instead, he describes in upbeat detail attempts to go fishing while at sea, the quality of meals and the occasional movies that play on board. I read the letters through carefully several times, confirming that they were indeed addressed from Lieutenant John Van Ness Philip of the Fifth Division Marines and dated just before the invasion of Iwo. Only from his letter of January 29, two weeks or so before D-Day, do I understand.

In that faded blue letter, my father began as usual asking for news of his younger brother Nick, whom he had just written advising him to take up a specialty to stall being assigned to the Pacific. He was very worried about that possibility and went on at some length to persuade my grandfather to advise Nick of the same. Before closing, however, he changed the subject: "At last I am permitted to say that we are at sea and that we are going into action. Where or when I am not really certain myself, though the scuttlebut has been flying about, naturally, and we have certainly planned long enough and thoroughly enough. . . . After I have been in action, I will be permitted to write you about the many places I have been since coming here. Your devoted son, Van Ness jr."

Only two days earlier, he had sent a similar, although markedly more descriptive letter in which he alerted his mother to the news of pending action, but then did his best to reassure her. "Dear Mummy, After we have been in action, I will be able to write about many of the places I have seen. The sea is very calm, a pale blue in the bright sun, broken only by the white foam from the tow and the green wake. No whitecaps but small ripples atop the swell, which rolls the ship very quietly from side to side. It is quite comfortable aboard, the Navy chow the best I have had anywhere except at home since I joined the Marine corps. I hope all is well. My love to Daddy. With love as always, Van Ness jr."

ᴥᴘ

It was like my father not to complain or to want to worry his elderly father, but his complete silence on the issue of Iwo had been navy censorship. In his next letter, four days later, he again wrote of his great concern that Nick stay out of active service. Then he asked about recent reports from Talavera. My grandfather was serving on the Pan-American

Highway Finance Committee then and he and my grand-mother had closed Talavera for the winter and were living in Washington, D.C. My father reported that life on ship was not unpleasant, meals good and lots of work to keep them busy. Only that it was hard to keep track of days and time. They had to keep changing their watches as they proceeded. And then there was the annoying voice of Radio Tokyo, which they picked up on the air every day saying that MacArthur was being led into a tremendous trap.

Only in his close did he again mention his situation. By that point, they were close to Iwo, some 750 miles from Tokyo. "Dear Daddy, I suppose you are up on the news and realize why this letter was so long in getting to you. Re-member, I will always write when I can, if only a few lines, so expect to hear from me again soon. There will also be a time when I can tell you where I am, where I have been, what I am doing."

By February 11 he could see Tinian Island from the ship and he described it to his mother, carefully withholding the name.

Dear Mummy,
Soon I will be able to write and to explain many things. . . . This island is more formidable than some I have seen, but it is new and strange in a way—differ-ent shades of green and different shapes from the other islands of its size, though it is misty and overcast with some rain and the view is none too good. Still quite warm, though, and peaceful, with hundreds of lights twinkling on shore.

The ship rolls impatiently at anchor in the swell, and the little boats have the devil of a time coming up to the gangway, and launching themselves off for the mail and messenger runs, etc.

I hope you and Daddy are in good cheer and health and finding everything is satisfactory at Talavera.

The war is personal to us all, of course, as you say, but

it is good to look over the big picture and see how well it is turning for the best, and realize that happier days may not be too far off. My best to you and Daddy,
    your devoted Van Ness jr.

Then it was February 15, less than twenty-four hours to D-Day. As if in preparation, my father sent his sixty-five dollars of spare cash home to his mother via registered mail, telling her that he had "no way to spend it and I fear it getting lost." Again my father wrote of everything he could think of that would entertain his parents. He described how marvelous it was to stretch his arms out into open ocean on the occasional times they were allowed to swim off the small boats, and the great beauty of the South Pacific, "calm, bright sunshine, a fresh breeze on deck, and only the gentle motion of the ship in the swell. Lagoons fringed by coral reefs and little islands that seem a pleasant oasis." Perhaps D-Day had already been announced for quite suddenly, before he closed, my father burst into an uncharacteristically open disclosure of yearning for his parents and for Talavera. "How I wish that I could be there with you and Mummy, if only as few times as I got home last spring. But perhaps by next spring, who knows. I will be at least beginning to think of real possibilities of getting home."

On D-Day the sun broke cleanly over the blue horizon. Visibility perfect. Operation Detachment began at 0500. The men ate steak and eggs, traditional landing day fare. Then, by 0640, the guns of heavy transport ships boomed into action. While the prelanding bombardment continued, the Third, Fourth and Fifth Marine divisions got ready. The transports eased into their assigned areas, and at 0805, seventy-two fighter and bomber planes roared toward the island to attack the eastern and northern slopes.

At 0830 the first wave of armored amphibians, loaded with marines, headed for the shore. Each one had been allotted thirty minutes to reach the steep beach, a distance of four thousand yards. At 0902, only two minutes off schedule, it was H hour. Orders came bawling over a loudspeaker from the control ship for marines to get down into their boats. Minesweepers had already cleared pathways, carefully knifing the sand for mines as the marines crawled forward. The plan called for the Fifth Marines to cut off Suribachi and then pivot north. As soon as the Fifth splashed ashore, climbing up onto the black beach, the men began to run as they had trained, as fast as they could across the beach and toward cover. But something was wrong.

The sand on the beach was not at all like the sand on the Hawaiian beaches where they had trained. One step and they were ankle deep in black volcanic ash, fine as cake flour. They couldn't run. They could barely walk. Miraculously there was no fire from the Japanese. The marines struggled forward, more and more of them becoming mired like ants in honey. Only when seven battalions of marines were struggling across the dark sand did the Japanese rise from their hidden positions and open fire. Some marines panicked and tried to dig foxholes, but it was impossible, like burrowing into a bag of wheat. Soon, among urgent calls to the control ship for mortar shells, stretchers and plasma, there were cries for sandbags so that the marines, pinned down on a beach that was being raked by enemy fire, could build cover.

At 1130 Associated Press photographer Joe Rosenthal was still waiting in a landing craft. The waterline was choked with the wreckage of boats and vehicles trapped in the sand. He could barely see the beach so much black dust was being kicked up by shellfire. Enormous spigot mortar shells called flying ashcans and rocket-boosted aerial bombs were especially scary. Then there was Mount Suribachi, bathed in an eerie fog. In an interview, Rosenthal recounted: "I kept thinking. 'Here are guys who haven't lived yet. . . . If I'm killed it will be no great loss, but these kids haven't had a fair chance, and we know the odds. The odds mean that four or five of them are not coming back. . . .'" When his boat touched the shore, Rosenthal stood up and snapped two pictures of "kids" racing down the ramp lugging their mortar carriages behind them. A few minutes later, onshore, he saw a picture that for him seemed to sum up the nightmarish quality of the landing. A dead marine was lying on an uphill slope, his gun ready, frozen in the act of charging forward. Struggling past him were newly landed marines, one of whom could have been my father. Rosenthal crept up the beach until he could get an angle on the shot. Then, just as a marine lurched by, he clicked the shutter. By nightfall the press plane had left for Guam carrying his film. By Wednesday his image of the dead marine standing guard for his comrades as they ran through enemy fire was on the front page of every major newspaper in the United States.

Regular airmail was not allowed in combat zones, but soldiers could send and receive V-mail, brief personal letters reduced onto microfilm to save precious cargo on ships and airplanes, then developed and enlarged to fit a 4½- by 5-inch sheet of paper. My father's first V-mail was just a paragraph that he sent his mother. "Dear Mummy, I am fine, unscratched and in good health and intend to stay that way. . . . Hope you and Daddy are both well. You must not worry over what you read in the newspapers, it is always exaggerated. Be sure that Nick sticks to that sea duty. It is fine, as you know. All my love to you and Daddy, Van Ness jr."

Three days passed before he could write again. This time he sent a V-mail to his father, urging him to ignore the newspaper accounts of the invasion and repeating his concern that they try to keep Nick from active duty. "No air mail facilities but I wrote Mummy yesterday I was O.K. and well. We are enjoying fine hot meals, hot coffee, butter, etc. . . . My main worry is that you and Mummy will worry unnecessarily from reading exaggerated accounting by newspapers. . . . You know I can take care of myself and will continue to be O.K. love to you and Mummy and Nick, steer him to sea duty by all means. VN jr."

In the next V-mail to his mother, sent out the same day, my father tried to make light of his situation: "Rumor has it that our General has bet someone $1,000 he would get us back to the States within a year."

What he did not tell them was that his colonel, operations officer and sergeant major had already been killed and that the fighting was not yet over. He also did not mention that his battalion had actually been part of the heroic charge up Mount Suribachi to plant the American flag or that on D plus 5, or February 24, while pursuing two powerful cross-island defenses, hills 362 and 362A, he had been wounded in the head by shellfire.

Only my uncle, still stationed at Parris Island, knew that my father had been hit. As soon as letters came in, one arrived from my uncle, who assured my father that he would honor my father's request not to tell their parents about what my father had called his "Hollywood Wound." Nick went to assure my father that if he were assigned to Princeton that summer, he would visit Talavera on weekends as my father had done, that my father should not worry about the place. Again, he asked my father about his hit, but my father didn't seem to answer that either, for in letters that followed, my uncle repeated the question and commented that their parents had written to say that my father's surviving Iwo had changed their whole view of life.

213

On March 11, my father wrote again but still did not mention his hit. He seemed intent upon deflecting his parents' concern and made fun of the newspaper coverage of the war.

Iwo Jima, March 11

Dear Daddy,
All is well and I hope you have been getting my letters. When you get this letter of course, it will all be over long since, as it is almost over now, and you and Mummy will not be worrying anymore. . . .
    I have seen mainland news accounts reported in our paper over here. The latest one to give us a good laugh

was about nurses and doctors being rushed to Pearl to devise means to protect us from the "deadly sulphur fumes" of Iwo. This is ridiculous. While the dust does get in our weapons, the hot sulphur smoke coming out of the earth is often one of the comforts of this island as it keeps you warm at night and literally furnishes steam-heated foxholes.

. . . I hope all is well with the fruit and that the pruning is coming along okay. No doubt the snow is melted by now. All my love to you and Mummy,

your devoted son, Van Ness jr.

Only in a letter to his uncle Hoffman, written that same day, did he describe something of what he had been through.

Dear Uncle Hoffman,

I have seen plenty of action. We are the "George" company of the 3rd and the policy around here seems to be "let George do it" for my company has seen more time on the front lines than any other company in all 3 Divisions. Now we are in a rest area. The big Japanese mortars and artillery are pretty well silenced. . . .

Those Marines in the assault platoon certainly have guts—I never believed such courage and heroism as I have seen right before my eyes time and time again. Well, I will tell you about it when I see you. . . . I have not told Mummy and Daddy about the action and perhaps won't for a time.

Your devoted nephew, VN jr.

Only on March 27, when guns on Iwo finally went silent, did my father send some news of what he had survived. His letter, written on Red Cross stationery, not the usual marines' letterhead, implied that he was in a "resting area," if not a hospital. As usual, he started with assurances: "Dear Daddy, I hope that you and Mummy are well and have been getting

ANOTHER WAR

my letters, and of course realize that Iwo Jima is a thing of the past for us now." He went on to describe recent skirmishes with Japanese who had come out of hiding to try to steal their water and K rations, but nothing serious. His main complaint was with what he considered media mongering by the Twenty-eighth Battalion, which was photographed planting the American flag on Mount Suribachi, although his battalion, the Twenty-sixth, had fought with them to gain that ground. "Our battalion took the last pocket of resistance on the island—a fact which will probably not be recognized afterwards by anyone but us, as the 28th Marines, the Suribachi outfit, had a company right behind us (which was supposed to be on our flank) which rushed up as soon as we had taken the last hill and planted the flag on it in the name of the 28th Marines right in the middle of our leading companies—It seems they had a lot of cameramen along and after Suribachi, wanted to leave no doubts as to who were the champion flag-raisers on the island. So, if you see the 28th again, you will know the true story."

He did not admit, even then, that he was wounded but wrote about the strange, hollowed-out feeling of returning to life after Iwo: "Now that it is all over, it will seem strange to go back to the old routines—wearing uniforms, holding inspections, calling captains and majors 'Sir' or 'Captain'— all the things so utterly foreign to what goes on in action." He added that it would take him some time before he could see a Japanese person in civilian clothes and not instinctively grab for a rifle. He wondered if he would ever be able to smoke a cigarette without cupping his hands around the tip to hide the glow at night. Some of his comrades were exhibiting classic effects of shell shock: "It is probably lucky that none of us goes to civilization too soon after these operations. Everyone would think us crazy. I know only last night somebody sleeping next to me in a nice safe bed with sheets woke up screaming bloody murder and woke everyone up." The marine had apparently been dreaming that a

215

Japanese had jumped into his foxhole. He could not stop screaming for a long time. This was all my father said about life in the camp, except to repeat his strange disbelief that he had come out alive.

Looking back on it curiously though, I know all of us still here can only reflect that we will never again have the right to complain, no matter what befalls us in the future. We are lucky, that is all, and it is hard to understand why luck runs as it does.

I hope you have good reports from Talavera. I know we can look forward to a good year to make up for the "hail luck" of last. We are due for one. Hope the Mexico business goes O.K. Anxious for news of Nick. My love to Mummy as always.

Your devoted son, VN jr.

For the first time upon my reading the letters, it hit me with some force that I was reading about my own father. I knew those words. I had heard them myself, or something similar, because when I tried to ask my father about the war, all he would ever say was something mumbled about how he never understood how he had come out alive. "I just came back and the others didn't. That's the thing, the only important thing." Not talking about his wound had become a habit, so that even when his children asked about his being shot, he would wave his hand dismissively and say, "What I got was nothing. There were lots of soldiers braver than me." Talking about Iwo at all seemed to make him angry, and he refused to associate with anything to do with World War II veterans. At one point he had written his uncle Hoffman that he intended to save his helmet with the four bullet holes in it as a souvenir of Iwo. But he had either changed his mind or disposed of the helmet when he returned. For him, that time was over, and he didn't want to think about it, especially not in terms that made it seem heroic. But he hadn't left the war behind, not really. Like thousands of men who came back from World War II to found the blue dream of the American suburbs, he was haunted by it. For the first time, holding his thin letter, tender as a new leaf between my hands, I felt I understood something new about my father. The sadness that could creep up on him at odd moments was a form of survivor's guilt. He had survived Iwo Jima.

On Easter Friday, my father attended services (later his parents received a letter from the marine chaplain to say that their son had attended Good Friday service) and wrote to his mother. He thanked her for sending him a compass, a camp stove and heat tablets, apparently things he had requested, and described in detail how good the meals were on Iwo, which he called the Rock. "Always when things were not too active, the front lines would get hot coffee twice a day, often with doughnuts and white bread, so all in all the living conditions were not what I expected."

He asked about Talavera and the place and responded that he had not been able to check on the status of a friend's son in the Twenty-eighth Battalion because censorship did not allow them to mention casualties. "If he were wounded, I wouldn't be able to say." As usual, one of his main concerns was the status of his younger brother, who by this point was working hard to try to get V-12 status and enter officers' training: "I am particularly anxious to hear about Nick. I do hope he has gotten the best that luck and opportunity could afford, over and above his own earnest efforts."

Again, his letter was written on Red Cross stationery, implying that even as late as April, he was in a resting area, but neither my grandmother nor my grandfather queried him about his location or condition. Only my great-aunt Lee, clearly suspecting something, tried to get him to reveal his situation. On April 8, she wrote innocently: "It was wonderful to get your letters of March 28 and 29 and know that you had actually left Iwo. . . . I can understand your not wanting to write much about details of your experience on that '7 miles of hell' as the correspondents put it, but I would like to know what you did about sleep! It seems you would have to catch a few winks to keep up the fight . . ." She sent him news of Talavera and how they were all on the usual spring tenterhooks because of the coming bloom: "This week we had a cold snap again for two days and the question of damage to the fruit trees is acute."

In her next letter, along with sending him the great news that Nick had made the V–12 and the sad news of President Roosevelt's sudden death, she raised the question of his status: "Where ever you are in your 'rest area.' It is wonderful to know you are enjoying the luxury of sleep and cleanliness and rest. And yesterday came the news from your mother that Nick has made V-12. It brought some cheer into the terrible gloom in which we have been since the news of the President's death stunned us Thursday evening."

Only gradually did she disclose how worried they had all been, how they had spent the first terrible days before his first V-mail arrived listening to the radio every hour. In her next letter, her usual description of the land and the trees at Talavera soared with relief: "It is like the spring when you were born and the apple blossoms and lilacs were in bloom. Your father actually picked some apple blossoms and took them to your mother in the hospital. She was more impressed than she would have been by jewels."

She included a letter from a cousin, Bill Whitney, stationed in France. But as she ended, she admitted that they had all been trying to figure out where he was by the speed at which his letters were reaching them. They were reaching Talavera in two days, as fast as when he had been stationed in California. She closed: "PS I can't figure out at all where you are. Can you mention any clues?"

My father was probably not allowed to mention his location at this point, and he stubbornly and poignantly refused to reveal that he had been wounded. He would rather write about the latest news of Talavera. At times, reading his looping hand, I thought of his great-uncle Lieutenant John Van Ness, who, while chasing confederate ships off Mobile, was constantly thinking about Talavera and worried about affairs on the farm. In between brief descriptions of ship life, my father spoke to his father about the labor shortage caused by the war, about the falling price of apples, about the frost and early bloom. Even then his faith in the land was complete. "In the meantime though, I don't see how we can help but have better luck next season than we did last."

Miles from any tree, still at sea in the Pacific, my father clearly cheered himself up by thinking of spring in the orchards, even mud season. "All goes well, and I am looking forward to the next mail which should not be too long from now, to hear about the latest word from Nick and your and Mummy's spring plans. I imagine now that the country is thawing so that you or Mummy or Nick have been able to get the Chevrolet out in the orchards."

Only a week before his birthday, as April came to a close, did my father reflect upon what he had been through. For the first time, he alluded to his own father's war experience in the trenches of World War I:

> It was fine to hear about the place looking well and Danny in fine form. I trust that there is no frost damage. It is grand to return here, but the associations only make us think more keenly of those who will not see it. I know you can appreciate this from experience. . . .
>
> Our own Colonel was killed, also our operations officer, and the Sargent major, and the executive officer evacuated—all within 48 hours of the landing of the battalion. . . .
>
> But it is over now and I hope there will never be any more Iwos for anybody.

On August 6 an atomic bomb decimated Hiroshima. Three days later another bomb destroyed Nagasaki. Within twenty-four hours the Japanese surrendered. VJ-Day.

On April 22, 1946, my father was released from active service. Three weeks later he received what was probably a form letter of official thanks from General A. A. Vandegrift, the commanding general of the Marine Corps.

My dear Lieutenant Philip,
Your readjustment to the life of a civilian has, I hope, been fully accomplished, and with as little difficulty as you experienced in adapting yourself to military life when you came on in active duty.

No one is more familiar than I with the essential role which you of the Reserve assumed in the war. Together we accomplished our missions, however difficult they may have been. Together we developed the Marine Corps into the finest of all fighting forces. It could not have been done without you. Your patriotism and your fine devotion to duty have been an inspiration to the Officers and men who shared the responsibilities for final and complete victory.

. . . We always think of you as one of our own.

Please accept my personal and official thanks and my best wishes for your continued success.

Sincerely yours,
A. A. Vandergrift
General, USMC
Commandant of the Marine Corps

By the time my father arrived back at Talavera, the apples had bloomed and a fine crop of button-sized fruit could be seen throughout the trees. My father folded his wool jacket and pants, and one of his better khaki shirts and placed them carefully in his wooden U.S. Marines trunk along with his hat, his medals and various papers. His Purple Heart medal and Purple Heart ribbon for wounds received at Iwo Jima had been tucked into a separate envelope. He wrapped the entire package in newspaper. Before he closed the trunk, he threw in his dog tags and another mysterious pair, not his own. Then he closed the lid and dragged the trunk up into the barn loft. He did not place it with the other trunks of family things, however: the Civil War correspondence of his great-uncle and grandfather or the boxes of books on Christian readings collected by his grandmother and great-grandmother. Instead, he pulled the trunk across the aisle to a corner under the eaves where it sat, collecting mice droppings and bat guano, for the next fifty-three years.

That fall my father entered Harvard Business School, where he completed a master's in business. When he returned, he went to work as the editor of the *Princeton Herald*. There he met a vivacious young reporter with glossy dark, almost black hair and a wide smile. As with all the young women he met then, she dressed like a movie star, the most notable influence being Joan Crawford. Even her hair, cut so that it swept the shoulders, was gently waved and parted to one side Crawford style. She wore the latest fashions, tight-waisted dresses with padded shoulders, strangely reminiscent of military wear. Her slender legs touched the floor in high-heeled pumps. She smoked. Now that the wartime shortage was over, she wore silk stockings all the time. She loved a good time. In fact, she had been living on something of the wild side, cohabiting a brownstone in New York City with several other women and men. They joked that their establishment was a commune. No, the young woman my father fell in love with was definitely not a rich debutante, although she had gone to Vassar.

She was the daughter of a Princeton professor. Both her parents were from Virginia and had soft Culpepper accents and a strict Baptist view of the world. But my parents negotiated these differences. They were in love. With my mother's natural appetite for risk and my father's love of tradition, they balanced each other like yin and yang, light and dark. In Cary Grant fashion, my father's tall, broad shoulders filled his well-tailored jackets. He sported a fedora ever so slightly tilted at the brim. In my mother's closet were emerald evening gowns, a color that made her eyes flash. On what was then a wild open beach in Jacksonville, Florida, my father proposed. In 1952, they married and joined the rest of the country in trying to forget the war.

By 1957 two of my older brothers had been born, and a third baby was on the way. My father had risen in his chosen career of business journalism to become the managing editor of a magazine titled *Industrial Distribution,* published by McGraw-Hill. His younger brother had also done well as an agricultural engineer working for a large international firm. Together the two brothers pooled resources and bought a brownstone on East Eighty-fourth Street in Manhattan. My family took the downstairs apartment with its backyard, and my uncle and his family the slightly larger upstairs apartment with its grander front entrance. Both families were happy with the arrangement. By the time my sister and I were born, joining our three older brothers, we had three cousins living upstairs and kids all up and down the block to play with. My parents rarely locked our door. If we came home from school and didn't feel like playing at home, we walked into someone else's house. Everybody's mom was always home.

Every Friday without fail we drove to Talavera, where my father and at that point his younger brother Nick were running the farm. My grandmother lived at Talavera and managed the house. The orchards planted by my grandfather now produced twenty thousand bushels of apples and pears. Both brothers were clearly knowledgeable about the orchard business, for when one of them had to be away, the other kept him up-to-date with detailed information about sprays, blossom counts, pollination, picking and shipping schedules and many other details of ongoing farm work. It was the heyday of postwar technology and a typical curculio spray was four parts lead arsenate, three parts Ferbam and four parts DDT, chemicals that would not be banned until the 1960s. Willard Swartz, my grandfather's valet, then the general handyman at Talavera, had retired, but his nephew, a young man named Mike, had begun doing some work on the place.

In addition, my father and uncle had hired a headman named Adam Keeler, who oversaw and did much of the orchard work, bringing in extra workers to help with big seasonal jobs like winter pruning. During the harvest a crew from Jamaica, led by a crew leader named Reginald Small, drove up from Florida in a blue school bus to pick and pack out the crop.

As early as 1957, however, a pattern began to emerge whereby my father was at Talavera overseeing work and my uncle was traveling. When a sudden freeze threatened the crop, it was my father that my grandmother wired at his editorial office at McGraw-Hill: ALL APPLES SAFE IN BARN BEFORE LAST NIGHTS FREEZE. Most of the letters that I found were written by my father to his brother. On February 17, 1959, my father wrote to my uncle, away on business in Chicago: "Dear Nick, I spent yesterday with Adam—pruning about half way through no. 7, or more, and Adam wants to finish it before pushing brush. We have spent nearly $1,000 on the work for 1957 following harvest—but if he gets other work done economically we had best go ahead with it I think." The farm seemed to be paying its bills and supporting the house, but only barely, for my father went on to discuss their decision to buy a new sprayer and ways they could finance it temporarily by using personal capital. "Delicious are sold but only half paid for. Macs selling very slowly. We are shipping some this week. . . . Please let me know about gas papers, expense account and the literature on the sprayer. Yours, VN"

By 1963 letters from my father to his brother about farm activities were being sent to Kuala Lumpur, where my uncle was working. We no longer trooped upstairs to play with our cousins because they were living in Malaysia. My uncle had an active interest in affairs at Talavera, and my father wrote him regularly and received detailed letters in reply, but my father had assumed de facto responsibility for the farm and increasingly for management of their shared brownstone in

223

Manhattan. My uncle had tenants who lived in his half of the house while he was away, and my father served as land-lord.

My father did not complain about his increasing workload of their shared property, nor did he seem to consider how work spent maintaining Talavera was time he did not have to build his career. Within a year he had convinced his brother to purchase the farm just south of Talavera, a 150-acre fruit orchard that they call the South Place. They closed the deal in December. My father was thrilled with the decision, fig-uring that their total bushel capacity had just been expanded to close to fifty thousand. They would still produce some of the old favorites like Baldwin and Northern Spy, but most of the production would be in the popular new breeds: Royal Red Delicious, Rogers McIntosh and the newly developed Ida Red, a cross between a McIntosh and a Rome. They would also market young pears and plums.

But it was much more than the commercial opportunity that excited my father about this purchase. Our farm now stretched for almost a mile south along Route 9H, the Old Post Road, toward Claverack—all original Van Ness lands. The north and south sections of the first Van Ness farm, founded in 1732, had been reunited. The original Van Ness house had been sold to new owners, but the land and the original barns were back. My father clearly felt he had ac-complished something important by restoring the farm to its original size, for in his papers I found a press release typed by him which began "Historic Farm Reunited" then briefly outlined the farm's eighteenth-century founding and more recent past.

My uncle also seemed to have been excited by the pur-chase, although that summer hail thrashed through the or-chards, scarring the fruit so that the best price my father could get was eighty cents a box for hail-hit Macs, but that seemed good to them at the time. Not enough profit to ser-vice the large mortgage that they had taken to purchase the south farm, but even so, their excitement over the new land

persisted. The following fall my uncle sent my father a detailed letter outlining improvements he thought they should
make to the land on South Place. These included the plowing, debrushing and seeding of meadows and the bringing in
of new water by enlarging the existing pond and digging
out some swampy aquifers. Before they could start on these
improvements, however, they faced another bad hailstorm,
which again ravaged the crop.

By the fall of 1966 my parents had begun a new marketing strategy which they believed would help solve the farm's
financial problems. It was called Pick Your Own. Instead of
paying a crew to pick and pack the fruit, then paying a dis-
tributor to store and ship it, my parents planned on having
people come to the orchard to buy the fruit directly. If all
went as planned, they would triple their profits and cut out
the high costs of middlemen entirely. My uncle endorsed the
idea, calling it their bright hope. But since they had had two
bad years in a row of losses from summer hail, he thought
they should not concentrate all their land investment in fruit.
His suggestion was that they begin plantings of oaks and
maples along the road frontage and think about selling sections of the land, at least the more valuable road frontage
property.

Here I begin to read a division of thought that grew over
time, eventually dividing the two brothers. For my father,
Talavera and now the older Van Ness lands of the South
Place were not just home, but the family homestead, their
place in the world, their identity. He didn't seem to mind doing the maintenance work of upkeeping while his younger
brother was off making his fortune in the larger world, because he was the older son, and keeping Talavera together
was his duty, just as it had been his father's before him. He
couldn't think of the land as an asset because for him it
wasn't. Since it could never be sold, it had all value and no
value at the same time. He believed in farming because he
believed that the land would never let them down. It was his
great strength and his Achilles' heel. They had just righted an

ancient wrong—the sale of the south section of the farm by cousins at the turn of the century—and he couldn't embrace thinking of the land in terms of development. But far away, involved in large-scale international development projects, my uncle could.

By 1969 my father and his brother had sold most of the road frontage property, but they still needed cash to finance improvements on the land. They decided to sell the old Van Ness barns and fifty acres of land around them. Within weeks of their being put on the market, four doctors from New York City bought the old barns to make a weekend retreat. I remembered that year as an especially exciting time because my cousins had returned from Malaysia and the family was together again. Talavera was in constant commotion. Every day Betty was on the verge of quitting and my father or my uncle, both of them charming and handsome, would convince her to give it one more day. When Mrs. Patzwahl, the local woman who did errands for my grandmother during the week, drove up in her baby blue Impala, we were ushered out of the house. Miraculously, the house was cleaned, and fresh flowers filled the vases in the dining room, the library, the parlor, the south hall. When I look at pictures of that time, I see that the house was even then in need of repair. But I never noticed the worn rugs or the fading wallpaper. The mysterious rhythms of the house, rhythms that had to do with caring for my grandmother and caring for such an old and large house, were strange but comforting.

I didn't know any of the land's long history then. But I must have overheard something or at any rate felt my father's enthusiasm because I vividly remember the day the four doctors arrived at Talavera to visit. They had already agreed upon the land deal. As one of the four doctors later recounted, "We met at the Princeton Club in New York. I'll never forget it. Your father and your uncle came. They were both wearing tweed jackets. We had a concern because in the deed they specifically stipulated that we could not develop the land for any commercial use but there was no such constraint on their land. Our lawyer had told us to have this changed. But when we mentioned this concern to your father and uncle, they looked at us sort of shocked. 'This land has been in our family for over two hundred years,' they said; 'it will never be developed.'" Apparently the four doctors were satisfied, because by the end of the conversation they had agreed upon the price and the terms. The old Van Ness barns became the 4 Docs Place.

The day the doctors arrived was a rainy day and cold. I remember this because I had gone out riding anyway, and now I was back inside, deliciously warm. Lunch was creamed chicken over rice. For some reason we all had been sitting in the parlor, plates on our laps, eating, when the doctors arrived. I remember the warm room, the hot food, a fire in the grate, my brothers and sisters, maybe my cousins too all around and the rain pouring down outside. Above the black marble mantelpiece in the parlor hung a large portrait of William of Orange dressed in slate-colored armor, a long white wig curling down from the top of his head to the bottom of his breastplate. For years I assumed he was some sort of ancestor, like the other portraits that lined the house. Especially as the long Dutch sword that rested on the baby grand piano on the other side of the room was just like the one in the portrait. Until they were told that having a portrait of William of Orange was an eighteenth-century Dutch fashion, most visitors to the house thought so as well.

227

I remember the doctors stopping and staring at the portrait, peering out in some kind of disbelief. I don't know that what they felt was awe. Perhaps they were simply perplexed. Here were people living in a suspended state of history, caught like ants in amber. Maybe it was comical even to see us all there acting like gentry while we ate creamed chicken on plates seated cross-legged on the floor, on our already worn rugs.

I didn't care about my ancestors or William of Orange. The portraits looking down on us were simply extensions of the house, of my parents, of everything I took for granted. I was busy eating my lunch, trying to figure out if I could get away with saddle soaping my tack there in the warm parlor after everyone had gone.

But something made me look up, and when I did, I saw the doctors there, hands in their pockets, heads upturned. Their voices were hushed, almost as if they were in a museum, and perhaps it was that which made me take note. I remember looking at them while they looked at us and feeling for the first time a sense that we were different from other people and that somehow that difference, which had to do with the old portraits and the way people stared at them when they came into the house and sighed when they looked up at the white columns outside, had to do with the past, a past that made us special. I knew as well that to talk about this would have made my father frown. Talking about yourself was rude, and anyway, you didn't have to. Talavera spoke for us all.

The sale of the barns didn't seem to bother my father. The land was what mattered, and now he and my uncle were running almost two hundred acres of it in fruit. By 1969 Pick Your Own had proved such a success that within a few years the entire crop was sold directly to customers who came to pick. In his own career my father made a bold move, leaving the steady paycheck of McGraw-Hill to found a specialized business newsletter titled *Modern Distribution Management,* which he published biweekly. From now on, when I walked home from school, my mother was away at a job and my father was the one at home, writing in his office.

A year later something wonderful happened. The heirs of the man who had lent my grandfather four thousand dollars in 1914, a loan that had never been repaid, called my father to say that their family wanted to give my father the portrait of General John P. Van Ness.

That July 4 my father and mother drove down to the river estate where the painting had been hanging for more than fifty years, wrapped it gently in a blanket, placed it in the backseat of our old VW sedan and drove the general home.

Once the portrait had been returned to the dining room at Talavera, the room seemed to glow. Even when oil prices soared and the recession hit, causing apple prices to crash and small farms to falter all across the nation, my father did not waver in his belief that the land and the family would make it through.

But in 1973, when my grandmother died, a cavern opened. My father and uncle disagreed on the future of Talavera. My father envisioned a land trust, keeping Talavera together and preserving the land for the next generation—my brothers and sister, my three cousins, me. My uncle wanted to divide the estate. My father was clearly not prepared for this. All the years of caring for Talavera while his brother was away had set a dangerous precedent. He must have assumed that, as had been the case in previous generations, he and his brother would work together to keep Talavera intact or that if one stepped out, he would do so in a way that did not threaten Talavera's continuity. Even Aunt Bessie's histrionic sale of 1912 had been done with the full knowledge not only that her brothers could afford to buy all the family possessions she put up for sale but also that they would. It seemed likely that she and Gaston had felt they got the better deal when they unloaded any responsibility toward Talavera for a dollar.

But this moment of generational transfer had no precedent. My father and his brother went back and forth about possible lines of division. My father wanted Talavera, and my uncle wanted the brownstone in Manhattan, already a valuable income-producing property, although nothing like the multimillion-dollar real estate holding that it would become. The division should have been easy, but it wasn't. They couldn't agree on how much land should go with each house. Finally, my father proposed that they make two equal parcels and flip a coin to see who got which one. He figured that way they would both work toward a division that was fair. But then my uncle told my father that if he got Talavera on the flip, he would sell it. My uncle must have known the effect that his words would have on my father. His words

229

were like lightning. From that point on, my father agreed to almost everything my uncle and his wife wanted in order to be the one who inherited Talavera.

My father could not imagine what had come over his younger brother. But my uncle was already unwell by that time and perhaps even then knew that he had cancer. He was driving such a hard bargain that by the time my father took over ownership of Talavera, our family resources had been so diminished that years of hardship followed as my father and mother doggedly set out to preserve the family place.

My father was the third generation of men named John Van Ness Philip to leave a career in the larger world to return to Talavera. But while Lieutenant John Van Ness had come home to follow the moral agenda of nineteenth-century scientific agriculture, expanding the farm and the estate, a process that fifty years later, my grandfather echoed when he too retired from a rising career to return to Talavera, my father was heading back on different terms. He left New York City and moved his publishing business to Talavera, not to seek his fortune in agriculture but to preserve the farm from disappearing altogether. Yet from that point on, he followed the family tradition of men named John Van Ness by concentrating more and more of his time, effort and energy into restoring the farm.

Soon my family was packing up and moving out of our house on East Eighty-fourth Street in Manhattan. Rugs and furniture, silver and portraits were being carried out of Talavera. Then my uncle died. For my father, it had been loss after loss, and it was not over yet. Soon after my uncle's death, his widow sold their share of the family land to a developer. The bulk of the original Van Ness farm, which my father had tried to preserve twelve years earlier, became Orchard Estates, a 1.5-acre sudivision of prefabricated houses. It felt like the end of the farm, the end of the family.

But the following spring the land woke up as it usually does and sloughed off winter. The apple trees burst into bloom. Another season began. And it wasn't the end of the farm after all. In some ways, for my own family, it was a new beginning. My father replanted the orchards with a hardy semidwarf rootstock to try to make the farm, now half its size, profitable again. The era of Paris fashions and gants de suede was long gone. That summer one of my older brothers woke at 5:00 A.M. to drive the spray rig through the orchards. My sister and I weeded and watered baby trees. We headed off to boarding schools to finish high school and, on vacations home, pruned and pulled brush and helped plant more young orchards. Within the next five years, my brothers, my sister and I were at various stages of entering or finishing college. With my father concentrating so much of his time on the farm, income from his newsletter declined. Even with my mother's job, they didn't have enough money to pay for Princeton, Columbia, Vassar and Smith, the colleges we all attended. We got scholarships, held down jobs and took semesters off to work, then went back to finish. This had become our life now. Good harvests and bad. On my eighteenth birthday, we celebrated in the April wind by planting an orchard of Japanese Mutsu trees, a new variety that my parents thought would sell. When thunderstorms shook the French wallpaper loose in the dining room, my father, getting stiffer now, climbed the rickety wooden ladder and hammered it back on.

231

Talavera was not sold. The apple trees produced, and the farm survived. But there was a price. Like his father before him, my father spent too much time alone at Talavera. My mother was there on weekends, but we needed the income from her job, so she continued her office job in Manhattan, boarding Amtrak for Hudson every Friday. In the evenings, before catching the news, my father liked to sit for a while in the dining room, facing the portrait of General John P. Van Ness. Even when it was cold, he sat there, hunched in his tweed jacket, taking some sort of strange comfort in the portrait before him.

I didn't like his sitting there. I could tell by the way one of his large hands was fumbling with the dog's soft retriever ears, and the other was wrapped around a drink, that he was thinking too much about the past, brooding, sitting alone, as *his* father had done, following that other family tradition, of stiff evening drinks.

It was terrifying to watch the father I loved become someone else when he was drunk. But in some ways it only made me love him more. What I hated was the sadness that, loosened by the alcohol, would slide over him, so that his talk became sentimental and maudlin. "You know, I love you all so much. . . . You do know that, don't you?" All the things he felt and couldn't say rose up to the surface. Just as bad was his guilt the next day, a force that made him leap out of bed in the morning so that long before anyone else in the house, he was already bent over his desk, writing as if he had gone to bed at nine instead of at two.

For years I connected his drinking to the portraits. I didn't know any of Talavera's past then, but I could feel it all around me, and it felt like a prison sentence. I was jealous then of Talavera, which, like some aged and imperious diva, furiously past her prime, demanded so much of my father, so much of us all. Because I had no real knowledge yet of the long past that my father saw himself part of, I didn't understand how so much of that past was a history of military service and land—the sword and the plowshare—and that for a long time, drinking had served to mediate the inevitable conflict between the two. Or, even more confusing, how for my father, the lean, aristocratic face of General John P. Van Ness, like the stern visage of Catherine Douw, could be like the evening light, streaming in through the soft gauze of the long curtains, offering him solace.

Strangely, this direct hot wire that my father had to Talavera and the family's past there seemed to make him modest rather than proud. It was as if like people who work outdoors or who live in direct contact with the wilderness, living with all that history, he was forced to realize his own insignificance on a daily basis. As a teenager I had begun to feel Talavera's influence too, only I fought it. So much history flowed in and out of the house, swirled across the land, that the balance could become swayed, so instead of just keeping you from becoming conceited, it made you feel irrelevant. It took me years to be able to stand between Talavera's columns and not feel that the past was something grander, better, more important than the present. Sometimes I even wondered if sitting there alone, my father wasn't stumped by the past too. But for a while anyway, the face of his greatuncle there on Talavera's wall seemed to offer him moments of peace and resolution.

But unlike a mountain or a river, a house, even one that has lasted so many generations, is a risky place to find solace. Within two years, my uncle's widow, who by then owned the Ammi Phillips portraits of my father's great-grandparents Colonel Henry G. Philip and his wife, Catherine Douw, sued for half ownership of the Gilbert Stuart portrait of General John P. Van Ness. When I asked my mother about the event, for I knew enough never to try to discuss it with my father, she said that they had hardly taken the suit seriously, assuming that they would win. They had a letter written by the heir of the man who had wanted to give the portrait to my father, stating his father's intent, and since the loan had never been repaid after so many years, they had assumed that their family owned the portrait and could give it to whomever they wished.

Even without that letter, my father could not believe that there would be any question that the portrait belonged to him. General John P. Van Ness, his great-uncle, was one of his namesakes. That the portrait was intended for him was as natural as the fact that because his brother's middle name was Worthington, he had been given their grandfather's pocket watch. Initially, my uncle had wanted the portrait to be included in the things they divided, but just before he died, he had written that he had changed his mind and considered the portrait my father's.

My parents did not think to use my uncle's letter of understanding in court. They hired a local lawyer who offered them cheap rates. My father refused to do more than make sure that

233

when the day came, he remembered to show up. This was his mistake. The prosecution came well prepared, arguing on the basis of New York State debtor-pledger laws that the subjective intent of the donor was irrelevant. Rather, they argued, the donor held only possessory interest in the portrait and thus had had no right to give it in the first place. It didn't matter that he had had the portrait for more than fifty years and that the loan had never been repaid. The court now considered the portrait part of my grandfather's unsettled estate.

Friends and relatives urged my father to appeal, but he wouldn't. Going to court over a family matter had been shameful in the first place. He wanted it to end. The portrait was put on the market and bought by a well-known collector who hung it in his Hudson River estate. My father was relieved that General John P. Van Ness would remain in the Hudson Valley, but he never went to see the portrait in its new home.

My mother moved the portrait of lovely Eliza Worthington, my father's grandmother, into the empty space between the windows. She found a decorator who specialized in period restoration and showed her the many layers of hand-blocked French wallpaper in the room. In exchange for copyright use of the original 1812 patterns, the decorator had the pattern reproduced and gave my mother enough wallpaper to redo the dining room and the parlor. My mother had the bright new paper put on the walls. My father went back to sitting in the library.

When I began my search through Talavera for papers and letters that might open up the family's past, my father's wooden army trunk was one of the first things that I found. The day I located it was hot and muggy, and I was ready to quit my prowling through the dust-ridden dark when the green trunk caught my eye. Glimmers of light were streaming over it from the small dovecote holes under the eaves. I could just make out the letters printed neatly on the side:

"J. Van Ness Philip jr. Lt. US Marines." Of course I made my way toward it, pushing through the piles of broken metal garden furniture.

I opened the box slowly, curiously afraid. When I pulled back the dusty layers of newspaper, I saw my father's wool uniform, the manila envelope with his Purple Heart medal and ribbon, then a small brown book in which he had listed the shoe and uniform sizes of all his men, then a pocket-size army primer on conversational Japanese and a folder of discharge papers. As I lifted these things, his dog tags clinked against the bottom of the trunk, and right then I decided to close the trunk. I didn't want to know any more. I was overcome with a desire to repack the trunk, to leave the barn, to let my father's war years lie, to be done with my quest for the past. That was when I heard the second clink. Dog tags. But not my father's. I picked up the silver tags and fingered them, reading the name embossed in the thin steel: Robert Calvin Smith. I could feel my throat go dry. Who was this person? It was as if I had discovered the secret clue, the final piece that pulled the story together, something, but I didn't know what, that explained everything. I was as shocked as if I had just discovered that my father had had a secret lover, this marine, Robert Calvin Smith, whom he had never mentioned, but whose tags he had carefully packed away in his trunk.

When I asked World War II veterans about the mysterious dog tags, ex-marines answered that they were probably the tags of a buddy, the man with whom my father had shared the war until that man had been killed. When they heard that my father had been at Iwo Jima, they speculated that Robert Calvin Smith had been killed there. My father would have been twenty-two, his short hair bristling, sweat pouring down his sides, waiting for the order to leap ashore.

In late August, when my father was hospitalized for the last time, we had a brief, urgent talk about the farm. I arrived at the hospital just in time. My father was storming down the corridor, his IV clanking behind him. He had his boots on and was looking for someone to check him out.

"Where are all the damn nurses," my father exploded when he saw me. "I'm getting out of this hospital, and I mean now."

It took me some time to convince my father to let me page his doctor. We went back to his room and my father agreed to get back in bed and rest for a moment while we waited for his doctor to arrive. I had brought my father a box of sugarless chocolates and I opened it and offered him one. I sat on the edge of his bed, and we ate chocolates and waited. My father was in a single with a large window on one side, but still the bitter smell of hospital disinfectant filled the room. We talked about how the crop was looking, then my father interjected.

"One of you needs to get involved in the farm."

I nodded slowly, stiff with apprehension. My father continued.

"You could make a go of it because you would not assume that you know anything. You'd research it and learn about it just like you were writing an article." My father stopped to take a breath. "Fruit growing is all new ideas now, it's changing fast. You all have to realize that. What we did made sense, but that was then. The farm has to make money, otherwise you might as well forget it."

"Dad, I know, but . . ." I stopped, then took a breath and blurted out a rush of words, "Dad, I'd love to run the farm, you know that, but I want to write. I don't know if I can do both. You of all people know how hard it is."

My father didn't say anything. He nodded.

"Let me think about it, I mean, let me try to learn about it this year. If I could spend a year learning about what is involved, I don't know, maybe I could make it work."

"Okay."

I continued to sit on the edge of the bed, stunned. My father had never spoken so directly to me before. Perhaps he had talked to my brothers and my sister this way, provoking us to decide upon our commitments, but at that moment I didn't think so. What I thought about was all the time I had spent helping my father on the farm as a young girl, as a teenager, as a young woman. I thought about standing in the freezing winter wind, trying to learn how to prune apple trees. I knew then that it had been my first apprenticeship.

I closed the lid on the box of chocolates and looked at my father. He had shut his eyes and was leaning back on the stiff white pillow. His doctor walked in and began to speak. The doctor's words were swift, focused on one point. My father was going to die unless he could get more oxygen into his lungs. They didn't have any other treatments to try at the hospital, so my father could go home if he wanted, but he was going to have to accept almost complete rest. No more driving through the orchards in the pickup. If he would spend one more night so that they could check the oxygen level of his blood in the morning, they would release him.

My father listened quietly and accepted the doctor's terms. When it was time for me to go, he watched me leave in a mood that seemed content.

237
~

I went home and wept. I cried for a long time, for him, for myself. I knew then that my father was going to die. In that stammered response to my father I had uttered something I had always known but never said out loud. I had inherited his dream of holding on to Talavera. Like many people, I realized only with the death of a parent that I had been running from a childhood that I did not understand and had ignored. Instead, I had traveled, farther and farther west, until as Thoreau would say, I had finally arrived back where I started, in the east, my home.

First the study of ceramics, then work had taken me to Japan. But maybe it ran in the family, for like Aunt Bessie, I had loved my expatriate life there, had reveled in the sudden expansion of everything unknown. Also like Aunt Bessie, at every opportunity I had traveled: through Japan and China, Korea, then later south to Thailand and Malaysia, Indonesia, Bali, Singapore. When I looked back, I could see that all over

Asia I was fascinated by the things that reminded me of home. Asia in the twentieth century was synonymous with traditions trying to persevere, to adapt or simply not to be wiped out in the crush of everything new.

In Bali, I had met a prince swatting flies in the swirls of red dust left by a roaring bus. His gaze from his aluminum lawn chair had been regal, even despotic. If he was ashamed that his family's once-resplendent palace, half of it in ruins, was now an overnight stop for tourists, he did not show any signs of this. His dark eyes, the gaze that looked right through and beyond the scraggly tourists who came stumbling off the bus, knew who they were by what his family had been. He was a prince whom, in all his absurdity, I could not mock. He was too familiar.

The summer that my father's lungs gave out, I was working in Japan. In July I had traveled to a mountain in the far north named Osorezan. The Japanese believe that when you die, your spirit travels to this mountain. For forty-nine days your spirit wanders there, or longer if it becomes waylaid because of your misconduct in life. Osorezan is a topography of hells, each one a brightly colored mineral pool bubbling with hot spring water. Only after successfully passing through the mineral blue hell of avarice, the sulfur yellow hell of drinking, the orange hell of adultery and, the biggest hell of all, the blood-red hell of murder does the soul reach the shores of heavenly paradise, a large lake on the far side.

I watched pilgrims wandering through the mist, slowly navigating the paths of black volcanic sand. Contemporary pilgrims picked up maps at the entrance so that they could leave incense, food, liquor, water and sandals at the particular hells where they believed their loved ones might have become waylaid. Kneeling by the bubbling sulfur springs, they placed their offerings on the sand and prayed. Crows circled and cawed, waiting for the pilgrims to leave so that they could dive-bomb and pillage whatever food had been placed there.

I had come to Osorezan to watch the blind shaman

women who were allowed to set up booths outside the walls of the Buddhist temple there for four days each July. As part of their pilgrimages to Osorezan many visitors engaged shamans to contact the dead, tell their fortunes or give them advice about the advisability of various plans. A Japanese anthropologist had come with me to translate the shaman's rough Tohoku dialect into Japanese that I could understand, and I engaged a shaman, asking her if she could tell me something about my future.

The old shaman chanted and shook, then rattled her wooden beads near my face and, in bursts of rough guttural dialect, began to speak. "I hear a voice calling me, it is very faint, but I can hear it calling. It is calling you, it needs you to hear it, it is calling, calling. The voice is telling me, it wants you to go home, to go home. . . ." I didn't think much about what she said. I had listened to shamans doling out what often seemed like canned versions of the same advice to the lines of pilgrims that waited for hours to enter their white tents.

As I rode the train back to Tokyo, the next day, it wasn't the shaman's words that had me thinking. While I watched the landscape flash by, the rice fields glazed with sun, the sea's gray, broken edge, I wondered if the Japanese people, through centuries of superstition mixed with Buddhist and Shinto thought, had shaped Osorezan's fantastic landscape, towering and volcanic until it was in fact a pretty great rendition of hell. Or perhaps things had worked out the other way around, and the mountain itself had been what shaped the Japanese.

It took me all day to travel by train from Osorezan back to Tokyo. By the time I arrived, a fax was waiting for me. My father had had his first mysterious collapse. When I stared at the thin transmission paper, I saw the shaman as she had looked the day before, her thick wooden beads clacking as she rocked back and forth, her unseeing eyes staring straight at me as she told me to go home.

CHAPTER SEVENTEEN

In the Orchard

We are standing in the thick orchard grass, my mother, her dog, Danny, and I. My mother and I are hunting *Psylla pyricola,* the dreaded psylla fly. Danny is hunting mice. Despite the already hot morning sun, we are clothed in long pants and long-sleeved shirts. My mother wears a bent straw hat, and I wear a similar but more ragged version, frayed at the brim where Danny chewed the edge. Entering the orchards in June is to enter an insect kingdom. We need all the protection we can get. Even now the whirring and buzzing, clacking and colliding of wings and mandibles, so many legs and pincers, rises into a sea of sound. I listen for a minute while the insect noises build to a shrill crescendo, then just as suddenly subside. A crow's sharp rasp breaks the droning; a ground dove starts her long, gentle moan. Down by my feet, Danny scratches industriously in a patch of yellow vetch at the base of a tree.

My mother needs to know how many psylla flies are in her pears so that she can determine if and when she needs to apply a spray. Psylla is a predacious insect whose nymphs, encased in beds of sticky insect spit, called honeydew, devour pear trees. They begin by sucking the nutrients out of the leaves but then move onto the fruit. A pear where psyllas have been is not a pretty sight. Blotches of black mottle the surface, and the skin is as rough as sandpaper. Meanwhile, as they feed, the nymphs spread their honeydew, which is toxic to bud formation and thus destroys next year's crop as well. But psylla flies, which overwinter as eggs and hatch out with the first of the blossoms, are hard to kill. Even so, my mother is trying to control them with the mildest of chemical sprays. Four days ago, when she shook a limb and several adults came zooming out, she applied Mitac, a fairly weak insecticide. She hopes that it has done the trick. I have never seen a psylla fly, but my mother knows their wretched habits well. Last year over fifty bushels of pears from this block were so scarred from psylla that they had to be dumped. Nine hundred dollars of income gone.

"See anything?" my mother asks, pushing back her hat.

"Nothing that's moving," I say, and grab another branch.

"Get 'em, Danny boy," my mother says to the dog. Encouraged by her voice, he paws the ground harder. Spatters of dirt flick my calves.

"Check a terminal; they like soft new leaves," my mother says, looking across the tree. She reaches over and pulls down a young branch of sucker growth that is shooting straight up. I take the branch from her and position my magnifying lens over the young leaves at the tip, turning them so that the underside of the leaves comes into view. Two weeks ago this tree was a white froth of blossom. Now the leaves are as long as my thumb, and the blossoms that survived the sudden frost in early May have swollen into perfect doll-size Bosc pears. The leaf in my hand has a reddish tinge, so new that it hasn't produced much green chlorophyll yet, the cells still full of carotene. I stare down into the magnifying lens, and my view constricts to a red-green blur. Then the leaf comes into focus. Unlike the apple leaf whose underside is woolly with fine hairs called trichomes, pear leaves are as shiny and smooth as holly. The serrate leaf that rests in my palm is full grown with intricate yellow veins fanning out in all directions from the midrib. I start in the center of the leaf and move outward, scanning the leaf for insects. A tiny dark spot comes into view, and I move the lens closer. The spot sharpens. I see a black insect with an ugly, blunt head and lacy, transparent wings.

"Got one here, I think."

"They look like tiny cicadas," my mother says, her arm still extended, helping to hold down the branch. When I hear her description, I know that I am staring at a psylla, which, if left unchecked, will produce as many as eight generations in one summer.

"One, two, three, four." I begin counting off the number of flies that I see holding on to the leaf. Then I stop, amazed and horrified. My lens has come across a mass of orange eggs stacked in overlapping piles as if the leaf had grown fish scales. I lose count at fifty. Then I see a fly with what looks like a clear orange substance emerging from the tail. It is long and oval, already twice the size of the huge head: a female laying her enormous brood. Instinctively I shudder.

"What do you see?" my mother asks, moving closer so that she can look over my shoulder.

"I think it's psylla," I answer, not mentioning the egg-laying business, "and eggs."

"Let me take a look."

I hand her the lens and let go of the branch so that she can bring it down closer to her. She stares hard, then stops for a moment to push her straw hat back farther so that more sun falls on the leaf. She studies it again.

"Yes," she says suddenly, "those are psylla all right, and lots of eggs. Dammit, the Mitac didn't work."

"How many eggs did you count?"

"Too many." My mother let the branch snap back, hands the lens to me and starts to walk away from the tree.

She does not need to count the exact number of eggs to learn what she needs to know. The Mitac application did not work, and she now has a well-established infestation with at least two generations present on the leaves. If the problem were something like thrips, my mother could consider importing enough aphids or ladybugs to control them, but psyllas are the sharks of the insect world; no one eats them. My mother can try Mitac again or go for a stronger chemical like Pyromite, which will wipe out her beneficials—the ladybugs and predacious black mites she has been trying to cultivate for the past three years. I watch my mother walk back to the truck, swinging her stiff left knee as she crosses the thick orchard grass.

My mother is eager to get going and complete the scout. She sits in the cab of the truck, one hand on the key in the ignition, waiting for my return.

"Be right there, Mom," I call, and take a last look at the leaf in my hand. The past two weeks of rain finally let up, but since then the temperatures have been in the eighties. Around me the trees seem to heave like sweating horses, their hundreds of leaves pulsing with the force of energy being released.

243

I keep staring at the leaf beneath my lens, trying to visualize what a botanist must see. Deep in the mesophyll layers of the leaf, the football-shaped mitochondria are thrumming with the force of molecules splitting and rearranging. $6H_2O + 6CO_2 = C_6H_{12}O_6 + 6O_2$. Photosynthesis, the mystery upon which all life depends. Here in my hand, light is being converted into chemicals that will rapidly combine to form sugars—plant food. My mind balks. How can this basic fact of life be? A botanist, intimate with the chemical transfer of energy into food, the shattering of molecules and the forming of ions, probably sees this mystery before even the leaf. In the same way a physicist might see molecules racing at two thousand miles an hour where I see a match being struck. What we see depends upon what we know. Here in the orchard what I see is how much there is to learn. Later, tucked into bed with a heavy book on plant physiology across my knees, I will read about the complex chemical reaction called plant respiration, the carbon cycle and the oxygen cycle that makes plants the link between the living and the dead, the organic and the inorganic worlds. If plants stopped breathing, all life on earth would suffocate within a matter of days.

I take another deep breath, one of the sixteen I will take each minute, one of the twenty-three thousand that I require in the course of a day. I let the leaf drop and move my mammal bulk down the row and toward my mother, all fifty trillion cells of me, including the ones that must be expiring in the heat.

"Let's check the young pears," my mother says when I slide into the truck next to her. "The psylla might not have crossed the road yet. I'm not sure where they come from. The hedgerow, I think."

We drive across the road into block nine. This hillside orchard was the first orchard that my father replanted when he and my mother took over full ownership of the farm in 1975. I remember a windy spring day, me standing up to my calves in the newly tilled dark soil, trying to keep a guide string steady while my parents sited the rows. My parents put in mostly apples: Empires and Macoun, Ida Reds, Red Delicious and a scattering of Romes on the top of the ridge. But at the very top and bottom of the orchard, they planted pears—Boscs and Bartletts and Seckels—pulling out the Clapps, which ripened too early to sell to our Pick Your Own crowds. Orchard nine was also where my mother planted trees the first spring that she began managing the farm without my father. Along the top ridge, where some open space remained, she set out two rows of Harrow Sweets and Anjous, new pear varieties that she and my father had talked about planting.

My mother parks at the far end of the young Harrow Sweets. When we shake the terminals, psylla flies tumble out. Through our lenses we find eggs, some already into the nymph stage, the leaves tacky with trails of clear goo. But what bothers me even more than the psylla are the piles of green aphids feeding on the tips of the new growth and the tree's slender leader. On some of the terminals, the tiny leaves are so studded with green bodies that the aphids pile up upon one another like nursing pigs. At fruit-growing school this past February, my mother and I had listened to Cornell pomologists lecture about the importance of a young tree's first three years. Trees were not unlike humans in that the first three years of development were key. Whatever happened during that time would be reflected throughout the tree's entire fruit-bearing life. I can't stand looking at the infant trees so burdened with intruders.

"Mom," I almost shout, "what can we do? I see psylla everywhere, and aphids."

"Nothing," my mother says bluntly. "Wait."

"Wait?"

I am thinking, *How can we wait? The trees are being devoured.* And it is as if my mother can read my thoughts because when she answers this time, her voice sounds irritated. "You can't just kill psylla. It doesn't work that way. I don't know the timing exactly, we'll have to check, but you have to wait until they hatch into nymphs."

"But what about the aphids? Mom, we have to do something."

My mother sighs. "I don't think they're such a problem. There's always somebody ready to eat an aphid. Look, there goes a ladybug now."

I look where my mother points, and indeed, several ladybugs are climbing up the stem of the young pear tree in front of us. But three ladybugs seem no match for the crowds of psylla and aphids cutting into the terminals.

"Look for ants," my mother continues soothingly. "They get the aphids too. Look, there's an ant now. Attaboy!" She points to an ant traveling quickly up the terminal and gives a short chuckle before turning back toward the truck.

I check a few more trees and see many ants and several more ladybugs, but I am still worried about the young trees. As we head down the hill, I ask my mother how she knows when aphids are a problem.

245

"Oh, you can tell. You'll see yellow leaves curling. The tree looks sick."

"I see," I say. But suddenly I am trying to remember the times that I had scouted the orchards with my father. Had we ever seen aphids this numerous? When we did see pests, what sprays had he chosen? All the hours that I spent with my father in the orchards, but I realize suddenly how little I really had learned about fruit growing. My family seemed to have owned the land since forever, but as for actively working on it, that was a new story. We weren't a midwestern farm family. In fact, as far as I could tell, it seemed that my father had been the first generation to make the uneasy transition from gentleman to farmer or at least, the first generation to work the land directly in many generations. Even Lieutenant John Van Ness, who had dedicated himself to running the farm, relied on the yearly income from his inheritance to fund his many farm improvements. Women in the family had always been mistresses of Talavera, keeping kitchen gardens and overseeing the sale of butter and eggs, but my mother was, I believed, the first woman to run the larger farm as well as manage Talavera. Would we learn how to run this farm in time? Even if we could, should we be trying to raise apples on this scale in the Hudson Valley?

Two weeks ago our closest neighbor to the north set out For Sale signs. His orchards were on the market as five- to twenty-five-acre lots. It wasn't just our farm that was struggling. The entire fruit growing industry in the Hudson Valley was in a state of crisis.

My mother and I walk over to look over the Bosc and Anjou whips that my mother planted this past May. Several trees have curling, blackened leaves. My mother fingers them silently, letting the dead leaves crackle between her fingers.

"Fire blight?" I ask my mother, thinking again of fruit school, where a Cornell scientist had lectured extensively on the recent emergence of this disease in the Hudson Valley. Fire blight is a systemic disease that will kill a tree in one season if left untreated. The only cure is to cut off infected areas and bathe the wounds in a copper solution. Infected wood had to be burned immediately or the disease could spread throughout the orchards.

"Could be," my mother answers glumly.

"Mom, do you mind if I call the fruit agent?"

"No. Sure, that's a good idea."

જ્ર

We drive back via the sod, a square of orchard at the top of block thirteen in which we had planted the first Mutsu apple trees one April weekend. According to the family lore, this area just beneath the hedgerow had been cleared by hand by my grandfather, after his first year at Princeton. He had apparently been bullied all year, and he spent the summer bodybuilding to make sure that it not happen again. His self-imposed Jack Armstrong routine was to spend weeks clearing the land of trees and brush. It is almost impossible for me to imagine my grandfather sweating in the hot sun, working off his frustrations by cutting trees and underbrush with ax and saw. But then, despite all that I had learned about what he had done and where he had been, he had remained a mystery.

Back when my grandfather founded the first orchards, the farm produced apples with enticing, old-fashioned names like Opalescent, Baldwin, Wealthy, Spitzenburg, Newtown Pippin, Seek No Further, Northern Spy. They were early apple breeds that had been replaced on our farm in the 1930s by more contemporary stock like McIntosh, Red Delicious and Macoun. The oldest apple tree on the farm was a seventy-year-old McIntosh that my father kept for nostalgic reasons, but also for grafts. These he sent to the nursery, where they were grafted onto vigorous, fast-growing rootstocks for re-planting as semidwarf trees. We called the old tree the Captain Mac and kept it alive, although these days it is a gnarled and bent affair.

You never knew with apples what would become fashionable again. In the late eighties my parents had begun to plant small plots of "old-fashioned" apples for fun. Customers enjoyed rediscovering sentimental favorites like Greening and Northern Spy. These days you could special order gift boxes of these antique apples from catalogs like Williams-Sonoma that marketed country nostalgia. Balducci's in the Village carried "heritage" brands for twice the price of regular apples. But my mother was skeptical of increasing her antique orchards too rapidly. There were reasons why the older breeds had been replaced. Northern Spies, for example, had a tendency to bear biannually. Once the trees got into this habit, you had to put up with it, which meant a crop every other year, instead of fruit each fall. Also, trees take at least five years to mature and begin serious bearing. The enthusiasm for antique fruit could end as quickly as it had begun, leaving my mother with bushels of eccentric fruit to try to sell.

As we head down along the meadow, we pass block ten, a small grouping of Northern Spy and Greening at the edge of the meadow, one of our youngest "old-fashioned" blocks.

"Look at those trees. Dammit, something is wrong," my mother says suddenly, slowing the truck as we pass by. "Mites are in there, I just know it."

"How can you tell?" I ask, surprised by my mother's vehemence.

"Look at them. Those trees are just plain sick. They haven't been looking right, and I don't know why, I just don't know. It's not too wet there. They just never have been right. No, I'm afraid they were just too damaged by the time they arrived."

The spring that the trees arrived, a UPS strike virtually stopped deliveries for weeks. My mother's trees, boxed and ready to go from the nursery, had been stuck in transit so long that by the time she opened the boxes, new roots had sprouted from the trunk.

"Oh," I say. I had not noticed before that the trees were sick. As I drove by, they had seemed fine. One or two were crooked, but that wasn't unusual for a dwarf rootstock. Each limb was spread with new growth and a fine covering of leaves. But when I look closely, I see that none of them have much fruit growing on the limbs.

"Spies can't take much," my mother adds. "That's part of why everyone stopped growing them. And mites are bullies. They go for sick trees that can't defend themselves. That's just what bullies do."

We drive in silence around the bend and up toward the main pond. I am absorbing this new information when my mother stops the truck again, this time to peer into the woods that line the road on my side. Earlier in the spring this spot under the trees had been spotted with yellow turk's heads and the ivory tufts of wood anemones. It is also one of my mother's favorite spots for cutting the early pussy willows. When I ask what she is looking for, she answers, "My new cash crop. Ramps."

"Ramps," I say, amused. "Isn't that some kind of hillbilly food?"

"Was," answers my mother. "Now brings twenty dollars a pound, and I have lots of it."

Earlier that spring my mother had sent three hundred dollars' worth of lilacs down to New York City with a local berry grower who was making trips to the Union Square farmers' market. He had wanted more, but my mother didn't want to harvest any more blooms from the lilac walks that lined the west edge of the garden. Planted in 1857, when Lieutenant John Van Ness, inspired by Andrew Jackson Downing, had reshaped the gardens at Talavera along visions of the picturesque, the lilacs were now a cash crop. Instinctively, my mother was returning the farm to an older pattern of diversification. *Alternative agriculture, ethnic markets, direct marketing* were the new buzzwords at the yearly meetings of the Columbia County Fruitgrower's Association. That, and the one billion apples now entering the global market from China each year. The Asian markets had gone with these cheaper Chinese apples, and there were reports that Chinese Fujis were beginning to appear in London as well.

New York State had traditionally competed with Washington State for shelf space in East and West Coast supermarkets. But now the competition was global. Even with the cost of shipping fruit grown seven thousand miles away, large chain stores believed they could get a better deal with apples from China and New Zealand. Already most of the nation was drinking apple juice made from Chinese apple concentrate sold on the world market.

Our customers would be those who could afford the higher price of food grown locally with a minimal use of pesticides. My father had predicted that the New York State apple industry would lose its markets unless it radically reorganized. Only gradually were growers realizing that if they were going to survive, they were going to have to work together and develop a plan for regional marketing. Meanwhile, my mother had plans to supplement apple sales by planting raspberries and gooseberries, maybe late-blooming strawberries as well. Now lilacs and ramps. No significant income, but it all helped pay the bills.

"Look!" exclaims my mother suddenly, and reaches over to point toward the woods. A large dark bird walks out of the underbrush, its huge dinosaur feet jerking up and down in exaggerated, cartoonlike motions as it begins to cross the road: a wild turkey. Behind her ran six half-grown chicks.

"How grand!" my mother exclaims, and for the first time since we have been in the orchards, her face beams.

Unlike most farmers, my mother delights in the presence of the wild on the land she farms. For her, the orchards are a meeting ground of things she should not control and things she believes she must.

Western civilization has romanticized the beauty of agrarian life since the time of Virgil, but all fruit growers know that during the early summer months what they are engaged in is war. A Darwinian struggle, if you will, but one that nonetheless relies on brutal tactics, even softened by strategies like IPM. The very chemicals and fertilizers that we were using had been developed from domestic applications of military technology, spin-offs from major world wars. Parathion, used as a cover spray for many insects during the sixties, had been derived from nerve gas. The nitrogen fertilizer that we needed to increase fruit production could be traced back to a World War II process for making explosives.

But even in this state of "war" with insects and disease, every time I drove over to scout the orchards with my mother, I found myself falling back in love with the land. It was not hard to do. Apple and pear orchards in April, May, June are a sanctuary of sun and green. No wonder the Roman poets eulogized the orchard as prototype of that first garden, a counterpart to urban confusion, the great human mess. But the fact remained that much of our work as fruit growers was hardly lyrical. Unlike the Roman hero Cincinnatus, whose world was neatly divided into the roles of warrior and farmer, establishing that division for Western literature, my mother's life on our farm was a constant war. She couldn't trade her sword for a plowshare because her battles happened on the land. They had to do with figuring out how to make broken-down machinery keep running, how to kill off waves of insects and disease, how to anticipate changing weather, fickle markets, and her worst enemy of all, the bottomed-out price of apples and pears.

I loved scouting the orchards with my mother, getting to know the trees in that way, but I was suspicious of our cultural romance with the family farm. If we assume that agriculture is an inherently good practice and way of being on the land that is noble, then we have to ask an uncomfortable question. Just where does this romantic idea come from? For that matter, who gets to have this kind of relationship with the land in the first place? Thomas Jefferson's vision of the new Republic was as a democracy of independent yeoman farmers, but that history of landownership would not include women for a long time.

In Columbia County, farming is still a man's world. When my mother and I take our seats at fruit-growing association meetings, a sea of worn visors turns to stare at our white stick-on labels that read "Philip Orchards." She is the only woman fruit grower in the county, and although several of the growers are accompanied by sons, we are the only mother-daughter team. We are not unwelcome exactly, just not what anyone expects to see.

ఴ

Two days after our scout, the county fruit agent arrives and diagnoses possible fire blight in the young pears. He takes several leaves to send to the experimental station for testing. He recommends that we spray the psylla as soon as possible with Pyromite, a much stronger chemical than Mi-tac. Reports are coming in that Mitac hasn't been working this season; possibly the psylla have become resistant. He suggests we try using Agri-Mek next season when we put on the oil spray to coat and suffocate overwintered mite and psylla eggs. Agri-Mek not only is a contact killer but has a kickback as well, meaning that it is absorbed by the vascular tissue of the tree and will be there waiting to poison any new insects that begin to feed. The only problem is the cost.

Agri-Mek sounds like the answer to all our problems. As I watch my mother listen to his recommendations but say little, I am overcome with a sinking feeling. I knew why my mother hadn't gone with Agri-Mek: It was too expensive, and she had not wanted to spend the extra $1,000. She was trying to make do on an undercapitalized farm that couldn't pay all its bills. Only the week before, we had confronted another tractor breakdown. The John Deere needed an engine overhaul that was going to cost $500. Meanwhile, we would have to rent a tractor at $250 a day. My mother had hoped to get by this year without borrowing against the harvest, but the John Deere's collapse erased that hope. Last week she went over her outstanding bills to calculate her debt load and then called Production Credit to get the necessary paperwork moving for a $10,000 loan.

Tractor disasters were a familiar story at Talavera. There

had been three tractors on the farm when I was growing up, a powerful red 2010 that pulled the spray rig and pushed brush, a green John Deere with cheerful yellow trim that my father hitched up to the cutter bar for mowing and a rusty old red Case that was used for odd jobs. What I remember most about them was that they were always breaking down. To me, tractor disasters were a fact of life on a farm. So was being late for wherever we were going if the weather was good and my father could get in a few more hours in the orchards. We would be all dressed up and waiting on the porch, ready to head out for a family outing, when someone would realize that my father had not been getting ready all that time but was still down at the barn . . . working on a tractor.

My favorite had been the Case with its long old-fashioned nose. It looked as if it belonged in a junkyard, but I liked the way the tin can tilted to one side over the exhaust pipe, keeping the rain out, the way the grid of tree wire that covered the radiator had rumpled into an abstract pattern. I could still see over the hood when I slipped down a little to get my foot all the way down over the clutch. Most of all, it didn't bolt away from you like the fast 2010.

When I was fourteen, my father decided that I should learn to mow. That my brothers and sister and I work on the farm was part of his vision of running Talavera as a family business and part of his training for me as well. It occurred to me now that part of my ostensible rebellion against girl-hood—my obstinate tomboyishness that went on and on—had another dimension. From the time I had been little, my father had been giving me lessons in competence and self-competition usually reserved for boys.

At first I was thrilled to handle so much raw power. The John Deere moved with a smooth, coiled energy even in first gear. When I engaged the mower gear, the blades whirred menacingly and ripped cleanly through the stiff orchard grass. Along the bar twenty serrated triangular knives were flicking back and forth with enough speed to cut even small bushes and scrub. I nosed the tractor into the waist-high grass and watched it fall. We nosed into a yellow chaos of drying grass and weed and left behind a rich green carpet.

But the whole time that I was mowing, I was worried that I would encounter a hidden stump or steer incorrectly into a small tree and get the mower stuck. Not long before, I had almost jackknifed the Case while coming up a steep hill with a load. The tractor had begun to slip on the incline, sliding back into the trailer, which immediately began to twist. Miraculously, I had managed to jam it into a lower gear just in time. But my near accident had given me a case of the willies that stuck. By the end of a mowing session I would slump off the tractor, too exhausted to speak. The meadow looked wonderful, a parkland of mowed grass, but I didn't feel the rush of satisfaction that I had figured I would. I had been terrified but was too proud to admit it, and I didn't want to risk letting my father down.

254

જીજ

By the time she calls me five days later, my mother has solved her tractor problem. She and Willi found a second-hand Ford that the dealership was willing to let her take on credit until the production loan came through. That morning she had sprayed for psylla, another round of Mitac. She hadn't wanted to use Pyromite because she thought it too rough on her aphids and ladybugs. To be safe from chemical poisoning, I will have to wait ninety-six hours until I can reenter the orchard, but then my mother would like me to do a scout. The timing of a psylla spray is key. Nymphs could be killed only when they entered their last instar and were in the hard-shell stage. But if you waited too long, they would hatch out, another generation ready to lay thousands more eggs within three days. The heat that week had risen to record highs, and it was still hot at five when I set out to walk through the pears. Every leaf tells me the same story: a carnage of withered black psylla bodies. Scattered eggs remain, but most of them seemed to have hatched out.

I walk on to inspect the young pears across the road. They had tested clean for fire blight. My mother now thought the damage had been caused by splatters of weed killer that Willi had applied to the bases of the young trees as mouse control earlier in the week. I turn over the young leaves and examine terminal ends. What I see surprises me. The aphid population is about half what it had been. But it is the apple trees in block nine that I find the most mysterious: no red mites, even in the Red Delicious.

Back at the house, as I sip iced tea and recount my observations to my mother, she grins when I mention the mites. "See what the beneficials can do!" she exclaims. "You have to give them time."

"I can't believe that they could have eaten so many mites. It's tremendous," I say.

"Yes, well, that's why I don't use Agri–Mek. You use that in the beginning of the season, and it kills everybody. Then you are just stuck with spraying away. I want the beneficials to do the job."

"Why did you wait so long with the Mitac?"

"I can use it only twice a season, so I wanted to wait until the population of psylla was the highest." My mother looks at me and smiles, "You don't go in to get the enemy until you see the whites of their eyes."

I say nothing but tell myself to remember this moment. My mother had been raised in an era when direct competition with men was not tolerated. She masked her competence, but when she set her mind to it, insects that invaded our trees didn't have a chance.

Still, running an orchard with an integrated pest management approach could end in disaster. Unchecked psylla could not only ruin a pear crop but hamper a tree's productivity in the coming year. Left to propagate, the shy and highly camouflaged oblique banded roller cuts a young tree's growth in half. No one wants to eat an apple after a snout-nosed plum curculio larva has hatched out, leaving a wide brown scar where it has bored its way out from the core. When the most serious and common pest, European red mites, get out of control, they prey on trees so rapaciously that it is not long before the leaves are completely sucked dry of nutrients and begin to yellow, a condition called bronzing. Severely bronzed trees lose their leaves and cannot store up enough carbohydrates for the winter. Come spring, the chemical reactions that triggered up through the xylem, telling the cells to initiate fruit, will not occur. Instead the cells inside fruit buds will vegetate in an attempt to replace the lost leaves and keep the tree alive.

By using IPM, my mother saved significantly on her spray bill. She also protected the environment from pounds of unnecessary toxins. The underlying philosophy was appealing. IPM was an insect version of *High Noon*. A farmer tried to pit the good guys against the bad guys and trusted that the good guys could win. There was truth to this. By our not spraying a continual regimen of toxic chemicals, beneficial insects flourished. These "beneficials" could have huge appetites for such pests as aphids, thrips, leafhoppers and, the bane of all apple growers, European red mites. The innocent ladybird beetle, *Stethorus punctum,* dines on mites three and four times a day then snacks on mite larvae. Her own alligator-shaped brood could eat even more. No one knew how many aphids the orange syrphid fly larvae ate in a day because no one had been able to keep count.

Only when my mother identified harmful numbers of insects like European red mites, rosy apple aphids, green aphids, leafhoppers, apple maggots, leaf miners, plum curculios, scales, coddling moths, oblique banded leaf rollers or psyllas on her pears would she spray. Monitoring the orchards in this way took time. Since mid-May my mother and I have spent hours each week tramping under the hot sun to study leaves for insects and disease. Each month brought a different insect plague and a different fungus or disease. Scab ascospores, which overwintered in the fallen leaves, were mature and ready to fly by the end of March. Right on the heels of the prime scab infection period came danger zones for powdery mildew and black rot. May is when the first generation of the insects begins to hatch out as well, the overwintered eggs of "rosies," or apple aphids, and mites and psylla.

My mother was willing to risk pest damage because she figured that what she lost in damaged fruit, she saved on her spray bill. Our orchard required six to ten tanks to cover completely, and one tank of spray cost up to two hundred dollars. But her decision to manage the orchards this way had as much to do with her attitude toward farming as it did with her desire to save money. One August day, when the spray representative advised her to go after her leafhoppers, warning her that they would fly out and bother her Pick Your Own customers at harvesttime, she answered promptly, "No, thanks, my customers like it wild."

ঞ্চ

Three weeks later at four o'clock in the afternoon I pull into the driveway right on time for the first of the July mite counts with my mother. Last week European red mites had flared in the two back orchards, especially in the Red Delicious, and my mother applied Kelthane, a fairly weak miticide that tended not to harm the beneficial mites like *Amblysieus fullacis* and *Ti pyri* that feed on the damaging ones. Today I have brought my fifteen-month-old son, Rhys, with me. When I stop the car, he throws down his bottle and shouts, "Oooh, oooh, oooh." Danny leaps up and down at the car, his long ears flying like sails.

We begin in the new land, a corner block of Jonagold, Mutsu and Marshall McIntosh trees. Most growers are scornful of Kelthane, thinking it not powerful enough, but even when fighting a July flare of mites, my mother wants to give her beneficials a chance.

My mother parks in the shade of a large pine tree. It takes me a minute to pull Rhys out, slap Skin-So-Soft on his arms, pull a hat down on his head firmly enough so that he can't pull it off and set his favorite toy, a yellow bulldozer, down on a shady patch of orchard grass. "Uh, oh," he says when I

257

put him down, and immediately he starts out, walking un-steadily toward the young trees where my mother is already standing, peering at a leaf. The grass comes up to his waist, so walking is hard, but he makes it to the young tree just as I do, then belly flops down into a tuft of grass and laughs.

"See anything?" I ask my mother.

She shakes her head. "You look."

I take the magnifying glass and pull a leaf out from a fruit cluster. The woolly underside feels like velvet in my hands. I peer down at the top surface first, beginning at the midrib and moving the lens carefully out over the leaf blade. The warm leaf is midsize, fully veined and clear of blemishes like apple rust and scab. My mother must have gotten the timing of the fungicide sprays perfect because this is a bad year for scab in the valley. No mites on the smooth leaf top. I turn it over and study the underside, where a dozen crumpled black mite bodies are stuck to the fine hairs. Near them is a sprin-kling of orange dots, at least twenty mite eggs.

"Kelthane worked," I say, "lots of dead ones, but I see a lot of eggs too. How long does it take for the eggs to hatch?"

"I'm not sure," my mother answers. "We can look it up back at the house. Did you see any predators? There's one that looks like a shiny black dot. Look for those."

"I'll look some more," I say, "I want to check some trees down the row."

My mother stays behind to keep an eye on Rhys, who has begun poking the dirt under the tree with a small stick. A brown ring surrounds the base of the tree where weed killer was applied earlier in the spring. All commercial weed killers are derived from chemical weapons, such as Paraquat, which defoliated much of Vietnam, and I wonder if I really should let a baby play in chemically burned grass but decide to let him be. Down the row, I check leaves on the four quadrants of four trees. Each leaf tells the same story: a high concen-tration of dead mites but also a new generation of eggs that will hatch out, meaning another mite spray will be needed when they hatch. Mites are like psylla in that the eggs cannot be killed. I haven't seen any black dots or the delicate lacewings or grublike syrphid larvae, which also feed on mites. No ladybird beetles. I walk back and give my results to my mother. When he sees me, Rhys looks up at me excitedly, then turns his head back down to where he had been looking in the grass and shouts, "Buh, buh, buggh."

"What you got, baby?" I say, and bend down to look where he is looking. On a blade of grass near his foot, a large *Stethorus punctum* is crawling up the stem.

"Rhys found a predator," I say and point to the large ladybug that Rhys is now reaching out to try to grab with his small hand. My mother and I both laugh.

In the next block, the far end of number thirteen by the pond, we stop to check the Spartan trees. A cross between McIntosh and Newtown Pippin, the Spartan has never really caught on with Pick Your Own customers. This year we have a fair-size crop, but the set was so heavy that the size is small. We had thinned them with acid after petal fall, choosing a warm day. But there had been days of rain the week before, and the apples, still thimble-size, must have carbo-loaded in the cool nights before we applied the thinner. They held on despite the thinning acid, which usually makes the surface cells on the epidermis of the fruit stem constrict, causing the stems to fall off the branch.

"Dead ones?" asks my mother hopefully, as I leave the tree to walk back toward her.

"Live ones too, I'm afraid," I answer. "Twenty dead, but about five live on each leaf that I checked."

"The new generation must have hatched out." My mother sighs. She is losing her war with the mites. "We need another spray. Let's check the Ida Reds and Goldens on the other side."

I take Rhys onto my lap, and we bounce across the grass to the other side of the orchard, where a young orchard of Golden Delicious lines up in beautiful, even rows. Five years old, this block of semidwarfs produced a beautiful crop last season, and the fruit set was again good this spring. Unlike in the Spartans, here in the Goldens, the thinning took, so the fruit is evenly spaced, already the size of tennis balls.

This time my mother wants to get out of the truck and scout, so I try putting Rhys on the grass by my feet while I begin studying the leaves on a nearby tree. Each leaf has a scattering of dead mites and lots of eggs but no live adults. Then I begin to see the baby mites, tiny crablike specks, their four legs already poking out of their rosy bodies. More and more of them. I had read that left unchecked, two mites become thirteen million in six generations alone. No surprise that mites are the most numerous animals on the earth. More serious for fruit growers is the emerging fact that they are becoming resistant to the only five pesticides approved for use to kill them: Kelthane, Apollo, Savey, Pyromite Vendex and Carzol. Of these, Carzol and Pyromite are rescue sprays, meaning that they are so powerful they can be used only twice during a growing season. If they are used more often than that, the mites could easily become resistant to the pesticide, leaving growers with no means of control. There were some new chemicals on the market, like Agri-Mek, but the best hope for fruit growers and the environment alike was for the valley to achieve biological control through the cultivation of mite predators.

"Babies," I say when my mother returns. She bends down to sniff the piece of clover that Rhys is holding up for her to smell.

"Lots?" she asks.

"Baby mites galore," I answer.

"Baybee," Rhys suddenly says emphatically, as if to join the conversation. He holds up his arms and chants, "Baybee, up, up." I ignore him and try to finish examining the leaf in my hand. His small fists begin to pound my calves. Then he stops. "Baybee?" he asks inquisitively. When I look down, he gives an enormous chipmunk grin.

"Okay," I say, "you win." I scoop him up and balance him on my raised knee while I do my best to keep studying the leaf by placing it on a bare spot on a nearby limb. Rhys screeches with delight and pulls a fistful of my hair.

"Fruit set looks good, Mom," I say, letting the leaf drop and turning to my mother.

"Yes," she says. "But I don't know whether to blame the spray rig, which hasn't been working properly, or Willi, or myself. This mite situation is bad. Bronzed trees . . . it's shameful."

"You'll get them this time. I'm sure you will," I say, and although the sight of the trees with yellowing leaves had startled me too, I believe that she will. We pile into the truck just as a familiar rumble sounds along the road. As soon as he hears the noise, Rhys scrambles up until he stands his full height against the truck door to get a better view.

"Traktah, traktah," he shouts excitedly. Soon we see Willi on the new blue tractor driving by. Now that the terminal buds have set, he can begin the summer pruning. My mother turns the key in the ignition, and the truck roars to life, then heads forward with a jerk. We are soon racing along the orchard rows. It occurs to me that these trees, which, through their mysterious ability to photosynthesize light into food, link the organic and the inorganic worlds, have also forged another kind of link, a new way for me to be with my mother. Not inside the house making beds or preparing one of the many meals that seemed to keep us perpetually busy there, but here, bouncing along in a silver truck, outside, in the orchards.

"Look at that size," I say, pointing to a large Ida Red as we pass it by.

"That one's headed for the fair," my mother says decisively. She strains to see over the top of the steering wheel as the silver truck bounces along, her straw hat tilting like a windmill.

261

〜

We had won. When my mother and I walked into the apple booth at the county fair that fall, we saw a huge purple ribbon clipped to the sign for our farm. We could hardly believe our eyes. Philip Orchards had been designated the grand champion fruit grower for Columbia County. We had received blue ribbons for individual fruit categories before, but never had we won so many blues that we came in first over all. My mother was typically wary of accepting praise, but she couldn't hide her delight either.

"We just took the prize because so many farms got knocked out with hail," she said when we went to look over our displays of apples and pears lined up on the shelves around the room. "But those Ida Reds, I just knew they would win."

It was true that my mother had been lucky with the weather. Only a month earlier the *New York Times* had reported that the July drought, then scourings of summer hail had destroyed the Hudson Valley fruit crop. Fruit growers were applying for federal disaster relief. My mother's was one of the few orchards in the county whose pears had not been completely shredded by the bean-size hail. Some of our fruit had been scarred, but overall we had a gorgeous crop. In fact, it looked as though we just might have a record harvest.

When I had driven through the orchards to do the fall check with our spray representative, Gil Lasher, even he had clucked over my mother's success. "She just got the timing right on everything," he said, giving one of his big belly laughs. "These orchards are clean, cleaner than I've ever seen them. Your mother got lucky with the weather with those psylla. The heat breaks 'em. They just can't take it. But she knew to figure that, and then she just got the timing on everything else just pretty damn perfect."

Gil advised us on what pesticide to use and as a service routinely scouted our orchards. A large, quiet man, he rarely paid this kind of compliment, especially because he was lukewarm about the pest management strategies that my mother was using. Once during the scout, I'd brought along a new IPM publication from Cornell, and he'd snorted. "I don't use IPM guidelines. I use my onboard computer," he had said, tapping his head to emphasize his point. "I look until I think I know what's there. Then I stop. Even when it looks like I'm not looking, I am. You've got to see the whole picture; then you can step back and look for specific problems."

Gil had been scouting orchards for thirty years, and he was good at it. I had watched him glance at a block of our trees from a distance and, just by the particular hue of green in the leaf canopy, predict with accuracy how many leaf rollers were there. As he would say, "By July I know what's out there. From that point on, it's all inventory." Although my mother didn't always follow Gil's suggestions, she knew she could trust him. Gil was too smart and too ethical to recommend unnecessary sprays to boost sales for his company. And he knew only too well how quickly growers were going out of business.

"Once I'm on the property, I'm working for the grower. The last thing in the world I think of is that I'm a salesman. The most important thing you can do for a fruit grower these days is make sure he survives. Then you have a customer next year."

On the way back from our late fall scout after the fair, we had stopped to look at a set of trees by the garden where I had released a colony of voracious beneficial mites called *T. pyri*. At the February fruit school, I had heard about an experiment that some scientists at Cornell were running to try to combat red spider mites with predators. Everyone knew that it was just a matter of years before the current population of red spider mites became resistant to the current sprays. Chemical companies were working furiously to develop new chemical weapons. Meanwhile researchers at Cornell were trying to reintroduce natural red mite predators to the valley to achieve biological control. You could receive as many as six hundred female mites for release if you wanted to become part of the experiment.

When the Styrofoam box marked "Living Organisms, Refrigerate Immediately" arrived, I set to work as soon as I could. The three hundred leaves with *T. pyri* on them had to be stapled to the shady undergrowth of apple trees that would become the mites' new home. My mother and I chose six Lady Apple trees by the garden because they tended to be hardy against red spider mites and were slightly isolated from other trees. The *T. pyri* could eat mold until they were strong enough to begin moving to other trees, where they would find plenty of red spider mites to eat. Meanwhile, the incubation trees would protect them, for the sprays that killed red mites would also kill the *T. pyri*. We would have to hold off on spraying those trees for the rest of the season.

I eagerly crunched numbers. Adult mites lived for twenty days, and the females laid one egg a day. Those eggs took one to three days to hatch out and matured in about thirty days. Then the process began again. You could count on at least three to four generations of mites in one season, and in some years, as many as nine. That was why they could become such an epidemic so fast. In two generations, my 600 mites would become 120,000, but by generation four, they'd be up to 48 million. I had a vision of my *T. pyri* spreading out over our orchards, feasting on the dangerous red mites for breakfast, lunch and dinner—saving us.

Gil wasn't so optimistic. Lab trials were one thing, but the field was another. He had looked at the trees and nodded, but then added, "I don't know about these *T. pyri* fellas, maybe they'll take off in the valley, but I can tell you, right now, the only predator I have any respect for is *Stethorus punctum*. Like this one right here." He had laughed, then pointed to the ladybird beetle crawling up his hand.

❧

After the fair the harvest began in earnest. Even the weather cooperated so that the first weeks in September were sunny and bright, perfect for apple picking. Except that pickers were not arriving. Every Saturday my mother looked at the thin trickle of cars pulling into the barnyard and frowned, remembering the days when so many customers came at once that the line of cars had reached almost out to the main road. The customers who did arrive couldn't believe the fruit. "It's like a candy store in there," one man said, loading bags of enormous Golden Delicious into his trunk. He still picked for his extended family, and his wife still baked pies.

The apples began to drop. My mother sprayed the Macs with Naphthaleneaccctic acid (NAA) in an attempt to hold them on the trees. NAA was an acid that kept the fruit from releasing hormones that caused the cells in the stem to constrict. When those stem cells constricted, the apple fell from the tree. But ten days later the sprayed apples also began to fall. Usually, Willi trucked bins of fallen Macs to a local cider operation and sold them as cider fruit. But the mill had closed after a recent E. coli scare. New pasteurizing regulations meant expensive new equipment that the mill couldn't yet afford.

By the time the first frost hit, my mother had calculated that only 60 percent of our fruit had sold. The ground under the trees was red with rotting fruit, our farm was ten thousand dollars short of paying its current bills and the barn shop needed a new roof.

That November, at our yearly postharvest meeting, when my brothers, my sister and I sat down to review the harvest and affairs at Talavera, tempers flared. No one wanted to admit it, but the Pick Your Own business was over as a means to market all of our fruit. Pick Your Own had worked during the seventies and eighties, but families no longer had the time to pick and store fruit. We had a loyal core of customers, many of whom had come to pick apples at the farm for two generations, but they came more as a form of recreation than as serious pickers. They picked a half bushel of fruit where their parents would have bought four or five. Some farms had adapted by developing what was called agritourism, offering hay rides and petting zoos and special programs to attract weekend customers. Other farms closer to the city had adopted a park mentality. You paid an admission fee to enter the orchards in addition to the price of the fruit.

Agritourism brought snorts of derision from my mother,

and I could see her point. When you worked hard all year to raise the best fruit you could, it seemed nothing less than demeaning to have to entertain your customers too. What was the line between agritourism and running a farm museum, a kind of Sturbridge Village of farm life? We wanted to sell fruit, not market ourselves. But the fact was, Pick Your Own was no longer profitable. Packing out fruit for stores was even more dim. Our closest neighbor had put his orchards up for sale, or rather the bank had. Three other farms had likewise folded. Down the road at the old Estok farm, Paul Estok carried a piece of paper in his back pocket with the previous year's apple tally. Ask him how business was doing, and he'd give you a lopsided grin, then pull out the paper, which showed that his entire crop, planted to help diversify his dairy—fourteen thousand dollars' worth of apples—had netted exactly two thousand dollars once the cost of picking, packing, storage and shipping had been factored in. His father had bought their-two-hundred-acre farm with four hundred dollars in the 1920s. The orchards, just south and west of ours, had gorgeous views of the Catskills, and it seemed as if a crop of houses would be going up there soon. Commercial fruit growing in the Hudson Valley was becoming a thing of the past. We were not the only farm whose books were coming up red. Most farms were being subsidized in one way or another: The wife of the farmer took a job, or the fruit grower did, or the land was bought by someone who made money in the city and enjoyed the farm on weekends.

Our farm was being subsidized by my mother's free labor and her inputs of cash, and it couldn't go on. More troubling, we didn't have a clear idea of how we would take the farm over when my mother no longer felt she was able to run it.

ꙮ

We spent a restless, anxiety-ridden winter. Only my mother, busy with the present tense reality of life on a small farm in an enormous house, seemed characteristically nonplussed.

She had kept the farm going for more than five years, and she was not ready to give up on it yet. Meanwhile, out in the orchards, the trees, irreverent to history, were already gearing up to produce next year's seeds, which would be genetically distinct, a completely new generation. While in winter sleep, they had chosen which cells would turn to flowers, which to wood so that when spring began, they were ready for those chemical changes that deep in the vascular tissue signaled the fruit buds to grow.

Before we knew it, the trees were in green tip, silver tip, tight cluster, bloom. As usual, those of us who could gathered to help my mother put on her yearly apple blossom picnic. This year something wonderful happens. A sudden heat wave has made the orchards too hot for the picnic, so we have gathered in the garden, backing the wooden trailer up to the cedar walk.

A few years earlier my eldest brother and my mother had widened the cedar walk and cut an opening in the eastern side so that right in the middle was a shaded area that looked out over the meadow, the pond and the upward swell of hills on the opposite side, a hillside now frothed with white pear blossoms and pink apple blooms. Because the spot afforded one of the best views of the farm, the family's dogs and horses had been buried there for some time. My father's childhood horse, Little Dan, had been buried there, as had his father's horse, Big Dan, and my horse, Peter, although luckily, I had not been there to watch the backhoe dig Peter's deep grave.

Lieutenant John Van Ness's formal gardens were smaller than they had once been. Instead of six garden beds of flowering plants and roses, my mother and eldest brother maintained only the long main bed and one other. Similarly, the terraced vegetable plots that had been there when I was a child had been mostly seeded over as lawn. We had a few raspberries growing at the bottom of the garden along with peach, cherry and plum trees, but the lines of grapes and berries had been discontinued. Still, one could see the outlines of the old plan. The long lilac walk, the cedar walk, the hawthorn hedges with their shiny thorns still outlined the whole, while the bottom of the garden area was now outlined with a bushy hedge of bridal veil. Here and there a carefully placed hemlock or spruce or white pine, now grown into a towering tree, broke up the symmetry of walkway and lawn. But still, walking south from the house you felt as if you were entering and leaving a series of green rooms.

As the picnic started, guests wandered across the lawns, enjoying the masses of purple lilacs, then slumped down in lawn chairs to escape the heat. We brought bowls and platters and baskets of food out and arranged a picnic on the trailer. It was while people were still gathered around it, helping themselves to the piles of food and glasses of lemonade from the silver punch bowl that Hari Kari had won, that a family friend walked to the edge of the garden and waited there. Beside him was an object draped in my grandmother's wool throw. Behind him the meadow dipped down and the orchards began, a haze of pink and white bloom.

He stood for a while until people noticed him and began to quiet down so that they could hear what he had to say. He had a gift that he wanted to give to Talavera in memory of my father. Ever since he had heard of how a piece of Talavera was missing, he explained, he had wanted to do something to try to bring it back. While we watched, he removed the blanket from a large, beautifully framed portrait of General John P. Van Ness. Everyone stared in amazement. There stood such a stunning rendition of the original Gilbert Stuart that had hung in the dining room it hardly seemed a copy. Someone shouted, "He's back. The general's back," and then everyone was clapping. I was astounded that someone else had understood how my father had been wounded by the portrait's loss and even more amazed that he had wanted to try to address that hurt. My eldest brother hung the portrait in the dining room between the two windows where the original had been. Immediately the room seemed to glow.

After all the guests had gone home, I walked through the dining room. Evening light was falling, and through the windows I could still see the pink haze of orchards. When I looked at the portrait, itself a work of art that had taken almost two years to complete, I thought about how in some ways the copy was even better than the original. A new story had become woven into that of Talavera, that of the portrait's return. All the stories that I had worked so hard to collect—Lieutenant John Van Ness, Tom, Catherine Douw, Eliza Worthington, my grandfather, my great-aunt Lee, my lost aunt and Aunt Bessie, Uncle Gaston, my father—seemed to reach out and hold me. I had begun my search for the truth about the past convinced that unless I did something, I would lose Talavera, lose my home. But the portrait's return crystallized for me the realization that what was here was more durable than I had thought. And it wasn't all up to me.

I had traveled a long journey to root out Talavera's past, to turn that past over, trying to make sense of previous lives, to weave those stories into narrative, giving them shape. Like any journey, the traveling out had been accompanied by a parallel journey in. I understood better now who I was and what that meant. I was not a fallen version of some previous generation because the idea that we had lived at Talavera like lords and ladies of the manor was a fiction. There had been periods of wealth, but we were my father with his grease-stained khakis and Brooks Brother jacket, just as we were my mother with her tilted straw hat, me with my magnifying lens and dog-chewed cap. The truth was, we never had been an elite, landed gentry for whom the farm was a passing distraction. That was a story of the Hudson Valley, but not our own story here. As much as it was *Talavera,* the house that anchored my family to this place, it was the farm.

Wealth and social position were a large part of the Van Ness legacy in the Hudson Valley, but it was not the almost mythic wealth of manor families like the Livingstons, whose river estates still lay along the eastern banks of the river just south of here. According to the earliest tax records, Catherine Douw's grandfather Peter Van Ness had been the richest man in Kinderhook by the end of the Revolution. His brother David had built a similar fortune south in Red Hook. Both of them acquired their wealth as merchants and traders and had built fine houses. Peter's sons had gone on to political acclaim. General John P. Van Ness became one of the first mayors of Washington, D.C., while his brother Cornelius became the governor of Vermont. But William's family had chosen the quieter path of carrying on the Van Ness lands in Claverack. His son, Judge William W., had been a distinguished lawyer and become prominent in federal-era New York politics but we were still a family for whom the farm was central.

I remembered something that my mother said when I asked her about the difficult years that followed my grandmother's death.

"Your father felt the land was what was important, not the house. It was why I suppose we concentrated on the farm and didn't worry as much about keeping Talavera up as we might have. . . ."

Her voice had trailed off then, part apology for the peeling wallpaper, for the yellowing curtains. Then she burst out chuckling, "This was built as a foolish house back then and it's still a foolish house now!"

We both laughed. What she said was so true. William W. had built his elegant, exotic mansion as much to display his wealth as his patriotism. He probably never noticed that by the time you shuttled food from the kitchen to the dining room, it was cold.

To me, Talavera, our foolish house, was the keeper of previous lives, but the land had been the constraint that had shaped them.

What a relief it was to accept who we were and had been. It didn't mean that I too now had to commit to staying here. But it did mean that if I left, I would know what I was leaving, and that knowledge seemed to equip me with a way to make a choice. I didn't want to live under the shadow of regret. Perhaps the most important lesson offered up by Chief Keesieway was not to become seduced by one firelock gun. If we sold Talavera, or developed rather than farmed the land, our burden would be lifted. But each century of my family's tenure here had revealed the same truth: Once you stopped working the land, you lost your connection to it.

Meanwhile, when I looked across the dining room and saw General John P. Van Ness's aquiline profile, I had to admit that Talavera had not given up all its secrets. They still swirled around the house like dust motes, bloomed and fell, falling, like the apple blossoms, like the falling evening light. And while I sat there, watching the light fall, listening for the far-off silence of the river, I was glad for all that I did not yet know.

271

Sources

RESEARCH FOR THIS BOOK BEGAN IN 1995 with the discovery of a cache of unsorted family and farm papers located in the house and barns at Talavera. Systematically removing, cleaning, stabilizing, then sorting these papers to create an archive took two years. The resulting collection, now called the "Philip Farm and Family Papers," includes photographs, correspondence, genealogies, farm and house ledgers, journals, accounts, assorted business papers and agricultural literature. Together with a collection of family papers that had been removed from the house in 1975 and acquired by the New-York Historical Society in 1980, these papers tell the story of the Van Ness and Philip families in the early political, social and economic life of New York. The two collections also describe the continuous ownership of one farm by one family for almost three centuries, making them a unique case study of agriculture in the Hudson Valley.

Within the text, these primary materials are indicated by quotation marks rather than traditional footnotes. Most of the letters and diaries of Lieutenant John Van Ness, William Henry, Martin Hoffman, Catherine Douw, Eliza Worthington, Herman Hoffman (Hoffman), Elizabeth Stark (Bessie), Gaston Pearson and the early letters of John Van Ness (1866–1949) cited in this book are located in the "Philip–Van Ness" collection in the New-York Historical Society. Most of the later correspondence of John Van Ness Philip (1866–1949), along with farm journals and my father's letters and papers, is drawn from the private collection "Philip Farm and Family papers."

One of the most difficult areas of research was the story of Tom, Thomas W. Johnson, the freed slave who fought with Lieutenant John Van Ness in the Civil War. Not surprisingly, family correspondence that mentioned Tom never mentioned his full name. I assumed that the will of John Van Ness's father-in-law might deliver some information about Tom, but my first task was to find it. I fi-

273

nally tracked down the name of Laura's father, John Johnson, by looking in Maryland newspapers on the day of his death, October 6, 1856. I then discovered that he had died intestate. Through perseverance, luck and with the help of a particularly knowledgeable staff researcher in the Maryland State Archives, I was able to uncover letters of administration that his widow, Mary Johnson, had received on April 6, 1858. Checking the administration accounts for that date revealed the inventory of John Johnson's estate. There, under household accounts, I found Tom's listing: "Negro man Tom slave for life 21 years of age." He was valued at $850.

Once I had verified Tom's identity, I was even more determined to find out, if I could, what had happened to him. He was not listed among family members and servants in the 1865 population census for Claverack. I began to look through the U.S. naval records of the Civil War. There I finally found his full name, Thomas W. Johnson. He was listed as one of the "landsmen" wounded in a skirmish with the *Wilder* in an official report filed by the captain of the USS *Cuyler*, Captain Winslow. *Official Records of the Union of the Confederate Navies in the War of the Rebellion*, Series I, volume 17 (Washington, D.C.: Government Printing Office).

Other key sources of primary materials included: Columbia County Historical Society, Kinderhook, New York; Columbia County Agricultural Society, Kinderhook, New York; Columbia County Surrogates Court, Hudson, New York; Columbia County Clerk's Office, Hudson, New York; Hudson City Clerk's Office, Hudson, New York; Hudson City Library, Hudson, New York; Library of Congress, Washington, D.C.; Maryland State Archives, Annapolis, Maryland; Municipal Archives of the City of New York, New York City; National Archives, College Park, Maryland and Washington, D.C.; New-York Historical Society, New York City; New York State Library, Albany, New York; private papers of Anna Post; private papers of Julia Philip.

In addition to the primary research sites listed above, a book of this nature requires broad reading in a number of areas. While this book was not written to stand as a definitive family or farm history, through the writing of it I was soon propelled into the following subjects and fields: American history, landscape studies and cultural geography, African-American history, landscape gardening and architecture, art history, pomology, agricultural history, horticulture, fruit growing, the women's suffrage movement and beekeeping. It was particularly important to read widely about the Dutch history of the Hudson Valley, the role of Columbia County in the founding of the new republic, the intricacies of the manorial system in colonial New York and the complex land transactions between the Mohicans and early Europeans in the valley. Luckily, some excellent research has been done on the Livingston and Van Ness families in early New York, which provided me with critical background.

Acknowledgments

Funding for research on this book was received from the American Association of University Women and the Colgate University Research Council, Furthermore, the publishing program of the J. M. Kaplan Fund and the National Endowment for the Humanities. In 1999, the Columbia County Historical Society served as a sponsor for this project.

For help creating the archives, I am indebted to Helen McLallan of the Columbia County Historical Society, Carl Peterson of Case Library at Colgate University and to my sister, Katherine Philip Chansky, a professional archivist. I am grateful to Margaret Heilbrun, the director of the library at the New-York Historical Society, for help tracking down acquisition records for the "Philip–Van Ness" collection. For help in researching the often shadowy and incomplete history of eighteenth-century land holdings in Claverack, I am indebted to the work of Ruth Piwonka, a consulting researcher who specializes in Columbia County. Maryland State Archives researcher Rob Barnes helped to find the missing clue that connected the pieces of Tom's life. Colgate reference librarian David Hughs helped track down Johnson genealogies.

Several individuals allowed me to interview them. I want to thank Mrs. Nancy Testa and Captain Ronald B. Moser USN-RET, for many great conversations and for help researching Lieutenant John Van Ness. Special thanks go to Anna Post for deciding that "it was time" and for generously allowing me to use her story. I learned a great deal from conversations with spray representative Gil Lasher and Steve McKay, educator at the Cornell Cooperative Extension Service of Columbia County. Thanks also to Dr. Jan Nyrop and Peter J. Jentsch, researchers active with the exciting "*T. pyri* Project," which aims to achieve biological control of European red mites in the Hudson Valley.

A number of people read my work at various stages along the

way and their encouragement and insight were golden. Thank you: Bobbie Bristol, Teresa Carbone, Jenna Laslocky, Angela Miller, Susan Packer, Kirk Savage, Christine Stansell. My great friend, Elizabeth Thomas, generously read my work with her famed red pen in hand. Wonderful support came from Joan Davidson and Mike Gladstone. Thanks go to my agent, Kim Witherspoon, who never had any doubts and to my editor at Viking, Ray Roberts, for believing in this book from the first pages on.

I would like to acknowledge the dedicated individuals and organizations, working with energy and vision to ensure that the rural landscape of the Hudson Valley endures for future generations.

My mother deserves all praise, not just for keeping the farm going, but also for her generosity and patience. I want to thank my brothers and sister for their trust as I poked around in our shared past. Finally, it would never have been possible to write this book without the great love, courage and unwavering support of my husband, Garth Evans. Along the way, our son Rhys, kept us both laughing.